Advance praise for *The Package Deal*

"In her sweet, funny, and immensely engaging book, Izzy Rose reminds us what it means to be a true family. I wonder if she'd adopt me."

—Cathy Alter, author of *Up for Renewal:*
What Magazines Taught Me About Love, Sex,
and Starting Over

"Here's to Izzy Rose and *The Package Deal*: clearly, she's turning into not only a Fairly Good Mother (the most any of us can really hope for) but—even more important—a Fine Southerner as well! Her jump-on-off-that-cliff bravery and her might-as-well-laugh attitude are all the proof I need."

—Jill Conner Browne, *The* Sweet Potato Queen

"You don't have to be a stepmom to love *The Package Deal*. Even if you've 'shot a tiny human out of your birth canal,' every one of Izzy Rose's hilarious observations will ring true, every nugget of her hard-earned wisdom will be treasured. As funny as it is tender, as idiosyncratic as it is universal, *The Package Deal* is a sweet-tart of a valentine to all mothers who cobble together families as best we can."

—Sarah Bird, author of *How Perfect Is That*

"*The Package Deal* is a wonderful read. Not only is it wickedly funny, [but] Izzy Rose's memoir contains great wisdom about how to embrace the unexpected and remake your life. You don't need to be a stepmom, or even a mom, to enjoy this fabulous book."

—Stacie Cockrell, Cathy O'Neill, and Julia Stone, authors of
Babyproofing Your Marriage

"*The Package Deal* zips along with insight and wit and raises the timeless question, How much can we change for love? And is it worth it? In Izzy's case, the answer is 'A lot!' and 'Yup!' Vivacious and honest, she doesn't tout unrealistic perfection but a doable heartfelt accommodation—her book is a must for anyone even contemplating stepmotherhood, and for anyone who wants a good laugh and cry and some of that Texas Rotel dip!"

—Laura Shaine Cunningham, author of eight books,
including the memoir *Sleeping Arrangements*

"If you are a stepmom, are about to become one, or know one, you simply must read this hilarious and heartfelt memoir. Even if you're not a stepmom you'll enjoy it thoroughly—it's that good. *The Package Deal* by Izzy Rose offers a glimpse into the brave heart of a woman who takes on another woman's children with courage, honesty, and humor. Pour a glass of red wine, dish up a slice of gourmet cheese, and curl up with *The Package Deal*—the perfect tonic for any stepmother's soul."

—Jacquelyn B. Fletcher, award-winning author of
A Career Girl's Guide to Becoming a Stepmom

"Izzy Rose's memoir, *The Package Deal,* captures the bittersweet life of moms and stepmoms with wit and wry humor . . . a poignant story every woman can relate to!"

—Jane Porter, author of *Easy on the Eyes* and *Mrs. Perfect*

"Izzy Rose nails how it is and what it feels like to be a new stepmom. There's nothing like that shocking first year! She moved from an exciting career in a perfect location with built-in best friends to *what?*—a strange place with no friends, no family, and the expectation of raising someone else's half-grown kids. Like many of us, Izzy was uprooted by love, and she portrays beautifully the strong love between her and her fiancé. It's that force that propels them to the next level of connection and confidence that makes it all worthwhile."
　　　　　　　　　　　　　—Susan Wisdom, coauthor of *Stepcoupling*

"Everyone knows that giving birth is both excruciating and joyous—and that painkillers are an option. *Not* everyone knows that becoming a stepparent is the same way, except that there's nobody standing next to you, offering up the opiates. This is a hilarious, honest, heartfelt look at what it means to take on a family that isn't your own. I'm a stepmother myself, and I can tell you, Izzy Rose rocks it."

—Maria Dahvana Headley, author of *The Year of Yes*

"An unvarnished and ultimately reassuring look at the terrors and triumphs of creating an instant family. Soul-baring, brave, and genuinely hilarious. Highly recommended!"

—Jennifer Marine, coauthor of *No One's the Bitch*

"A laugh-out-loud memoir packed with good advice . . . a much-needed resource for the fledgling or soon-to-be stepmother."

—Sally Bjornsen, author of *The Single Girl's Guide to Marrying a Man, His Kids, and His Ex-Wife*

"*The Package Deal* is good comic relief from a master of poking fun at herself and lightening the often bizarre challenges of stepmotherhood with humor."

—Cherie Burns, author of *Stepmotherhood:
How to Survive Without Feeling Frustrated,
Left Out, or Wicked*

The Package Deal

The Package Deal

My (not-so) Glamorous Transition from
Single Gal to Instant Mom

Izzy Rose

THREE RIVERS PRESS • NEW YORK

Library of Congress Cataloging-in-Publication Data

Rose, Izzy.
    The package deal / Izzy Rose.
      p. cm.
    1. Stepmothers—Family relationships.   I. Title.
HQ759.92.R66 2009
306.874'7092—dc22
[B]   2008050292

ISBN 978-0-307-45433-1

Printed in the United States of America

Design by Ruth Lee-Mui

10 9 8 7 6 5 4 3 2 1

First Edition

For Susan, my Mama Bird,
and
to the three sweet men who turned my world upside down

AUTHOR'S NOTE

This is the story of a California gal who fell in love with a Southern guy, married, became a stepmom, left her career, and hauled off to Texas all in the same year. Did everything in these pages really happen? According to me, it did. You see, what you're about to read is not an affidavit—it's my candid point of view. If you want to know how others experienced this time, you'll have to ask them.

For that distinction, names have been changed to protect the innocent—those who didn't necessarily know that TV people like me listen for good sound bites, remember them, and like to repeat them for laughs. And while *this* news promo producer values accuracy, I also consider myself a storyteller, so in an effort to make this memoir one you can easily pick up with one hand and finish before your next birthday, I have reordered some plot points, condensed the timeline, and combined a few minor players.

Regardless of these changes, I assure you this is the true, messy life of a very real stepmom. Best enjoyed with a sense of humor and, perhaps, a bottle of wine.

All your life
You were only waiting for this moment to arise.
—"Blackbird," John Lennon and Paul McCartney

The Package Deal

Introduction

I can do this.

For God's sake, I'm in my mid-thirties. I'm a certifiable grown-up. A successful professional who has survived the pressure of big-market TV newsrooms and demanding on-air talent for over a decade. I'm an independent woman with my very own one-bedroom city apartment that I can actually afford—and it's technically not in the ghetto. I'm super savvy about mass transit (tickets, tokens, transfers) and can parallel park on any slanted street in San Francisco. And I'm fearless, but not stupid, about venturing out after dark for essentials from the corner market: wine, fancy nuts, and tampons. I'm a big girl who's got a handle on sophisticated city living.

There is nothing I cannot do. At least, that's what I'm telling myself right now.

The truth is, the big question on my mind is whether I'm as gutsy and bold as I feel. Can this single, stylish, confident city girl remain courageous and in control as she meets some very adult milestone moments head-on? We're talking career change, cross-country move, and buying my first house, one large and sturdy enough to lodge my instant family. Oh, didn't I tell you? I'm getting married—to a divorced man with two kids.

That's right. Say good-bye to single! Hello, instant mom.

Instead of throwing up at the thought of losing my personal freedom in the face of increased responsibility, I remind myself that there is something like fifteen million stepmoms in the country today. I just never planned on being one of them.

Thankfully, I have one advantage going into this new arrangement. I understand what it's like to be a stepkid because I am one. My parents divorced when I was nine, and both remarried when I was ten, so while I might be an amateur as a parent, I speak the extended-family language.

But becoming a stepmother? To two adolescent boys? How do you prepare for that?

JUNE

Welcome to the Party

I've always preferred the window seat. When I'm flying, I can look down at the curl of the Colorado River or the tippy-top of the Sierras and immediately feel grounded. I know where I am. I know where I'm going. But today I'm stuck in the middle seat, thirty thousand feet in the air, with my boyfriend's two kids on either side of me. How did I get here?

The Young One is hogging the view, and he's been prattling on since his little buns hit *my* window seat. He's explaining to me how a plane stays up in the air (something I've never understood), complete with diagrams on the backs of gum wrappers with captions like "thrust" and "lift." I've got more than two decades on this kid, and I feel like there's nothing I know that he hasn't already mastered. He's full of data, history, and lore. Not only that, but his memory is flaw-less, and he doesn't hesitate to show it off.

Against his father's request, The Young One has hauled a stressed, thirty-pound backpack onto the plane. He's already pulled out a biog-raphy of Abraham Lincoln, *How Stuff Works* (see page 2 for the aerodynamics of your basic 747), and *The Field Guide to North Amer-ican Birds*. I feel super-simple devouring the latest *People* magazine. Doesn't the kid know the rules of air travel? You catch up on celebri-tology, not useful information.

The Tall One has no problem blocking out his younger brother's chitchat. He's been writing in his journal since we got on the plane. He insisted on bringing four on board with him. "Different books for different thoughts. I need them all," he said. I didn't push it. He's a private guy—and likes to keep it that way. He can be very introverted (almost monklike) and then, all of a sudden, he'll surprise me with some witty retort that cracks me up. But he's also a teenager, so his charm comes in waves. Still, I figured traveling with him would be relatively painless. Although he doesn't share my shallow interest in *People* magazine's "Style Watch" section, he at least understands the quiet rule.

I realized pretty early in this relationship with Hank and the kids that I'm not a big fan of noise. Yes, I like the unrelenting sounds of the big city outside my front door, but I don't like a lot of chatter in-side my apartment—and I don't like sitting next to a Chatty Cathy on a five-hour flight.

"Did you know that spearmint gum helps with the oxygen flow in your brain?" asked The Young One. He offered me a stick from the bottom of his backpack.

"Can't say I did." I passed on the gum and said, "Let's play li-brary."

He looked at me suspiciously. "How do you play library?"

"We don't talk. It's very quiet."

"And then what?"

"That's it. No talking."

My boyfriend, Hank, seated across the aisle and drugged on Dramamine, snuggles with the poor stranger next to him. While I was stuffing my carry-on with magazines, my iPod, and snacks, he was counting how many snooze pills he had left over from his last trip. He checked out an hour ago and until he wakes up I'm on my own with his kids, who've got me sandwiched in row 22.

I can't breathe.

Hank, a Southern boy, invited me on this adventure to meet his family in Memphis. I must say I find his redneck roots amusing and somehow exotic; plus, I could hardly pass up an opportunity to travel, especially to somewhere that gives me an excuse to buy new summer sandals and indulge in eighteenth-century cocktails.

When he suggested we take a trip together to the South, I was all over it. "The home of the mint julep! When do we leave?"

He was pleased I accepted and booked four tickets. This is what dating a man with kids often means: We seldom go places as a couple. We go as a gang. So here we are, on our first family vacation, and I've been a good sport until now.

I'm stuck. I can't move my arms. I think I'm having a claustrophobic fit. What's that smell?

Let me be frank: Traveling with children is a bit of a chore. *Welcome to the party, honey.* Is that what you're thinking?

I'm well aware that I'm not the first person to come to this conclusion. I've been on plenty of planes, sitting across from rattled parents with wailing babies, and there is nothing about that ordeal that's ever looked rewarding. Or remotely fun.

Juggling a tween and a teen has a different set of challenges. Ten- and fourteen-year-olds don't shed as many tears as babies do, but they still lose their share of liquids—from the armpit region. Two hours in and the trip to Memphis was getting a little, how should I say, *funky*. If smoking were still allowed on commercial flights, I would have torn the ripe T-shirt off The Tall One and torched it in the plane's bathroom.

Instead, I threw off my seat belt and squirmed my way safely over him and out into the aisle.

"Ouch! What are you doing?" he said.

"I have to use the restroom. Unless you want me to stay put and pee on you?"

"You're weird." He went back to his journal-writing and I headed to the back of the plane.

In my moments of anxiety about adding half-grown kids to the romantic mix, I often seek out a bathroom mirror where I can give myself a good talking-to. In the plane's lavatory I told my sallow reflection that tolerance is a favorable quality—*It'll erase years from your green face*—and moreover, I'd heard that a self-centered lifestyle is ultimately unfulfilling. *If I love this man, I have to accept that his kids are along for the ride.* I searched my own eyes for conviction. If I wasn't ready to accept the vacation-package, I ought to let this man go and get back to traveling alone.

I don't want to let this man go.

I think what's always scared me about having kids is that they'll bring out the worst in me. They'll just be doing what kids do (tracking in dirt, licking the floor, or screaming until their lungs bleed) and I'll get agitated and become that mean lady who stuffs them in the oven.

I'm not a witch who bakes kids on high. I can do this. I can be the kid-loving type.

I forced a cheerful smile, unlocked the door to my confessional, and headed back to my seat with renewed strength.

The boys were knocked out, so I wedged myself in between their bony frames. Once I had enough room to exhale, their warm (albeit stinky) bodies felt quite cozy, and when The Young One—clutching his favorite stuffed animal, the lobster—nestled up against my shoulder, I thought, *Okay, maybe this isn't so bad.*

Hank woke up just in time to see our dozy display of affection. He looked at me with a playful grin. "You okay? Want to switch spots?"

I delivered my best nonchalant, "Nah, I'm good." For the most part, I had no need for rescuing yet. Surely I'd be able to get through baggage claim before my next panic attack. I mean, *come on*; I work in a television newsroom. I get paid good money to maintain my calm when other people are erupting into hysterics.

Hank and I are TV producers. We've both spent the majority of our careers working in news promotion, writing and editing those captivating on-air spots that tease and, yes, sometimes exaggerate the top stories of the evening news. Instilling fear in viewers is a popular tactic. (*Tonight, a shocking discovery: We'll reveal how your loved ones could die suddenly from a seemingly harmless household product.*) It's very sexy and important work.

I admit, condensing a top story into one neat little package (fifteen skimpy seconds) infuriates many, but it titillates me. From a creative standpoint, what's not to love? Dramatic music (think driving violins), emotional pictures (slowed down for heartbreaking effect), and a dynamic voice track (Darth Vader on steroids) make for good television and an entertaining day's work. In my opinion, the best promo producers are the most passionate and energized by the art (good journalism is just part of the job). A successful promo will connect with viewers on a base emotional level in the first five seconds of a spot. We call this "the hook." And once we've got you, it's hard to look away.

Which leads me to how Hank "hooked" me in the first place. When I first met him, I immediately noticed three things: (1) The man had the sense to completely shave his head once he started to go bald; (2) He was confident enough—or lacking vanity enough—to wear Cliff Huxtable–inspired sweaters that his mother *(I pray)* must have sent him; and (3) He said exactly what was on his mind—the good and the bad.

I was intrigued.

Hank possessed a quality I haven't often encountered: He's unabashedly honest, a straight shooter who isn't afraid to shoot. Many people think that Southerners are just the opposite—a little too sugary and, possibly, insincere. Not Hank. In fact, he's been accused of having a harsh manner, but I prefer to explain it this way: He doesn't hand out compliments unless he's truly impressed. The thin-skinned don't like this at all. It makes them shaky. I admit that when we first met, I was both offended by and oddly attracted to his rawness.

For example, on any given day he'd blast into my edit suite and criticize the spot I'd just spent hours cutting. "It's just not working for me. I think you should start over." *Just not working? Who does this guy think he is?* Then he'd plop down in front of my keyboard and start re-editing my project with sickening competence. *I hate this guy, I'd think. I wonder if he's any good in bed?*

On other days, he'd catch me off-guard with his softness. I'd march into his office prepared for battle only to find him in tears over some contrived lost-puppy story. *This guy is a mess!* I'd hand him a tissue and he'd ask me to sit down, saying something like, "I've been meaning to tell you, your writing is fantastic. You're the best producer I've ever worked with."

Hank was a surprise.

He came into my life just around the time I was craving a man who wouldn't be afraid to throw me up against a wall and tear my clothes off (after obtaining the proper permission, of course), and then tenderly adore me. I wanted someone with an imperfect balance of hard edges and soft spots. Someone unpredictable who would challenge me and keep me interested for a while.

I think what I'd hoped for was a relationship that tested my intellectual and emotional depths, but not necessarily one that called for a complete lifestyle overhaul.

Yet here I was, flying through the air with my grown-up boyfriend and his two kids. In little more than a year, I'd given up much of my single-minded independence and become part of a pod. A part-time-family-unit thing. And honestly, I wasn't entirely sure where it was going.

We landed in ninety-degree heat. I'm from the northern part of California (land of wine and fog, not celebrity-spotting), so my glands began a suffocated protest as soon as we walked out of the airport. As a general rule, I don't like to expose a lot of skin; my legs are morgue-white, so shorts are not a regular fashion choice. On the other hand, I find long pants unbearably sticky if the temperature climbs higher than sixty degrees. I instantly knew that Memphis would call for bravery.

Hank's folks live in South Bluffs, a community with cobblestone streets, stately fountains, and, in June, blooming azaleas and magnolia trees. The house that Hank's father designed overlooks the Mississippi River, with views of the "New Bridge" connecting Tennessee to Arkansas. I was so busy taking in the unfamiliar scenery that I hardly noticed the thick band of sweat gathering around my waistline and the tiresome bickering between the boys over whether the Mississippi River is longer than the Nile.

Of course, Hank was right on them. "Boys. Enough! We're here."

We'd stopped in front of a well-manicured house, and there she was—Hank's mama. Red hair, big jewelry, and electric blue eyes. Margaret the Methodist minister was coming toward the rental car and waving up a storm.

"Hi, y'all. Come here. Hug your Grand-mom."

I soon learned that, like her son, Margaret is a bit of a contradiction. On one hand, she's a dynamic feminist (female ministers aren't exactly dropping out of pecan trees in the South), and on the other, she's a proud member of the God Squad who values the proper order of things. Case in point: She requested that Hank (age forty-two) and I (impure since sixteen) sleep in separate rooms. I found it charming (*This must be the Southern way,* I reasoned), and unpacked my high heels and hair products before sneaking into Hank's room for a sliver of downtime.

I climbed up onto his four-poster bed and said, "I just have to lie here for ten minutes. Just ten minutes of quiet."

Hank chuckled at my premature exhaustion. "Take your time," he said.

Hank explained that his daddy, Hank Senior or Big Hank, was downstairs working on the Rotel, so I had at least a brief respite before I had to emerge fresh as a daisy and turn on the charm.

"Is the Rotel an appliance?" I asked Hank as he unzipped his suitcase. My Southern ignorance amused Hank. "No, it's dip, baby."

Popular Southern Recipe: Rotel Cheese Dip

> 1 *can diced Rotel*
> 1 *lb. browned ground beef or Wolf Brand Chili with no beans*
>   *(optional)*
> 1 *lb. Velveeta cheese*

Cut up entire package of Velveeta and melt in a Crock-Pot. Add one can of Rotel. Mix in ground beef or chili. Serve hot with tortilla chips.

But what exactly *is* Rotel? I still don't know. You'll have to look it up . . . or ask The Young One.

When Hank finished unpacking all the contents of his bag, he lay down beside me on the rose-colored quilt. "Are you ready to go downstairs?" He kissed my forehead and looked into my eyes.

"You're sweet," I said.

"I'm sweet on you."

Now, how scary could Hank's parents be when they'd produced such a gentleman?

"Okay—let's go. Is there any Southern etiquette I should know about? Like, should I curtsy or use a hanky?"

"No." Hank grinned. "It's just my folks."

I was very self-conscious about impressing Mom and Dad because, obviously, they'd be observing my relationship with their darling grandkids. Even though their mother was still very much in their lives, because I was Hank's new gal my relationship with the boys was important. *Were we bonding? Did they like me? Did the mere sound of my voice strike terror in their hearts?* I was certain they'd be looking for cracks—the kind that could split Hank and me apart.

I worried that if they looked close enough, they would see what I'd revealed to my girlfriends many years ago: I'm missing the mom gene. Truly, I'm not making this up. Wouldn't you agree that any woman who maintains that newborn kittens are more lovable than tiny humans has a maternal defect? I had hoped that I'd eventually grow up or grow out of this phase, but as I sat on Margaret and Big Hank's lovely sofa, I held my breath with my fingers crossed, hoping she wouldn't nudge me to praise her crowded collection of framed grandbaby photos. I'd already complimented her elegant display of antique ornamental plates and her elaborate arrangement of sweetheart roses. Wasn't that enough adulation for the first day? Snapshots of tots dumping food on their heads or taking baths in the sink I can't even pretend to like.

And believe me, I've tried.

I've historically been that woman at baby showers who looks completely awkward handling the baby-safe products and doll-sized socks. I feign enthusiasm and participate in the chorus of precious-isms, but usually what's going through my mind is *I'm just not feeling this.* And, *Is there rum in this punch?* Once the baby games begin, I'm either draining the punch bowl or escaping through the bathroom window.

A decade ago, so many of my friends were getting married and starting families. It was the mid-twenties surge and, honestly, I wanted no part of it. I had no problem with them moving forward with their adult ambitions, but couldn't they see I was still a kid? A kid of divorce, to be exact—which left me feeling a little iffy about the idea of playing house someday. I didn't want to end up like my parents, living in Splitsville.

My girlfriends persisted. "When do you want to settle down and start having babies?"

"Um, never?"

So everyone was astonished when in my mid-thirties I started to hint that I might have met the eternal lover of my loins. And that his baggage included two sons.

"You're dating a guy with kids?" my friends mocked me. "Do you know that will make you a stepmom?"

"Whoa, Nelly," I said. "Let's not jump ahead of ourselves. No one's getting married."

Don't get me wrong; divorce may have made me more cautious than some, but like every girl, I've always loved the idea of finding that one person who gets me, worships my hips, and doubles over at my jokes. What I've never subscribed to is the pressure to settle on a near-perfect match just to make everyone else comfortable and even out the number of place settings at dinner parties.

Yet here I was, south of the Mason-Dixon Line, with a man I was so crazy in love with that if asked I just might throw caution to the wind and slip on an overpriced princess gown and walk down the matrimonial runway—and in front of all my smug girlfriends, too. Still, I wasn't allowing anyone to rush me. I was going at my own pace—slug-slow.

That went for the boys, as well. We were taking our time getting friendly, and that meant I wasn't super lovey-dovey with them. What was the hurry? I figured we'd get there when it was right, and without my forcing it. Still, I worried that Hank's parents would mistake my guarded attitude for neglect. *I've never seen a woman so cold!* they'd say. *It's like she's afraid to touch them. What's wrong with her?* What's wrong is that I'd been where the boys are now. When my parents divorced, my dad started dating right away. The women he brought home who wanted to snuggle me and offer preteen fashion advice got a thumbs-down. Their eagerness was transparent. *You don't love me,* I'd think. *You're just hot for my dad.*

I did not want to be that lady.

But just because I didn't pour on *l'amour* didn't mean I wasn't planning to grow closer to the boys. Getting approval from Hank's little men was my ticket to stick around. I'm no dummy. I know how it works. Nothing kills a love affair faster than disgruntled children who wish the girlfriend dead.

Plus, the guys are really quite likeable, which was an unforeseen kick. I grew up in an all-girl household, so the last time I was around boys their age I was kneeing them in the groin during recess or ducking as they aimed for my head in dodgeball. Hanging with the same types as a thirty-five-year-old woman was much less threatening, at least physically. In the scholastics department, they both have me sorely beat. Thankfully, as a television producer, my knack for storytelling is well developed, so we spend a lot of our time together keeping it light and swapping fact for fiction.

I'd been able to slide into the role of "Daddy's girlfriend" without much protest, an achievement, I realized, that not all women dating divorced men can boast. Still, even after a year, my policy was to never get too comfortable. I figured our relationship was built on tentative ground—no telling what'll set off their little broken-home hot buttons. Better to play it safe.

I didn't think I could explain all this to Big Hank and Margaret without a confusing round of Q and A, so I just sat quietly on their leather sofa, staring at the bowl of hot cheese, trying to suppress a stomachache. Hank was sitting next to me in a fantastic orange paisley dress shirt, fancy jeans, and wingtip shoes. Since we'd started dating, his wardrobe had improved dramatically. I'm pretty sure the day he wore a bulky red cable-knit sweater to the office and I called out "Hey, Santa, where ya been?" was a pivotal moment in his decision to update his look. Margaret and Big Hank sat across from us. They were a handsome couple, finely dressed and well spoken, and Hank was an attractive combination of the two.

"So, tell us about your family," Margaret said. "Hank's told us a little bit—you're from the San Francisco area. You're probably not used to this heat."

"It *is* rather warm here." I smiled. Despite Hank's urging to act casual, I sat on the edge of the sofa with my knees locked and my ankles crossed. I spread my cocktail napkin over my white linen pants.

"We have a pool here." Margaret looked at her son to give her the green light. "Wouldn't that be fun—get the kids together and take a dip?"

"Maybe later, Mama," Hank said. "We just got here."

That's exactly right, I thought. *Let's stall on that one. Don't these people know I don't do exposed thighs?* I couldn't think of anything more awkward than getting to know Hank's family with my lapsed bikini wax on full view. It was important to get the conversation back on track. "My whole family lives in California—mom, stepdad, stepsisters, dad, his girlfriend, my grandmother."

"I see," Margaret said. "So your dad didn't remarry?"

Um. How much did I want to explain here? He had remarried a woman named Crystal, but they'd divorced when I was sixteen. I wasn't sad to see her go. She used to wear my jeans without asking, and she didn't believe in underwear. My friends and I called her Gonorrhea Girl behind her back (one of my passive-aggressive stepchild ways).

I decided to simply tell Margaret, "No, he isn't married right now, but he's got a really great girlfriend."

There was a pause in the conversation. I shifted on the couch and Hank dipped a cracker in the Rotel. *Why was this so hard?* My nerves were getting the better of me, and where were the mint juleps? I looked down at my ridiculous posture—an *uptight* bore. Thankfully, The Young One strolled into the room and broke the mood.

"Tell them one of your disgusting jokes, Izzy. She's really funny, Grand-mom."

And that's all it took. I let my breath out with a laugh (I think I'd been holding it since Colorado) and for the rest of the day I was able to be some version of myself, and Hank and his River City crew seemed sufficiently amused.

Memphis is a fascinating town, chock-full of heartbreaking history and artery-clogging food, and trust me, thanks to Margaret, we did it all. I understand what it means to hyper-host. When friends or family visit San Francisco, I turn freakish. I make lists and prioritize with highlighters. I take it as my responsibility to make (er, force) people to love my town as I do. It's exhausting (for everyone, I'm sure), but

I don't know how else to do it. For me, being in charge means providing a detailed itinerary (with corresponding maps) and keeping everyone on a caffeine high.

The beauty of visiting someone else's town is getting to take a backseat and let go. So I did. I sat right between Hank and The Tall One as we drove through Overton Park (the Central Park of Memphis), to Sun Records (birthplace of rock and roll), to Beale Street (where the Blues got its start), and, of course, to Graceland (where die-hards are still waiting for the return of the King). Every time the sweat pooled underneath my clothes and my skin started to expand or my energy began to fade, I'd remind myself, *This trip is not about personal space. Or napping.* But after seventy-two hours of getting in and out of the car, posing for group photos, and discussing the location for our next family meal, I needed a break. And a big-girl drink to go with it.

We were back at the house freshening up before the next activity when Hank suggested it. "I think we should go out tonight. Just the two of us." I was so relieved. I fell into his arms like a true Southern belle.

"Oh, thank heavens," I said in a mock plantation drawl. "It's not that I don't like your parents, but I can't talk any more, and we don't have to do everything together, do we? I mean . . . that's not healthy. Is it? Plus, aren't you tired? I feel like I'm going to pass out on the floor right in front of your mother if I have to keep talking, talking. And I can't eat any more fried chicken, and no more bacon buffets. I need a drink, a real one, like bourbon. And it's not that I don't want the kids around, but honestly—"

"Shut up," Hank teased and kissed me. We left the kids with their grandparents and slipped out the front door.

The evening air was oppressively wet and as hot as it had been at noon, but I felt flirtatious and free. We were finally alone. *How delicious!* When we boarded the late-night wooden trolley and headed downtown, I was simply happy, and things got even better when we walked through the doors of the legendary Peabody Hotel.

I'm a sucker for hotel grandeur, and the Peabody did not disappoint. The Grand Lobby has polished marble floors, Cinderella chandeliers, and an exquisitely romantic cocktail lounge. A massive floral arrangement sat atop a splashy fountain, which I soon learned was home to the famous Peabody Ducks. The real kind. In fact, Hank explained, bona fide quacking ducks march down their own red carpet every day, jump into the lobby fountain, and swim around for hours while tourists take pictures. It's a Memphis thing.

Finally I got to order a mint julep (your basic mojito, but with bourbon), and when Hank excused himself to go to the restroom I called my stepsister and left the following message: "Gigi, you would LOOOOOOVVVVVVEE it here. It is so elegant and they have the best bar snacks ever." Gigi and I have been rating the nuts and pretzels at bars since before we were old enough to drink.

Since we were having such a ravishing time sipping exquisite cocktails and gawking at the hotel's haughty clientele, I hardly noticed when (into our second round of drinks) Hank lunged down on one knee. But when he pulled a ring out of his pocket and asked me if I'd please let him be my husband, I spilled all the Cajun nuts on the hotel's fancy floor and yelled, "ARE YOU SERIOUSLY KIDDING ME RIGHT NOW?"

"No." He smiled. "I'm not kidding."

I thought, *Oh my God, this is that moment* . . . the moment when a man asks you to marry him . . . and all I could say was, "Really?" I wanted to pause the scene so my emotions could catch up with the action. *A man has just asked me to accept diamond jewelry. He has chosen this very second to be the one—the significant, life-changing one.* I sat there with my mouth wide open, unable to react, watching the picture process in the present. Would this moment replace the

lifelong fantasy version I'd been simultaneously cherishing and pushing away as implausible? *Remember this moment,* I told myself. *Hold
on to it.*

I looked around the sparkling lobby and back at Hank, equally
dazzling and still on one knee.

"I can't believe you got me all liquored up and now you're asking
me to marry you."

"Is that a yes?"

"Put that damn ring on my finger."

JULY

Reality Bites

When Hank announced our engagement to the boys the next morning and they didn't punch their fists through the wall or start cutting
themselves, I was relieved. I wasn't *really* surprised, but then you can
never really know how hormonal kids will react. The Young One
said, "I was wondering when you were going to get around to it,
Daddy." The Tall One stoically nodded his approval.

For the first time in my life, I'd met a man who'd convinced me
that marriage could be fun, or at least worth the risk. And when the
kids responded positively, it seemed that Hank's proposal was coming from three men, not just one.

Still, I couldn't help but feel a bit of anxiety about moving forward;
how does an independent single woman learn to handle a ready-made
family overnight? And we're not talking about sweet-smelling babies

who look like you, but someone else's nearly full-grown kids! It's one thing to be the girlfriend. Becoming a stepmother is an entirely different gig.

But in the fairy light of the Peabody the night before, Hank had given me the confidence to believe that I could do anything. I trusted him when he told me we'd be wonderfully happy and that I'd make an amazing stepmom. I accepted the challenge with a wide, tipsy grin. When I met this man, I had television to produce and a single lifestyle to enjoy. *Who could want more?* But then this Southern beau came along and hooked my heart, so even though he came with strings attached, he had me. And I wasn't walking away.

But of course it wasn't just Hank, the boys, and me. There was Hank's ex-wife. And her new husband. And their two kids. In California, June and John don't live far; she works as a morning anchor for a competing TV station in San Francisco, and he's a TV cameraman. Yes, it is a small world. But not that small: Hank, June, and John's cozy arrangement is very much by design. From the beginning, they agreed that in the interest of keeping their family together, it was all for one and one for all (in other words, until death do us *all* part). If one of them got a better opportunity in a different media market, they would all move. Over the years the arrangement has taken them from San Antonio to Memphis and, finally, to San Francisco. This bunch doesn't stay anywhere for very long, and when they go, they all go together. *Really,* truth is stranger than fiction. I call them the traveling circus.

Like every divorced couple with kids, Hank and June have made special accommodations that work for them. They share the kids, which means I share Hank. I've accepted that I can't and won't always come first. That's not to say that my designer skirts don't sometimes get ruffled. Many an evening I've been stood up for dinner because, at the last minute, Hank has the kids. *What can I say?* I've developed a love/hate relationship with patience.

Here's how it works: Half the week, Hank and I leave the TV station well after dark and duck in for dinner, usually somewhere between Broadway and Market Street, where we retreat to an intimate corner and pretend no one else in the world exists. Then we head back to my apartment, where we get tangled up until the alarm goes off.

The rest of the week, Hank attends to dad duty and I go about my very comfortable Izzy-centric lifestyle. I meet my city-dwelling girlfriends for cocktails and savories at all the new restaurants, and in addition to discussing the latest earthquake predictions, the newest plan to solve the city's homeless problem, our fluctuating careers, and age-defying skin-care products, we often debate the demands and rewards of dating men who are already daddies. It seems that many of us—women who have pursued career over commitment and promotion before parenting, and who have waited until our thirties to marry—are in the same boat: We finally meet an eligible bachelor, but he's hardly single.

So, I wondered, how would things change now that Hank and I were engaged? For starters, would we move in together right away? And if so, what would that mean to my relationship with the boys? *Would we still get along?* Things could dramatically change once we started acting like a family.

Newly engaged and back in San Francisco, I stared out at the Bay from my second-floor gym windows. I pushed and pulled rigorously on the elliptical machine. Sweat poured down my back as I pondered life under one roof. *Where to begin this life of eternal bliss?*

I'll be honest: I liked living in my own apartment. My bachelorette pad had *three* walk-in closets (which is unheard of in the renting world). Sure, there was only one teeny-tiny bedroom. And, *okay,* you couldn't really open the refrigerator door all the way without its bumping into the kitchen table. But it was my home, where the only dirty socks were my own.

Hank's airy artist's loft was bohemian-chic and extra roomy. But it had only one bathroom. Three guys. One girly me. You do the arithmetic. I mean, it was okay for the occasional overnight, but not for the long term. Plus, with regular gunshots and crack-crazies in the street, it was hardly the ideal neighborhood for hosting a block party or introducing myself at the corner liquor store as the new step-bitch in town.

It was clear: If we were going to consolidate our furniture and start buying soap in bulk, we'd need a much bigger place, with more than one working toilet. "In San Francisco?" our friends mocked. Hank and I realized that unless we suddenly landed rock-star salaries, our chance of finding what our growing family required was unlikely. We'd be lucky to find a cramped and dismal fixer-upper. Or worse, we might have to join our friends who'd given up and moved to the suburbs, only to find themselves miserably . . . *suburban.*

"Perhaps I should just stay rooted in my single apartment until we get married," I said to Kate over after-work drinks and wasabi peanuts. Kate was a good friend and TV colleague. She, too, was accustomed to her single lifestyle. She'd lived in a one-bedroom apartment that she adored for years and, like me, she'd recently gotten serious with a divorced man with two girls.

"And save yourself until the wedding night," she teased.

"I know it sounds a bit antiquated," I mused, "but I'm just not ready to give up my place and move into a group home."

"It's absolutely not old-fashioned. If Jacob and I end up engaged, I'm not giving up my apartment until after the wedding," she said. "This is what women are *doing* now. In fact, it's fashionable. This is your last chance to live alone . . . until it all falls apart or you're widowed."

"That's encouraging." Was Kate making a joke about the fact that half of all second marriages end in divorce?

But I had to agree. If I had only a few more months left to live alone as a single gal, I had to relish every moment. But was it appropriate? After all, I wasn't technically single; I was engaged. "Are you sure it's not selfish?"

"Don't move," she said. "Not until you have to."

And with that, my mind was made up. I would beat the system: live independently *and* get the guy. What a deal.

But as it turned out, none of this fretting was necessary.

I knew from the get-go that dating Hank and company meant the possibility of a serious move; not just a simple address change within the same zip code, but a major relocation that suited the collective needs of the traveling circus. I just never thought it would happen so soon. Silly me. Hank, June, John, and I were four ambitious, career-minded adults who all happened to work in the same transient field. Someone was bound to be offered a better job at some point and want to take it. And that's exactly what happened.

Hank got an offer.

"In Texas?" I reeled. We'd barely been back from Memphis long enough to announce our engagement, and now this? Was I ready to leave my city before my next cup of coffee? Things were moving fast.

I imagined giving up the romanticized image of my city self: the professional woman who felt oh-so-*Cosmo* walking through the city's financial district on her way to work, tall heels click-clacking, cable cars ringing in the distance, juggling latte, the *San Francisco Chronicle,* and my faux Prada purse.

Of course, because it was my future husband suggesting the move, I thought it only fair to honestly assess my situation: While I love this glamorous picture of myself, my city life doesn't always look like this. There were many days when I'd be taking shortcuts through grungy side streets, stepping over rotting chicken parts and used condoms, and then waiting with the hostile, coughing masses to crowd onto the BART train. Those were the days I'd reapply my Purell hand sanitizer more than my lipstick. During the long commute home, I'd think, *This city-living shit is overrated.*

But every urban area has its ugly underbelly. That's something you just accept when you live in a big city. And I decided many years ago that the grime was worth the beauty. Cities can be hard and cruel, but for me the intense sounds and smells, the soulful energy and passion I witnessed every day, invigorated me. I was at home in the Bay Area and had no truly compelling reason to leave.

But now it wasn't just me.

I had never been to Texas, but I had a strong opinion about Lone Star living, and it wasn't favorable. It's like how my mother feels about Las Vegas: She detests the place and bashes it without hesitation, but has she ever actually been there? No. And she has no idea what she's missing, unlike my stepsisters and I, who adore Vegas for its twenty-four-hour room service and rooftop bars. My Texas prejudice was similarly not grounded in experience, so I allowed myself to entertain the thought. I made a pro and con list.

The cons were considerable. Suddenly, loving Hank wasn't just about becoming a stepmom; it also meant moving halfway across the country and leaving my family, my cool urban landscape, and my career. *Gulp.*

The pro list looked like this:

1. We could buy a house.
2. With a driveway.
3. And more than one bathroom.

4. We could actually afford the mortgage.
5. I could reinvent myself.

I wrestled with number five. Reinvent myself? Okay, but is that necessary—now? I'm thirty-five. I've kind of just figured out who I am, and I actually like myself. Shouldn't I reserve an identity upgrade for midlife, after I've made more mistakes and I'm lugging around some serious regret? And what about my career? I'm finally making a large enough salary that I don't have to charge groceries to my credit card.

Could I adjust to becoming a wife, a mother, and a *Texan* all in the same year?

I needed some convincing.

So Hank and I revised the list. Here's what we came up with: We weren't really moving to "Texas" (flash to James Dean stretched out in a desolate rural landscape on a movie poster for *Giant*); rather, we were relocating to *Austin,* a town we'd heard was something like Berkeley: hip and artsy, the breeding ground of strong opinionated women like Molly Ivins and Ann Richards. Austin was swarming with musicians, liberals, and physically fit people. "Listed as one of the most athletic cities in the county," my mother enthused after doing some supportive research. We'd also read it was a safe city for the kiddos, yet still sophisticated and musically vibrant, so it would satisfy our intellectual and cultural curiosities—minus some of the Bay Area's sketchy mean streets. What's more, I could try out a new wardrobe, one that reflected the Austin scene: Western glam and country funk.

Above all, it would be exciting. That's what got me. I'm always up for an adventure.

Hank called a family meeting. Sitting in June and John's chaotic, kid-filled living room, Hank appealed to June, who had been making recent hints that she was itching to leave California and move back toward the equator—somewhere hot and affordable, even if it meant a small town with a rinky-dink TV market. He presented his case for Austin, and she was open to it. Texas fit her criteria. Yet June wondered if there was somewhere else that might suit us better. Before I knew it, Tampa, Atlanta, and the Cayman Islands were all on the table. *Wait a minute*, I thought, *the world is* not *our oyster*. My head was spinning. *This is crazy.* I looked around the room—at June and John, whom I hardly knew; at the gang of kids running in and out of the room; at Hank, whom I had just agreed to marry—and I thought, *How did I end up here?* It's hard enough making intelligent decisions for myself. Three weeks into a marriage proposal and I'm participating in group decisions affecting the careers of three other adults and the emotional needs of four kids I haven't known as long as most of my shoes. *Am I insane? Am I really doing this?* I wondered. Sensing my unease, John offered me a Bud Light. I sucked the can dry. After a strained two hours, my new gang agreed to hit the road again—this time, bound for the Hill Country, where we would set up our own version of life on the ranch.

The Plan: Hank and I would go first. The boys would follow in a month and their mother, John, and the wee ones would arrive shortly after that, or as soon as June found another TV anchoring position.

When I got back to my clean, still apartment later that night, I called Mom and asked, "Do you think I should really do this?"

She gave me the same piece of advice she's given me throughout my life: "Go with your gut."

"I feel like I'm going to throw up. Does that mean I should stay in California?"

"Sweetie, I can't decide for you. This has to be about you and Hank."

I was on the verge of tears. "The thought of moving away from all of you makes me sick. If only you'd come, too, then I'd be fine."

"I'm sure Hank would love that," she teased.

"He *would*. He's very nervous about asking me to leave my family behind. He knows how close we are."

"Of course we'll all miss you terribly, but you're just a quick plane ride away, and as long as you don't move next to George and Laura, I'll visit as often as I can."

That night I had fitful sweats. I woke the next morning exhausted and clammy, yet resolved. "Fine," I grumbled out loud as I turned on the shower. "I'll do it. I'll move to bloody Texas."

As I stood under the hot water, I patted myself on the back for coming to my own conclusion independent of everyone else's opinion. While I wasn't elated to plan my life around Hank and June's preference for Southern living (at least we weren't moving to Biloxi), there was no way I was going to trade in the Pacific for some dusty corner of Texas unless I was convinced there were real advantages. I would have preferred to uproot my life for New York or Paris, but Texas called, and I decided that I'd make it work for me. Was I feeling a little pressure? Sure. Was I worried I'd turn resentful? A little. Was I devastated to leave my world behind? Of course. Was I exhilarated by the newness of it all? Absolutely.

Friends and family suggested that maybe I was biting off a teensy-weensy bit too much, even for a wannabe overachiever like myself.

"That's a whole lot of new," said my therapist. "Are you sure you want to take all that on at once?"

Apparently, mental health professionals keep an eye out for patients experiencing one of the following line items on the "Stressful Situation" list:

1. Getting married
2. Adding children
3. Relocating

4. Changing jobs
5. Unexpectedly losing a family member

She pointed out that number five was the only thing between my first nervous breakdown and me. "Not all the excitement at once," I joked. *Death can wait.* But she had a point, so I forged ahead before I could turn back.

Change is healthy, no?

I began wrapping things up. I tearfully resigned from my job, began packing, and made an emergency appointment with my hairstylist. (Who leaves town with an outgrown haircut?) I sat in Nicki's chair and told her the complicated details while she snipped my hair.

"So, when are you going?" she asked.

"Soon. At the end of the month. It's madness," I said. "Here I was, thinking I'd be preoccupied with planning an over-the-top wedding. That's not even on my mind now. I've got too many other things to worry about. Like finding a Texas stylist who doesn't want to tease my hair."

"Good luck with that." She snickered. Nicki is also a native Californian and shared my opinion of Texas. "So, when's the big day?"

"Our moving day?"

"No." She laughed. "Your *wedding* day."

"Oh." I stared at my tousle-headed reflection. "I have no idea. Let's just focus on my bangs."

There were moments when I was so consumed with leaving town, my job, and my family that I completely forgot about our engagement. I'd look down at my left hand and be startled to see a line of diamonds dancing across my ring finger. *Oh, yeah, that's how I got into this mess,* I'd think. I was thrilled to be marrying the man of my dreams, and I expected that my life would change, but my long-delayed engagement was getting ignored. *Where's my party?* I shouldn't be consumed with anything other than such wedding worries as *Am I actually going to wear a traditional wedding gown with a bow on the ass?* I left the salon and marched straight down to Walgreens, where I bought my first bridal magazine. I thought, *I can be a self-absorbed bride just like the best of them!* I sat outside and tore through the pages until panic set in. What if Hank and I get all the way to Texas and the stress of forwarding our mail and sharing hand towels drives us apart? What if we sling deplorable insults at each other, like *Whiten your teeth! Your incisors look like candy corn!* and have to call off the wedding? What if we split up before the boys even get there? I forced a gruesome daydream: I'd be jobless and alone, away from my old family, abandoned by my new family, eating greasy pig-belly tacos on a lonely park bench with big, ugly hair.

I had a solution.

"What do you think about getting married *before* we leave San Francisco?" I suggested to Hank as we sauntered toward the Ferry Building. It was an unusually warm evening, so we'd decided to take the boat home.

"In the next two weeks? How are we going to pull that off? Plus, I thought you wanted a la-de-da wedding?"

"How about a pre-wedding, just to get the legal stuff out of the way, and we'll save the big deal ceremony for later?"

This was my logic: I explained that except for my panicky moment flipping through *Modern Bride* magazine, I wasn't overly concerned that our relationship would fall apart, yet we did have some potentially challenging trials ahead that a marriage license might ease. And the TV station had just done a series on health care and how vulnerable one can be without insurance—like me! I was moving to Texas without a job. What if I got stung by a scorpion? I returned to my dire daydream—I'd be jobless, alone with bad hair, and dying on a park bench.

I said to Hank, "Let's just bite the bullet. Make the commitment now, before we leave and buy a home and the circus comes to town. Then on those days when I want to run away, I won't. And you won't. We'll be married and we'll be in this together and you'll be bound by law to stay with me no matter how crazy I become." (Crazy seemed to be already happening, seeing as how I'd gone from avoiding the state of matrimony to wanting to enter into it twice within the same year.) But in case this wasn't a strong enough argument, I added, "And if I become terribly sick, I can get medical attention from professionals. Unless you want to change my bed pan?"

"First of all," Hank said, "you need to lay off the melodrama. Second, don't you know I love you because you're already crazy?" Hank is a practical man. I think it was actually the issue of health insurance that sealed the deal.

"So, you're in?"

It took me only a week to pull it together. By the following Friday we were walking through the heavy golden doors of San Francisco's crown jewel: City Hall. We were fifth in line to exchange vows at the top of the stairs in the building's royal rotunda. With our traditional wedding celebration postponed until we were settled in Austin, I chose to postpone the white, as well. I wore a vintage cranberry-red dress with three-quarter sleeves, a suggestive neckline, and a high, gathered waist to celebrate the occasion. I found it at a consignment shop on Fillmore Street for fifty dollars, and together with the matching patent-leather chunky-heeled Mary Janes and velvet jacket, the dress felt as urban-chic as our downtown nuptials. Hank and I sat snuggled together in the marriage-license holding tank studying the suggested vows.

"So, are we going to read these, or do our own thing?" I asked. I was getting nervous. Maybe this was a bad idea. Not the marriage, just

moting vasectomy reversal. Things get really strange once you leave
Bay Area.

Hank insisted we focus on getting to our new home with no lol-
gagging along the way. The man does not share my enthusiasm for
ross-country shopping. I welcome every pit stop or bathroom
reak as an opportunity to purchase tacky trucker hats and tallboys,
nd to chat it up with the broken-down attendant behind the counter.
Hank would rather keep the engine running and be back on the road
before the toilet stops flushing. He's big on efficiency. But at some
point we had to run out of road trip essentials: turkey jerky, Fritos,
smokehouse almonds, and bottled water. And when we did, Hank
agreed to pull off at some nowhere stop so we could restock and
stretch our legs.

We took the first exit, which dropped us right into a little town
filled with turn-of-the-century buildings, but no people. Several spooky
Dawn of the Dead minutes of driving around later, we found ourselves in front of a small grocery bearing a striking resemblance to the
general store in *Little House on the Prairie*. I left Hank in the gravel
parking lot filling up the gas tank while I wandered around inside. I
giggled at the oversized dills floating in the pickle jar, along with the
outdated candy section (Bit-O-Honey and ChickOnAStick). But the
deeper I got into the aisles, the less appealing and more remote this
place became. I suddenly felt very far from home. My chest tightened
up. *I'm not going back.* I heard a woman walk up behind me and say,
"Honey, can I help you with something?"

I turned around to find a sweet-faced, white-haired woman in a
blue store uniform. She sort of looked like my grandmother (although
my gram would never wear a blue uni; she was more apt to wear
lavender-colored sweats with a string of pearls). I started to tear up.

"No, thank you," I said. "I'm all set." But I wasn't. I turned around

the accelerated schedule. Our parents certainly thought so ("We're getting premarried this week—surprise!") and were a bit miffed that our
sudden announcement didn't afford them enough time to be present.
But with so many people already participating in our relationship, I
thought it was sweet that this moment belonged to just Hank and me.
But now, sitting on cold metal chairs, I really felt I could use some
parental advice. When Dad walked in I let out a sigh of relief. Just
hours before he'd rearranged his work schedule so he could be with us.
We needed a witness—and sometimes a girl just needs her father.

Dad joked, "So, Hank, you sure you want to do this? It's not too
late to back out."

"Yes, sir." Hank laughed. "I can't wait to marry your daughter."

"Okay," he said. "Don't say I didn't warn you."

Hank squeezed my hand. "When it comes to the vows, say whatever you want to."

I looked down at the sheet. *The contract of marriage is most solemn
and is not to be entered into lightly, but thoughtfully and seriously
with a deep realization of its obligations and responsibilities . . . marriage is a full-time job.*

I looked over at Hank in his Southern-gentleman clothes and
imagined seeing this man every day. "I'm ready," I said. And then
they called our names.

Before I knew it, a guy in a black robe was delivering the custom-
ary line, "I now pronounce you husband and wife." We were at the
top of the sweeping marble staircase, framed by columns, in a pool of
natural light pouring in from the tall windows of the rotunda. A small
crowd of Asian tourists had gathered below and were smiling up at
us and taking pictures. Dad looked proud, standing off to the side.
Hank and I gave each other a surprised and hurried kiss, and I
thought, *I'm glad we're going to do this again, because I have no idea
what just happened.* Still, I was overjoyed, and relief washed over me.

By the time we'd gotten to the first floor, another couple had taken our place. I was still in shock, and Hank looked similarly dazed. We stared at each other with wide eyes and squealed in unison, "Oh, my God. We're married!" Hank scooped me into his arms and blasted through the front doors and out onto the street. "I love you, my beautiful wife," he declared. We kissed for a long time on the front steps of City Hall, in front of buses and honking cars. Dad snapped photos until Hank announced, "I think it's time for martinis," and then the three of us headed off into the fog.

The following Sunday, Hank and I stood outside my one-bedroom apartment. I'd just handed over my keys to the landlord and I looked up at my window—curtainless and no longer mine. Hank's two cats and all my clothes were crammed into my four-door sedan. My furniture and the contents of Hank's loft were already on the road in a company-paid moving truck. It was time for us to leave town, and my family was lined up on the sidewalk and poised for an emotional scene. *Why am I doing this, again?* I thought. *I miss them already.*

Breathe. Don't cry.

"It's not irreversible," Mom said when I dove into her arms. "You can always come back to California."

We drove away and I forced myself to be strong. I stared out the window and choked back the tears. *This better fucking work out.*

AUGUST

The Calm Before the St

California and Nevada were behind us. It was late morning Flagstaff, Arizona, and we were heading toward the high desert, riding in comfortable silence and sipping coffee. I gazed out the window at the endless expanse of dry earth and open sky. My eyes fixed on a line of ladders, stuck in the dirt and perched on the horizon, reaching up to the clouds. They reminded me of a Georgia O'Keeffe painting hanging on my mother's office wall—pink ladders floating in a turquoise sky. I took seeing these now as a good omen and scribbled a description of the image on an empty scone bag.

Up ahead lay an open road and a new life. I felt good, present. A not-in-a-hurry-to-get-there-because-I'm-already-here kind of feeling. We passed a billboard welcoming us to Knife City, and then another

and walked down the aisle and out the front doors. Now I was really crying.

"Baby?" Hank was checking the oil. He came toward me and I smashed my runny nose right into his chest.

"I can't believe I left everything behind—my family, my life. What was I thinking?"

Maybe I did take on too much, I thought. Away from my place, my people, my corner grocery store, I was so alone. *Out here,* I thought, *I'm just Ms. No-Name.* I could die out here and no one but the buzzards would care.

"You'll be fine. You'll be great. *We'll* be great," Hank said soothingly.

Somehow that reassurance wasn't enough in my weakened state. Hank took me by the shoulders. *Was he going to slap me out of it, like in some bad-guy movie?* He looked into my squinty eyes. "You will do great things because that's just who you are," he said.

I'd be stupid not to love this man. Note to self: When I doubt my decision to turn my life upside down, remember these Hank moments.

I pulled myself together and looked him in the eye. "There better be more places to shop than *this* in Austin."

As I've mentioned, my understanding of where we were headed was a bit limited. I'd had my first encounter with "real" Texans when I was in my early twenties and I'd gone to Maui to escape the mainland constraints of my rough dorm life (free food and no parental control) and enjoy the aloha lifestyle. I landed a job at an oceanfront bar where I was mentored by Angela and Ginny, two raucous Dallas gals who welcomed me with well-oiled, open arms. Their signature drink, the Mind Eraser, and their stories about home resembled nothing I recognized. This Texas they spoke of—cowboy boots and rodeo trophies—seemed as far away to me as the Emerald

City, and once I got off the island I had no intention of ever making it there.

We arrived in Austin late on the fourth night of our drive. Step one was to check into the Extended Stay Hotel on the outskirts of town; step two was to haul in our overnight bags and start making generalizations: *Extended Stay Hotels smell like livestock in Texas.* As soon as the door locked behind us, I collapsed on the king-sized bed, and Hank was immediately beside me. "This is just temporary," he promised. "Steve will be here in the morning."

Steve was our real estate agent. I had spoken to him on the phone before leaving the Bay Area and he assured me that he would have a list of houses to show us as soon as we arrived in town. I had given him distinct guidelines: Put me in the suburbs and I'll put a gun to my head. I don't do cookie-cutter houses in cul-de-sacs; I want a house with character, something with at least three bedrooms and, for God's sake, enough square footage so I can hear myself think.

Steve was on it. When I opened the hotel room door the next morning, he squealed an enthusiastic "You're here!" and attacked me with a hug. He was in his late thirties—fit, tight jeans, tucked-in T-shirt—all smiles and hand-clapping.

"Where's Mister?" He was referring to Hank.

"He went to work."

"Oh, goody. I have you all to myself. Lady, we're going to get you out of this"—he lowered his voice—"*dump* in no time at all."

He was a little over the top, but he was the only person I knew in Austin, so for me, it was decided—Steve was going to be my new best friend. Plus, what an unexpected treat—I'd moved from San Francisco to brawny Texas and my new fab Realtor was gay. I felt right at home.

My new BFF had been doing his homework. He had found us at least fifteen houses to consider, all within five miles of downtown and all over thirty years old. On our first day out, I sat strapped into the passenger seat, map in hand, while Steve tailgated every senior driver he encountered.

"I'm right behind you, sweetie." He gave his white Mazda some gas and passed the Lincoln in front of us, one agile hand on the wheel, the other holding his caramel macchiato.

I confided in Steve my concern that once I'd seen Austin by morning light, I'd want to go crawl back under the covers. What if I hated it?

"I'm not worried," he said. He was excited to show off his town, and confident that I would love it.

Steve explained that Hank and I were staying on the east side of town, near the airport—"A growth area," he said. I suppose that was code for something else, because so far, it didn't look like anywhere I wanted to grow, especially old.

We headed down Riverside Drive and toward downtown. We passed chain restaurants, new condos, Mexican take-out joints, and the most concentrated number of pawnshops I'd ever seen. So far, not so good. And then we went around a bend and *pop!* There was the downtown skyline, and an indigo line zigzagging through the center of town.

Water.

I let out a huge sigh of relief. I'd agonized about moving to the heart of the country, where I'd be landlocked and smothered by the heat. "I might suffocate," I'd told Hank. "It could screw up my equilibrium and shut down my organs."

I've always lived near a major body of water—the salty and power-ful kind—and I realized now that I equate the blue stuff with freedom and possibility. So as soon as Lady Bird Lake came into view, I calmed down. It's not the roaring Pacific, but it's got movement. I could tell it was going somewhere, in a lazy kind of way.

"Looks more like a river than a lake," I remarked.

"You're a smart one," said Steve. "It *is* technically part of the Colorado River."

That's more like it, I thought. The Colorado is a serious river, not like the kind you see in old Westerns, where there's hardly any water and it's easy to cross on horseback. It starts in New Mexico and drains into the Gulf of Mexico. I no longer felt trapped. If my new life turned truly ugly, I could always paddle my way out of here.

As we cruised through downtown, I had to suppress more than a few chuckles. The building facades looked like they belonged on a shoot-'em-up cowboy-movie set. *Am I actually living here?* I thought. And, *Did that guy's T-shirt really read: TEXAS IS BIGGER THAN FRANCE?* And *Wait, there's another one: FUCK YA'LL . . . I'M FROM TEXAS!* Just when I started to feel like I was scanning the surface of another planet, we turned another corner and—poof!—we could have been in San Francisco, for all the cafes, boutiques, wine bars, art galleries, and tattoo parlors. And hip-looking people! I thought, *Okay, maybe I'll love it here.*

The neighborhoods Steve showed me were all within a ten-minute drive from the lake. Good boy. And one could find street parking without circling the block for an hour—even better. But the houses we saw were not what I'd had in mind. When Steve said we'd be looking at a lot of ranch-style houses, I didn't realize he was referring to an architectural style made popular in the 1950s—more like a garage than a hacienda. It felt like we looked at about three hundred of them, and in every driveway we pulled into, I imagined I already lived there. *Was I happy to call this home, or did I want to burn the sucker down?* It's that gut instinct thing again.

On day one, I felt nothing, although I did come to understand how much I favor beauty over practicality. The one house I was slightly moved by had major structural damage, but I made an argument for it, anyway.

"Check this one off the list right now," Steve said as soon as we walked through the door. "I shouldn't have brought you here. Look at this floor. I can barely walk on it without getting dizzy."

"But look at the screened-in porch! And the stone fireplace!"

"It doesn't even work."

"So?"

By the end of the week I'd settled in quite well to my new routine of house-hunting and local trash talk with Steve. I was antsy to find a house and finally unpack, but I didn't want our outings to end. We were having tons of bitchy fun, so I encouraged Steve to keep talking and tailgating. We wound our way up into the neighborhood above Austin's cherished Barton Springs, where the locals lounge under oak trees and float in natural spring water year-round. Steve showed me several funky bungalow-style places, which I could maybe imagine living in. Perhaps I was being too cautious—but isn't this the way prospective buyers are supposed to act? I'd watched my Bay Area friends struggle for months—sometimes longer—before they made an offer on a house. Could the home-buying process in the Lone Star State be that different? I could tell that Steve was getting fidgety. All morning he'd been giving me a look like he wanted me to click my heels together and cry, *This is it! There's no place like home!*

Finally we pulled into the driveway of another so-so ordinary ranch house, except this one had a hydrangea-pink exterior. Steve said, "This just went on the market, hon. Do you like it?"

Hmm. "Let's take a look," I said. There was something about it that felt good, and once inside, I let out a little squeal of delight. The house was all 1950s retro with terra-cotta tiled floors, gallery lighting, walls painted different colors, and an expertly xeriscaped backyard. Still, I remained uncertain. Had I found *the one*?

It was hotter than ten kinds of hell (my new favorite Texas-ism) and my mind was fried, so Steve steered me back toward the car and took me to Curra's, renowned for their smooth and creamy avocado margaritas and something called *queso*. What's that, you ask? "You will ab-so-lute-ly die," is what Steve told me when I queried. He was beside himself that I'd never had either treat. "Poor thing," he said, shaking his head.

The only other time I'd heard of *queso* was from a producer named Will with whom I'd worked in San Francisco. He was from Houston and an okay guy, but I simply couldn't get past his dedication to slamming the "oversaturation of pretentious wine bars in this city."

"What Frisco needs," he explained, "is a *queso* bar. *Queso*," he explained, is a hot creamy cheese dip you eat with chips.

"Like Fondue?" I mocked. "You *do know* that you eat that with bread?"

"No, it's not like Fondue at all. It's totally different. It's amazing."

Whatever. I scoffed at this barnyard fool; he obviously had no appreciation for the sophistication of my City by the Bay. Looking back, perhaps that judgment was a bit harsh. I doubted his no-brainer dish could command a steady line of patrons, but now, sitting at Curra's with Steve, I witnessed firsthand the fervor with which Texans consume the unofficial state food (not unlike my new Memphis family and their Rotel).

"Yum," I said. *Wait a minute—this tasted just like Rotel. Was it the same thing?*

"Told you so." Steve took a sip of his avocado margarita. "Soooooo, are we ready to make an offer?"

"Just like that?"

"Dear"—he gave me a wry smile—"do you want to stay in that extended piece of crap forever?"

"I like the pink one."

"Done." Steve promised to get back to his office (after one more drinky-poo) and start the tedious process of making Hank and me proud owners of Texas land.

I was new to the world of home ownership. I'd always lived in apartments, where moving in was simple: Pay first, last, and security, and agree to a modest background check—just to make sure you didn't plan on turning the kitchen into a meth lab. It turns out that in Austin, where the housing market is alive and well, buying a house is almost as quick and easy as moving into a new apartment—just with a much bigger stack of paperwork. Steve took us out for champagne cocktails and made multiple toasts to himself about how fantastic he was.

"So, Mister, do you love me or what?" Steve winked at Hank.

I said, "I'm just relieved to have a permanent address before my two new stepsons arrive. I don't want all of us sleeping in the same king bed for *any* extended period of time."

"Jesus." Steve sprayed me with champagne. "I completely forgot you're a stepmommy."

Hank shot Steve a look.

"Well, I didn't *forget*. I was just so busy finding your wife a place to rest her pretty head, I put the two young ones out of my mind . . . temporarily."

"That's okay," I said to Steve. "So have I."

My mother has always told me, "If you don't take care of yourself, you're no good to anyone else." I love this advice, which was why I was hell-bent on taking care of the following before the guys arrived:

1. Buy a house (check).
2. Find a hairstylist,
2(b). and a female gynecologist.
3. Join a gym.
4. Get a new therapist.
5. Make a BFF.

I believe this is a good starter list for any woman new to a town (with or without stepkids on the way). In the absence of friends and family, it's important to find people to take care of you (your lady parts included). And I was amazed at how easy it was as soon as I started asking around. And that's because Texans are friendly—alarmingly so. I'd heard about this Southern hospitality thing, and it turns out it's not an urban legend. Perfect strangers will open doors for you. Receptionists remember your name and use it like they've known you forever. Hurried professionals tolerate uncertainty in the salad-bar line, and DMV workers make time to chat. Naturally, I was a bit suspicious. Strangers were looking me in the eye. *What do you want,* I wondered, *a piece of me?* I had some adjusting to do.

I began to understand why Southern boy Hank used to complain about a lack of civility in San Francisco: "People are so standoffish in this city. They don't know the first thing about chivalry or good manners." I guessed he was right, but I really didn't know any different. *What do these good manners look like, and do I not have them?* I found myself thinking.

I'd spent the majority of my adult life in a West Coast city, so I was used to existing as one of the masses. A big city swallows you up, and I learned to find comfort in drifting around without much interruption. Honestly, I thought that was just how people behaved: You pick and choose when you want to engage; you don't give it away for free; there is no opening up just for the sake of conversation.

Well, they don't have this rule in Texas. These folks like to *talk*.

On day five, I was lying on my back, staring up at a poster of a waterfall, when my new gynecologist asked me all about my life—and I'm not talking about her responsibility to ask about intravenous drug use or my preferred method of birth control, but about my career and my happiness and my decision to uproot my life.

"So why did you decide to move Austin?" she asked my vagina.

This is getting kind of personal, isn't it? I wanted to open up and get to know people, but *come on*. Although, I had to admit, I was lonely. Now that we'd signed all the necessary closing papers on the house, Steve didn't come around as much, and Hank was going to work every day.

Which reminds me—where was *my* career? I soon discovered the cold reality that many working women know too well—once you get off the merry-go-round, it's not that simple to get back on. I was now unemployed and depending on Hank to keep me properly fed and imbibed. Plus, I was "expecting." My stepsons, that is. Very shortly the boys would be taking up residence with us; surely there was work to do on this front. My girlfriend Claire, back home, who had young boys, advised me to stock up on flushable bathroom wipes. What else? Put a basketball hoop up on the garage? Paint dinasours on the bathroom walls? I was at a loss, so I found myself spending endless afternoons in our new house, swatting at my worry moths and unpacking our combined loot—none of which required heels and a briefcase. I couldn't believe that just over a month ago I was producing big-time television and hauling in a decent amount of cash and now I was down to a hidden stash of quarter rolls for afternoon coffee and pedicures. Despite my mother's urging, I'd never been good at saving. How could I? Affording an enjoyable lifestyle in a city isn't exactly a money-saver. I had Suze Orman's book on being a fabulous woman who's smart with money, but it sat on my coffee table for several months before I opened it up, and then I was too busy to read it. I had social engagements to attend.

Unlike Suze, I hadn't planned for my future, so when Hank accepted the Austin job offer and we decided to move, I scrambled to find a well-paying job. But we were on such a mad dash to get out of town; there was hardly any time for a phone interview. After several rushed career-counseling meetings with trusted colleagues and friends—*Okay, I have only five minutes. What should I do?*—I decided to wait to look for work until after we got to Austin. Some called this foolish, others thought it daring, but everyone agreed—it was out of character for me to resign (if only temporarily) from my career. My work defined who I was: Izzy, the TV producer. Yet here I was: the little lady at home, polishing the silver and putting it away in its mahogany buffet. In the absence of a job, I decided to take up whistling. It passed the time, and I liked the idea of resurrecting a dying art (like calligraphy). Perhaps there was money to be found in making it stylish again.

Just this morning, Hank pulled out of the driveway, a luxury we never had in the Bay Area, and I waved a limp wrist from the front door. He looked back at his fashionable city girl, now wearing an oversize maroon fleece vest, something I found myself doing with disturbing frequency these days. (*Fleece in August?* Yes—to battle the triple-digit heat outside, Southerners [and this includes my husband] blast their homes, offices, and malls with subzero air-conditioning. "If I get pneumonia," I complained to Hank, "it's your fault.") Even I hardly recognized this pathetic Lands' End version of myself. I watched his car disappear down the block and looked down into my coffee cup, imagining myself filling it up with something stronger. *What if I become one of those stay-at-home vodka moms?*

I shuffled back inside the house and shouted, "How has this become my life?"

I called my ex-colleague Kate; she was drowning in work and low on sympathy.

"So, you have the house to yourself and you're wearing comfortable clothes? That sounds amazing."

I was standing in the bathroom in front of a full-length mirror, looking at myself in checkered pajama bottoms, with wild hair and chapped lips.

"I'm not sure you're seeing the whole picture," I said.

"Why don't you just take this time to figure out what you want to do next . . . enjoy the quiet . . . paint a wall . . . find yourself."

I found myself at Bed Bath & Beyond in the middle of the day.

Before I offend a large population of women who shop at this fine establishment, including my own friends and family, let me state that buying towels is a perfectly acceptable thing to do. It's just that after many years of working ten hours a day in the frenzy of a loud newsroom where someone's always shouting "We're LIVE in two minutes!" and where seconds mean everything and everyone's writing, editing, and running in a panic right down to the wire . . . Bed Bath & Beyond was just a little too quiet, unless you count that appalling smooth jazz piped in through the vents.

I will not let this be the sound track of my death, I thought. *I am better than this fleece vest.*

How many women have reached their personal breaking point at a mini-mall, standing over the scented candles?

I turned to the woman shopping next to me and said, "You know, I'm just not ready for total domestication."

She misunderstood me. "I'm sorry? I'm not sure what aisle that's on."

Well, I wasn't going to wait around to find out. It was time to get back to my career—or at least a respectable wardrobe. I put the window treatment down and whistled right out the door.

The very next day I updated my résumé and took a shower before noon. By two o'clock I hadn't found a job, so I began fretting about the boys moving in, and by three I was downright hysterical.

I'd been absorbed with the temporary loss of my earning potential, but the real challenge to my identity would be adding two young men down the hall. I mean, I didn't know how to be *married*—how was I going to manage kids? I started running around the living room like a cat caught in the wrong house. I was so accustomed to having my private space with a lock on the door. I feared that sharing the house with Hank and his sons would feel like an invasion. Where would I go when the noise got too loud? Where would I go to . . . escape? Plus, I'd heard the rumors—boys are hygienically grotesque. I stood motionless in my maroon fleece, paralyzed by the impending threat of dirt.

I'd already had many big-girl talks with my friends about leaving my scum-free life behind. "You can do this," my wise friend Beth told me. "You're thirty-five. Cleanliness isn't everything."

"Then why do they compare it to godliness?"

I understood that Hank came with two sons and that filth and chaos were potentially part of the deal. But now it really started to sink in. What's going to happen to all my pretty things? They've never even been exposed to *cat hair*. And what about my sanity? I can maintain the mess in my head only as long as my environment is orderly. Alarm bells went off. *Prepare for attack!* Could I ask the boys to wear gloves indoors? Should I wrap all the furniture in plastic?

"That's a classy look," my father teased. I decided to give Mom a break and lay my neurosis on him for a change. I'd called him from the cleaning aisle of Walgreens. "Why don't you just get rid of the furniture altogether and do the minimalist thing? That'd be easier."

"Thanks, Dad."

I'd read about a new sector of uptight professional couples who waited until their late thirties and forties to have kids. By that time, they'd made a bunch of money and dumped it into high-end interior design, collectible art, and signature pieces that probably competed with their children for attention. In an effort to preserve their "adult environment," they asked their kids to play in the basement. *Now, that is obsessive.* Plus, Steve hadn't been able to find us a house with a basement (that's more of a Midwestern thing), so that wasn't really an option for us.

I spent the rest of the afternoon unpacking boxes and strategically placing my favorite bowls, vases, and decorative dishes high on a top shelf where clumsy boy hands were unlikely to go.

By the end of the day, I was exhausted and out of hiding places. It was fairly easy to keep Gram's china protected by stashing it away, but what about the rest of the house? How was I going to keep order? Maybe I could rope sections off and hire a bouncer? And then it hit me, from somewhere in the back of my mind . . .

I'm afraid of losing myself. That's what this is all about. Not protecting my pretty things, but preserving my pretty, single self.

Thankfully, my preteen stepkid self provided some much-needed perspective, *Get over it, girl.*

Maybe I hadn't planned on becoming a stepmom, but I did indeed say "I do." The boys, on the other hand, had had no say in the matter. They didn't ask for a stepmom, especially one with controlling, germophobe tendencies. So, as much as I don't want kid grime all over my furniture, these boys probably don't want any more mess, emotional or otherwise, in their lives, either. *Stop worrying about what they're going to bring in through the door,* I thought. *Just open it wide and ask them to wipe their feet before coming in.*

So that's what welcome mats are for. I wondered if Bed Bath & Beyond had any.

SEPTEMBER

Setting the Rules

Hank and I stood at the airport on a Friday night, waiting for the boys. I was dressed for the occasion: signature ruby lipstick, my grandmother's 1950s jewels, and impossibly tall heels. I decided to embrace my new stepmom role and do this *mi casa es su casa* thing right by welcoming the boys in style. I'd made a reservation at a new, top-rated restaurant in a trendy part of town, and as soon as we got all their ragtag luggage in the car, we were headed that way.

I saw The Tall One first—or rather, I saw his hair; it adds a good five inches to his height. Even though every adult in his life has strongly suggested he'd look more attractive if he brushed it, he insists on maintaining the homeless look. Shuffling behind him was The Young One, weighed down by his two-ton backpack. He walked forward, head down, absorbed in his *SkyMall* magazine and dragging his stuffed lobster on the ground. They both look just like their mother—caramel coloring, dark curly hair, and almond-shaped eyes. Hank, who is cracker-white and bald, has passed on nothing of his looks, and I've joked that when the three of them are together Hank could be mistaken for their church counselor. I tried looking at them through the eyes of the other passengers and found myself thinking, *They are pretty cute kids.* Awkward, disheveled, and a bit orphanlike, but cute. Hank and I watched them for a moment until they spotted us and broke into giddy grins.

The Young One was in Hank's arms first.

Hank enveloped him. "Hi, baby, how was your flight?"

Baby. Hank uses this term of endearment for The Tall One, The Young One, and me. I adore him for it. I love that my Southern husband, strong and masculine, has no reservations about addressing his two sons with such sweet and gentle affection. Hank credits *his* father, Big Hank, who still calls his adult sons "darling."

Before The Young One could answer, The Tall One took the opportunity to break the tender-loving mood.

"He got in trouble for pressing the flight-attendant button too many times. And for talking too loud."

"Shut up," The Young One hissed.

I could see from Hank's expression that he was gearing up for a line of questioning that could lead to disciplinary action before we even left the gate. *Dear God,* I thought. *These two don't waste any time before raising their father's blood pressure.* I couldn't bear an argument within the first five minutes of their arrival, so I stepped in. I smiled wide and said, "Welcome to Austin, guys. Let's get your bags and go out for a celebratory dinner."

Stepmom Rule Number One: Kids do not appreciate fancy dinners as much as adults do.

It turns out the kids were tired and grumpy and not impressed with the exotic flavors of the Pacific Rim. (What did they expect? Steak and beans their first night? How cliché.) Instead of tuna tartar and wild mushroom dumplings, they wanted to go home and hit the sheets. What a couple of party poopers!

I couldn't even tempt them with chocolate crème brûlée.

"Sounds nasty," said The Tall One.

How quickly my welcome-home bash had become a bust! *I know they're exhausted, but you'd think they could shake it off. It's Friday night!* I tried not to show it, but I was disappointed that the boys seemed to have no appreciation for the chichi evening I'd planned. The current wait for a reservation at this restaurant was over two weeks! Hank paid the bill before I could finish my wine and we headed home. *Had my charms as Daddy's girlfriend lost their potency?* I guessed so. Both boys were out cold in the backseat.

When we arrived at the house, the guys trailed inside without interest. Of course—how silly of me to expect more! Had I really imagined they might take one look at the artfully decorated living space and gush "*Man!* This color scheme is amazing! I love the crown molding and your clever mix of antique and contemporary pieces!" Instead, The Young One said, "Izzy, I gotta go. Where's the bathroom?"

As soon as the boys were tucked away in their new rooms, I crawled into bed, restless and let down. I'd spent the last few days unpacking, organizing, and decluttering our collective stuff, preparing for the boys' big move-in day.

To understand the magnitude of this task, you need to know that when it comes to found objects, Hank's extremely sentimental and gets a little jumpy if you ask him to discard anything. Never mind that he's been hauling around unopened boxes of knickknacks for the past two decades. Actually, earlier in the week, I'd feared Hank and I might have our first married fight over a box of crocheted beanie hats he'd bought at a garage sale years before and refused to give up. He pulled one out of the box and held it up. "A hundred hats for a dollar!" he said enthusiastically, sounding not unlike The Young One. He thought this was a great deal. Actually, he was convinced of it. "They were hand knit by a guy in a nursing home." I took a deep breath. The hats looked like potholders, not something you'd wear on your head. What was I supposed to do with these? Hang them on a rack? Make a quilt? "Just leave them right in the box and store it in the garage," Hank declared. "Sure," I gave in. "Right next to the one with all the old wine corks in it."

Resigned to the fact that I couldn't sleep, I got out of bed and took a spin around our new home. In the faint light coming in through the front window, I saw that our house was beautiful. It was an aesthetically delightful mishmash of our furniture and art. Hank's dining room table sat alongside my gram's hutch. They looked like a matching cherry-wood set, even though his piece came from Memphis and mine from Pennsylvania. I'd created a "family" wall of old black-and-white photos to celebrate our entangled tree. A portrait of Margaret on her wedding day hung next to a shot of my mom and dad cutting their three-tiered cake. Hundreds of our books lined the walls, and my favorite cucumber-green couch faced out the front window, where I could sit and admire the twisted branches of our magnificent cedar elm.

I felt certain the boys would feel at home here. I was even more surprised that *I* already did.

Of course the boys hadn't noticed any of the decor. I'd gotten the house ready like two princes were coming to town. I'd bought five stems of overpriced royal blue hydrangea to brighten up the entryway when they crossed through the front door. I'd laid out fresh towels and lavender-scented soap in their bathroom (yes, they have their own), and I made sure we had proper kid-friendly refreshments at the ready. Yet not a peep of gratitude had escaped them. They just wanted to be directed to the toilet. *The little turds! I bet they didn't even flush!* I started to wish Hank had had girls. Girls notice the details.

And that's when that little voice cleared things up for me again:

Stepmom Rule Number Two: Don't act like a hostess, act like a mother.

These boys were not my guests, nor did their moving in qualify as a party. I was so busy ordering wonton chips at dinner that I'd overlooked the obvious: *This evening doesn't wrap up in three hours; they're staying for good.*

I tried to digest this, but I wasn't sure I could swallow it. The hostess act was so familiar, and the mom thing felt, well, unnatural. I reluctantly considered, *Perhaps I need to expand my role. But,* my ego whined, *I've always worked so hard at being the crowd-pleaser (with a notable fashion sense).* I stared out the front window, feeling quite moronic, like the kid I used to be: a nerdy adolescent in clothes that never quite fit, a girl who collected stickers, flunked out of Brownies, and played the clarinet. Badly.

I imagine it came as a big surprise to those who knew me when that I had evolved into an adult Miss Popular of sorts—an A-list invitee (okay, maybe a B-minus), a woman whose hobbies included going out on the town, and not much else. I credit my grandmother for this; she was a gal who never let her impeccable style get in the way of having a good time. At a young age, she impressed upon me the importance of social graces; setting a nice table and preparing huge amounts of food, even if it was only to invite the neighbors over to play inebriated blackjack. For years now, I've felt very much myself in my hereditary role as middle-class socialite, dashing out the door in high heels, hopping over cable-car lines, late for another BYOB soiree.

I went back to bed only to discover that Hank was still awake, too, fervently reading some political bestseller.

"What's keeping you up?" he asked.

"Nothing specific." I was too embarrassed to admit that my hopes for the evening had been dashed. I hadn't been elected hostess with the mostest. Boo-hoo for me. But what about the boys? Perhaps they were sleepless as well, wondering, *How has this become my life? What am I doing in this strange, unfamiliar house . . . in Texas?*

Perhaps I needed to rearrange my expectations of, and my approach to, these kiddos.

The next morning, Hank let me in on a little secret—his no-fail ritual for waking up his boys. He rifled through a box of CDs until he found what he was looking for. He put it in the changer, cranked the volume to ten, and hit play. "American Woman" by The Guess Who reverberated through the house. "American woman, mama let me be . . ."

Five minutes later, the boys shuffled out to the kitchen, humming along, and I was ready for them. I greeted them, saying, "Morning, guys. Welcome to your new home. Ready to get this party started?"

They ignored me and went straight for the fridge.

I waited a minute and watched them dig around. I continued, "Of course, I want you to make yourselves comfortable, but first, we've got a few house rules to discuss."

"Rules?" they looked over at me. What did this have to do with a party?

"Yes," I cooed. "This is going to be so much fun. Have a seat."

Earlier that morning I'd asked Hank to help me compile "The List." Maybe I was pushing it to have our first family meeting before breakfast, but I was in a hurry to make a point.

Hank and I were lying in bed when I said, "Since we're all living together for the first time, it's important we establish some ground rules, don't you think?"

Hank's head was buried in his pillow, but he uttered a groggy "Okay."

I jumped out of bed, started the coffee, and got my favorite notepad. (Hank is used to my early morning enthusiasm for making lists.) He rolled over, eyes still closed, and said, "What'd you have in mind?"

I was a smidge squirmy about setting the rules and regulations. I'd heard a stepparenting theory that discipline should be handled by—and only by—the bio-parents, and that I—non-bio—should stay out of it. I didn't like this advice at all. It made me feel completely powerless in what was supposed to be my home, too. *Should I just slap some tape over my mouth and lock myself in the closet until mealtime?*

I tested Hank: "Or maybe you should be the main law enforcer around here, and I should just advise you behind closed doors?"

"No. Don't be afraid to assert yourself. This is your house, too." The man is a gem.

I wanted to be sure: "Some of the articles I've read say that the kids will resent me if I try to parent them."

"They probably *will* resent you—and who knows for what. They're kids. They don't want anyone telling them what to do. Including me." Hank was wide awake now, and giving me a serious look. "Look, I want you to speak up. *I* don't want to be the bad cop all the time."

"Then kiss me," I ordered, and we came up with the following:

Izzy & Hank's House Rules (or, *Stepmom Suggested Rule Number Three*)

WE do not:

Run in the house

Leave doors open (one word: flies)

Make loud, disruptive, and inappropriate noise (yes, you know what
  that is)

Leave toys, books, backpacks, or shoes lying around*

Eat *anywhere* other than the dining room and kitchen (Hansel and
  Gretel got away with crumbs. You do not.)

YOU are personally responsible for:

Keeping yourself clean (no stinky clothes, bodies, or hair)

Making your own lunch (fasting doesn't count)

Managing your own laundry: wash it, dry it, put it away

Doing your own dishes (the sink is not your personal dumping
  ground)

We, as your parents, are not your maids or slaves. We are, instead,
responsible for giving you the tools to be personally accountable
and to succeed. We believe in you. Now get to work!

I know this sounds harsh, but it wasn't like we were sending them
to the basement.

We all signed the document (by the way, The Tall One has an impressive John Hancock), and I posted it high on the fridge. I felt
much better than I had twelve hours before. I was back in control.
Or so I wanted to believe.

"It's all about boundaries, isn't it? Living with kids?" I was talking
to Sarah, my new therapist, whose office is conveniently located half
a block down the street. In a crisis, I'm confident I could be beating
on her door in under ninety seconds.

---

*Parents reserve the right to apprehend any items found outside of your room and give
them away to more deserving children who won't leave them lying around.

She agreed: "Kids act like they don't want rules, but the truth is, they feel safer when they have them."

I explained that when all of us lived in the Bay Area, I didn't have much to do with their discipline. Why would I? Their mom made the rules at her house, and Hank made the rules at his. When I was staying over at the loft, I let him be the boss. I just smiled, stayed out of the way, and tried to keep the jokes flowing throughout dinner. If everyone's laughing amicably, I reasoned, no one's getting sent to his room. And I made sure Hank's drink was always refreshed, which seemed to help ease his temper about everyday annoyances like dirty gym socks in the kitchen or farting during a meal.

From what I could tell, this arrangement worked just fine from the boys' perspective. I recall about three months into my relationship with Hank, when I was standing in the loft's open kitchen chopping garlic and The Young One walked in.

"You don't live here," he started.

I thought, *Oh, great, this is where the kid tells me to leave and never come back.*

I smiled and said, "You're right."

"But sometimes you sleep over."

"That's true." I continued chopping. "Is that okay with you?"

He thought about it for a minute. "Yeah." And then he added, "Don't cut your finger." He turned and skipped into the living room. And that was that.

"But now you all live together," said Sarah, "and boundaries have shifted. Dynamics have changed."

Yes. And according to her, I get to enforce the rules like they're going out of style.

This feels a bit dangerous: transitioning from friendly girlfriend to warden. It's a tricky thing, parenting kids who aren't your own. *What if they tell me to shove it?* But they are living in my house, under my full-time care (at least until June gets here—which better be soon), so why wouldn't I assert myself? I didn't want to overdo it, though. This wasn't reform school; it was their house, too. Still, that didn't mean they could push me around. I practiced saying, "DO IT because I SAID SO!"

By the end of the week, I had worked up the confidence to try using my new commanding tone. Hank had just served up a plate of beef patties in the shape of Texas. He'd spotted them during his last grocery-store run and wrangled them right into the cart. They're called Bubba Burgers, and they also come in the shape of the U.S.A. *If only my left-wing veg-head friends could see me now.* Anyway, The Young One was wiping his boy grime all over my kitchen chair cushions. (Why hadn't I included proper napkin use in the rules?) I'd had these embroidered cushions for over a year, and even after hauling them across the country, they'd remained spotless. Within one week of letting The Young One sit his little cheeks on them, they'd turned into a soiled, smudged, and stained mess. I'd let it go at first. The voice of my mother lingered in my head, advising me to "pick your battles"; this had stopped me from shrieking in horror the first time I watched the kid pick up a saucy pork rib, lick his fingers, and go straight for the cushions to wipe them clean.

But now I could see the ketchup dripping off his beef burger, and I knew where it was going to end up. He took an oversized bite, leaving beef, bun, and gunk all over his face. He wiped his mouth with the side of his arm and I watched his hands move toward the cushion in slow-mo. Before he could do any more damage, I bellowed, "Use your pants!"

All three of my men looked at me with confusion.

"If you're not going to use your napkin," I explained calmly, "then wipe those dirty paws on your pants."

"That's gross," said The Young One.

"Gross?" I took a controlled breath. "I'll tell you what's gross—that nasty cushion you're sitting on. I've seen you smear pancake syrup, cereal milk, butter, and now ketchup on that thing. It's ruined. Consider this the last meal you eat seated in comfort."

I felt a little cruel making my first edict, but I also felt satisfied. When the meal was over, I removed the cushions from both The Young One and The Tall One's chairs and hid them behind the Christmas ornaments in the garage.

"There will be assigned seating from now on," I told Hank. "Parents get the padding, kids get the wood."

Stepmom Rule Number Four: Do as Madonna says and *express yourself*. Even if it seems ridiculous to others.

I could easily guess that establishing boundaries and rules was going to be one of my bigger challenges as a new stepmom. It helped that Hank supported me, not literally, but with a smile. I think he was relieved to let someone else dish out the tough love for a change, even if my behavior was a bit erratic. After the boys left the kitchen, he came up behind me and put his arms around me. "You're kind of psycho about those cushions, aren't you?" *Was it that obvious?* I was quickly growing impatient with the kids during mealtime, and who could blame me? We had sat down to family dinners for eight days straight and every time we did so, the boys fought over who had more food positioned next to them. ("Daddy, he's got the chicken *and* the rice next to him, and all I can reach is the butter!") I'd been forced to buy my first lazy Susan just to keep the peace. The wine was no longer an adequate coping mechanism. I needed a break.

I'm sure most experienced moms would find my exasperation with this routine family activity laughably premature. I can hear the mocking voice of one of my girlfriends, who has two kids (and a less-than-helpful husband), saying: *Eight days. Wow. That's all you can take? You'd better start thinking in terms of* years, *sweetie. You've got a lot of meals ahead of you.*

But that's just it! It was the monotony of setting the table and sitting down together *every single night* that was already making me nuts. I mean, how many meals can you share with the same three people before you grow bored with one another and slip and say jerky things you immediately regret? Already, my record for remaining tactful wasn't very good.

Of course Hank was used to the dinner routine. He'd been doing it for years. But I hadn't sat down to family dinner this often since I was a teenager living at home with my two stepsisters. I called my mom for advice. My stepdad, Stanton, a veteran newspaper reporter with a passion for the "goddamn truth," picked up the phone, and I knew he'd give it to me straight.

I said, "How did you guys get through all those family dinners?"

He laughed at me. "So the honeymoon's over, huh, kid?"

"You're hilarious. Seriously, our family had dinner together almost every night, and except for the times Mom busted us for dancing at the table or coughing up milk, I don't remember it being painful. So what's the trick? How'd you do it?"

"Alcoholism. I highly recommend it," he deadpanned. I heard his grin through the telephone. "You better talk to your mother, but she's not here. She's out with her girlfriends."

Girlfriends. That's what I needed. Or at least another stepmom to talk to.

"Surely, there must be a support group," I said to Sarah. Having been abandoned by Steve once he made his commission, I now thought of my shrink as my new best friend. Of course, I hadn't told her about her promotion in status because I was pretty sure she'd tell me I was getting too attached and launch into a discussion about how we need to keep our professional and personal lives separate. Therapists can be so prescriptive. "In California," I told her, "there's a support group for everything." I reasoned that there must also be a group for stepmoms.

Sarah said no. She had heard of no such thing.

"Really? No meetings in auditoriums with fluorescent lights and metal chairs?"

"It *is* a stepmom group you're looking for, right?"

I think, *If there is no local support group, then where are all the stepmoms commiserating?* Didn't I hear there are more step- and blended families in this country than ones subscribing to the old-fashioned nuclear model? If that's the case, where are all my stepladies, and why isn't this a mainstream discussion? Why aren't we on *Oprah*? I thought, *Surely my fellow sisters are not all battling it out with themselves in bathroom confessionals, as I do?* I envisioned millions of women muttering to their shower curtains, *How did I end up with another woman's kids?*

I left Sarah and walked home. I slumped down in Hank's worn leather chair, turned on the TV, and found myself scanning hundreds of cable channels, searching for a lively stepmom debate, led by a panel of experts, titled *Where Did My Old Life Go?*

Nothing.

Later I went looking for advice online. What I found wasn't very uplifting: Stepparenting sites droned on about survival secrets, coping mechanisms, how to experience more joy than pain, and just when we've lost all hope, how to start a one-on-one-dialogue with God to guide you through. *That's right. Help me, Jesus.*

Clearly, I had no idea what sort of miserable fate I'd signed up for. I figured it would be hard, but not war. Obviously, I didn't want to dismiss the attempts made by others to help, but at first glance the resources I stumbled upon were hardly encouraging. They were depressing.

Isolated. Underappreciated. Sacrifice. These were not words I wanted to use to describe my new life.

Enough! I thought. I called on my inner producer, opened up a promo script document on my PowerBook, and typed back in retaliation:

> *Burdensome and merciless.*
> *It's a grim and lonely road.*
> *How will she . . . and millions like her . . . ever survive?*
> *The Stepparenting Journey: To hell and back.*
> *A lifelong miniseries, starting tonight at eight.*

I got up, wandered into the bathroom, and looked in the mirror. If family dinners were already a challenge, what was I in for? I did not like this look of defeat on my face. I could see that if I wasn't careful, my two stepsons might inadvertently etch some very unattractive, very permanent frown lines around my mouth. Talk about resentment! I'd have to sell all their toys (and possibly their hair) to pay for Botox injections.

Until that happens, I pledged, *we're just going to have to laugh our way through it.*

I headed into the kitchen and opened up a bottle of California zinfandel (so what if it's only three o'clock; I'm not working). After my first slug, I recalled the summer my stepsisters and I were all in our early teens and my older stepsister, Piper, attracted a swarm of bees into her room. For several nights, Piper fell asleep to a strange humming sound coming from inside her wall. After many restless nights and no luck at identifying the source, she mentioned the buzz to her father, who investigated. When he discovered an extended family of bees living in the wall, he erupted in a panic, which turned into a battle royale when he uncovered a week's worth of dirty dishes and half-eaten sandwiches under her bed. He swatted and shouted something like, *"Clean this freakin' pig sty, goddamn bees!"* It was total chaos until the exterminator showed up. I'm sure Stanton wanted to ring Piper's neck. But instead of resorting to physical violence—good call—he settled on a lot of lip-biting as he caught his breath and calmed down (I totally relate; I've gone through an entire tube of lip-repair butter since the boys arrived). And that was it. The family moved on—until the next explosive event. I knew that if my stepdad could survive three girls, I would adjust to life with two boys. But I did need some company.

The next morning over coffee, I said to Hank, "I'm going to start my own online stepmom community."

"You're what?" He passed me a section of the *Times*.

"Yep. I can't seem to find any local group of women to talk to, which seems crazy to me. There's, like, five thousand mommy groups listed in Austin alone, never mind the gazillions of bio-mom chat groups online, but hardly a handful for stepmoms. What's that about? We don't *need* support because we're not *real* moms?"

"Good point," Hank indulged me.

"Right?" I was on a roll. "The tired perception that stepmothers are ill equipped and evil is wicked lame. How many stepmoms do you think live in this neighborhood?"

"I don't know, babe. Why don't you start knocking on doors and find out?"

"Maybe I will. I see a lot of kids around here. They can't all belong to matching DNA."

"Look out, ladies," Hank teased. "Feisty stepmom on the loose."

"And I bet I'm not the only one."

"What are you going to call it?"

"Call what?"

"Your community of desperate stepmoms." Hank was being sarcastic, but I was *desperately* serious.

"Don't mock me, mister. I've got the perfect name for it. I'm calling it Stepmother's Milk."

Hank put down the paper and looked at me like he'd eaten a bad tuna sandwich. "Milk?" He looked confused. "Milk makes me think of breastfeeding."

Oh, Hank.

"I'm a stepmother," I emphasized. "There will be no talk of lactating, suckling, or boobies in general."

He didn't look entirely convinced, so I explained that Stepmother's Milk could be a metaphor for how non-bio-moms nurture and care for one another while trying to raise someone else's kids. "You know, sometimes the best pacifier is the voice of another woman spilling the god-awful truth."

"Okay," he said. "I can dig it, but I still don't like the name. It's just not working for me." Like I hadn't heard him say that before.

Actually, the name Stepmother's Milk is not mine. It originated from a coping style my own mother developed when she took on Piper and Gigi in her mid-thirties. She was fortunate enough in those early years of strain and disillusionment to stumble upon a group of northern California stepmothers. They became fast friends and quickly recognized that just one hour of indulgent, brutal honesty together was an effective antidote for warding off stepmom insanity. On a regular basis they'd retreat to a neighborhood bar, order rounds of very strong cocktails, and laugh and groan over their similar "spilled milk." The Ramos Fizz quickly became their beverage of choice, as it was one of those cocktails that was socially acceptable to drink before noon. One wise woman in the group renamed the Fizz Stepmother's Milk and, over time, the name was expanded to whatever was in the glass. "I need some Stepmother's Milk" became basic code for "I need to get out of the house and away from my stressful life, now!"

A tradition was born.

Stepmother's Milk Ramos Gin Fizz

2 ounces of gin
1 tablespoon simple syrup
1 teaspoon lemon juice
1 small egg white
¼ teaspoon orange flower water
5 ounces milk or heavy cream
Seltzer water

Combine ingredients with 5 ice cubes in a cocktail shaker and shake for 2 minutes. Strain into a tumbler.

Three days later, I introduced myself to the unknown masses in cyberspace. I hoped that by telling my story, I'd draw out other women just like me who were looking for an intoxicating platform to vent.

I began writing . . .

As a mother, I'm a virgin. I'm a stepmother—a different breed of mother. Actually, I'm more like a *feeder,* because my unsteady parental worth and general acceptance (or scorn) is most often equated with the amount and quality of food I bring home from the organic market. Kids are such eco-terrorists these days—am I right?

She feeds me wild Alaskan salmon. She's good. She stays.

My mother, a stepmom to my two sisters, recently explained to me,

"We steps are women who have inherited children who, in turn, inherit us."

As the story often goes, we fell in love with someone who already had kids of his own, and suddenly they became our kids—kind of. And just that quickly, we're supposed to start behaving like an additional parent.

The rules of intuitive bonding can be a little tricky. After all, we did not carry these creatures in our swollen bellies, clean up their unoffending drool, or quietly read them *The Runaway Bunny*.

Instead, many of us were minding our own business, buying designer T-shirts, drinking double Americanos at sidewalk cafes, and taking our own sweet time finding the right man to marry. I didn't predict that once I found mine, he'd come with two small versions of himself and an ex-wife.

Not exactly the fantasy, but becoming a common reality for many of us.

I liken myself to the woman in some old childhood tale who opens her front door one morning only to discover—*egads*—that some bird with scrawny legs has dropped off a package. "Here you go," the stork says and flies off with a smirk before I can tell her she must have the wrong house.

Quite literally, I've been delivered the package deal.

And, as with most unexpected gifts, I'm excited, surprised, and a little apprehensive. Should I unwrap it? What if I don't like it? Can I give it back?

In many cases, we imagined having children one day. We just didn't necessarily expect half-grown kids to show up one Sunday afternoon dressed in jeans with holes in the knees. And want to stay past dinner.

Ladies, are you with me?

OCTOBER

Good-bye Fun Monkey

Finally! I wasn't alone! And not only that—apparently, my frantic stepmom behavior was normal. As soon as I started spilling, other stepmoms started *spilling back,* and some of them, like me, had already started their own online communities in both famed and obscure cities throughout the country. It was exciting and validating to hear from these ladies, but why hadn't I come across them before? I shared the news with my girlfriend Kate back home, who had since gotten engaged to her boyfriend, who had two daughters.

"*I've* never heard of any of these stepmommy bloggers," said Kate, who produced morning-TV news and prided herself on being up on the latest social trends.

"Well, they're out there," I told her. "Each time I write something, another woman pops out of the shadows with a similar story. Of course there aren't that many of us. The true babymaking network has us outnumbered." There was silence on the other end of the phone. I could tell she was skeptical. Either that or she had tuned me out and gone back to seeing what story CNN was running. "But here's the twist. A lot of women have started sending yours truly e-mails, asking for guidance. Like *I'm* some kind of expert. If only they had any idea how unqualified I am to give advice . . ."

"You're not totally unqualified." I had Kate's attention again. "You're a stepkid, too."

"Oh, yeah."

"See . . . at least you've got that going for you. Let's talk later. I have to go. An earthquake in Asia just hijacked my entire first segment for tomorrow morning."

How I missed the insanity and absurdity of the newsroom—the manic producers, the self-righteous directors, and the writers with ADD. Most of us are overly caffeinated, sleep deprived, and short-tempered. And because we're perfectionists at the mercy of the clock, we're constantly in crisis mode. Sure, it isn't for everyone, but sitting on the other end of the call with Kate, I ached for it.

I decided to shower, a daily event that I was beginning to push further and further back in the day. My hard deadline for personal cleanliness was five o'clock. That's when I picked up The Young One from his new after-school program, where we hoped he'd meet other kids who appreciated his love for the unconventional, like metal detectors and house trailers. (If The Young One had his way, he'd park an Airstream outside his bedroom window. His fascination with mobile homes is real, and I'm amused by it, even if I don't understand the appeal. "One of my future goals," he said last night at dinner, "is to own my own RV business. I'll call it Chrome Home.")

I left the house with my hair still wet and made the half-mile drive to his elementary school. The Young One was seated at a table by himself, surrounded by pencils and a mountain of wadded-up paper that would make an environmentalist cry. He heard me come in, looked up, and waved sheepishly. He went back to his sketchbook.

I signed him out from the attendance list and said hello to Patricia, the wiry woman in charge who recognized me as The Young One's keeper. Just a week into school and I was quickly becoming a regular. She said, "Can I talk to you for a minute?"

"Sure," I said, a little defensively. New to the parent network, I was self-conscious about procedure. I must have done something wrong.

"I need to talk to you about your son."

My son? I hesitated, unsure if I should correct her or let her think I was indeed the birth mother. Before I could make up my mind, she continued.

"He's a really smart kid." She looked at me.

"Yes?" *Where was she going with this?*

"But he gets really upset with the other kids when they don't share his interests."

Ah. Yes, I understood this one. I myself had disappointed him a few days before when I couldn't tell him how many species of albino animals exist in the world. But he already knew the answer! "And why," I asked him, "am I supposed to know this?"

I nodded and gave her the encouragement to continue. "Today he yelled at another boy because he didn't know what a Liberty gold coin was."

Liberty coin? Is that like a lucky penny?

Patricia continued. Her lips stretched uncomfortably tight. Her eyes bore into me. "I have to separate him when he's disruptive to the group this way. You know, he's a lot smarter than most of the other kids, especially the younger ones, and he has to understand that they're not necessarily interested"—she paused for emphasis—"in the same things he is."

Ouch. Patricia stared at me, her eyes asking, *So what are you going to do about it?* Me? I wasn't sure. I hadn't expected a confrontation today. I was just the kid's ride. So I took a breath to clear my head and tried to answer like a confident adult.

Wait a minute! Did she just say he *has* to understand? Who does this lady think she is? She doesn't get to stand here and tell me what's wrong with my so-called kid. I stood a little taller so Patricia had to lift her chin to meet my eyes. I held her gaze and then looked over at The Young One, sitting alone and scribbling away. I couldn't decide which one of them I was more irritated with. After all, it was The Young One's short temper and spirited intellect that had me standing here in front of Patricia, taking a disciplinary beating. I was very tempted to set the record straight. Listen, lady, whatever his problem is, don't blame me. I'm just the stepmom. You need to talk to his real parents. I haven't been around long enough to be blamed for his eccentric behavior or social immaturity. Instead, I dropped my smile and said, "I understand, Patricia. Thank you."

I could have played the stepmom card, but that would have been cowardly, even for me. Someone's got to stand up for the kid and, well, I was the only one in the room to do it. While I might not have influenced his crucial developmental years, I had to accept responsibility for the moment. If he's having a hard time adjusting to a new school, an unfamiliar town, or the fact that his parents live thousands of miles apart, I'm at least twenty-five percent accountable. I was, after all, part of the group decision to uproot and move his little life here.

When we got into the car, I said, "So, you had a tough day?"

"Yeah, I guess."

"You know," I said as gently as I could, "you probably shouldn't yell at other kids."

"But he was insulting the things I care about."

I smiled. *A commemorative coin?* "Yes, and that's going to happen, but you have to temper the temper or you're just going to be that weirdo kid who's getting in trouble all the time."

"Weird is good, Izzy."

Good for you, kid. Yes, it is.

When we got home, Hank was already in the kitchen, unpacking a bag of groceries in a mad frenzy and cluttering the stovetop with pots and pans. *Why is hardworking Hank making dinner? Why doesn't unemployed Izzy have it waiting? Is that what you want to know?*

I certainly could have taken time out from my angst-filled day to whip up a lasagna, but Hank is the family chef. It's his habit, and one that he enjoys. Every evening the man comes through the front door, drops his fancy messenger bag, rolls up his sleeves, and heads straight in to the kitchen and starts making dinner. Just watching him exhausts me. I've offered the poor workhorse an alternative: "Take fifteen minutes to sit down and unwind, and then I'll help you." Hank is all for sharing the culinary duties, but he wants to get right to it and get it done.

Hank's been a divorced dad, preparing meals for the two boys, for years, so it's no wonder he's become a master of efficiency. This doesn't mean he pops dinner in the microwave and puts it on the table three minutes later. Oh, no. My Southern man likes to cook and believes passionately in fresh ingredients, family recipes, and making food from scratch. When we were living in the East Bay, he and a Cajun friend would throw backyard parties where they'd roast a whole suckling pig and serve it with spicy beans and rice, fresh corn bread, and Southern greens. Even before Hank and I hooked up, I was taken by how sexy he looked glistening with pork fat and reeking of Jamaican rum.

Tonight he was making a mushroom omelet from one of his favorite cookbooks, *French Cooking in Ten Minutes,* and I decided to get out of his way. I kissed him on the top of his head. I'd give him The Young One's disciplinary update later. For now, I'd let the man cook.

I kicked off my shoes and went out into the front yard. It was pushing one hundred degrees, and guess what—it actually felt good. Sure, my appreciation for outrageous Texas heat may eventually wear off, but right now I'm diggin' it. Granted, it took me some time to adjust. (Remember the fleece vest? And for the first several months after our arrival, I carried around an "emergency" jacket, and stashed a scarf in my purse "just in case." I could be sweating and on the verge of heat stroke, but I clung to my California habits, to always expect a piercing gust of Pacific wind right around the corner. "Just wait," I'd pant. "It's coming.") Now I trusted that the warmth would linger—even into October—and had eased comfortably into Austin's No Jacket Required mentality.

It was dusk—that captivating sliver of time when, in my neighborhood, the cedar elm and oak trees are often silhouetted against a cotton candy and copper sky. Texas has some exquisite sunsets—and they don't get lost in the fog. I gazed out at the treetops stretching up from the base of the nearby greenbelt. I thought about my scuffle with Patricia and how she'd knocked me off balance. *I have no idea what I'm doing,* I thought. *I don't have parenting credentials.* I took a deep breath and watched the sky deepen into a palette of pomegranate and tangerine. I lifted my arms up toward the sky and into the warm air. *Stretch, Izzy—you can do this.*

Although I was still unsteady in my stepmom shoes, I knew that having a successful stepfamily was possible. Sure, my own stepkid chronicles had some strange chapters (like when we started stepfamily counseling with Sister X, a nun turned hypnotist), but there had been many magical moments, too, and I had to hope that the boys and I would eventually have ours.

* * *

A few nights later, as Hank took a sip of his fresh lime margarita, I thought, *This is not one of those moments.* Hank had just made a family announcement that he'd be flying to Miami on business for two nights. *Oh, really?* We were out with the boys at our favorite Tex-Mex joint and Hank had ordered his usual, the *El Presidente* (a caloric pile of beef, pork, and chicken). I bit down on a chip and said nothing. Was this my reward for having a sympathetic moment with The Young One? *Just because we're all stepkids doesn't mean I want them all to myself.*

"Believe me, I don't want to go, but it's a corporate meeting. All the big dogs will be there. I don't have a choice."

I knew the business and I understood the obligation. Of course he had to go. He'd have to sip cocktails with a bunch of suits, prove his worth, and probably do some boring budget presentation. But I wasn't going to let him off the hook that easily. What did this mean for me? Two nights alone playing mom? What if the boys turned wicked and burned me in bed? I dipped my chip into our family-sized order of *queso*. (The stuff is darn good, but should really be enjoyed in moderation. Hot cheese does not mix with hot buns, after all. I silently pledged not to make a habit of scooping it into my mouth.)

I asked Hank, "Where will you stay?"

"South Beach."

"Aha. Where all the women parade around topless and party down all night?"

That got The Tall One's attention. He shot a look at me and then turned to Hank to confirm this marvelous image.

Hank rolled his eyes. "I'm going to be stuck in a conference room all day, not out on the beach."

The first night Hank was gone, the toilet backed up in the boys' bathroom.

The Young One had been locked inside for quite some time, and when he finally emerged he found me in the living room and reported, "The toilet's clogged. It's not flushing."

Of course it's not, I thought. *This is what happens when the master plumber is away on topless business.*

Lucky for me, I had memorized Stepmom Rule Number Two (don't act like a hostess), or I'd be in their bathroom making it all go away. So I offered, "Did you try plunging it?"

"It's not working."

I wasn't going to budge. I may be the adult and the one in charge, but I am not plunging that kid's toilet. "Then get your brother to help you," I said.

The Young One solicited The Tall One's help and I could hear them discussing the matter at hand. "Oh, man, that's disgusting," The Tall One said. "What did you *do?*" I covered my ears and stayed on the couch. I was reminded of stepdad Stanton cursing at all three of us teenage girls for clogging our bathtub with long hair and Suave conditioner. He'd be bent over our bathtub with a wire hanger he'd turned into a plumbing snake, yanking out mounds of slimy hair and barking, "Next time, you clean it out."

"It's your bathroom," I hollered. "You guys take care of it, okay?" And then the phone rang. It was Hank.

"How's it going?" he asked.

"We're fine. I'm just thumbing through *Southern Bride* while your kids plunge their backed-up toilet."

I had a new stack of bridal magazines and I was playing around with the idea of a Southern wedding, if only because it allowed me to fantasize about a bachelorette party with a mechanical bull–riding contest. I figured it was open season for daydreaming, as Hank and I hadn't really discussed what our "real" wedding would be like since we'd left the Bay Area after our City Hall quickie.

"One more night," he promised. *Thank God, or I'll have to drop his boys off at an animal shelter and lie about it.*

"No rush. Seriously. I'm having a turd of a time."

I was trying hard to be brave and keep it light. The whole toilet incident was skating dangerously close to one of my big worries about full-time parenting: that I'd become one of those sour, middle-aged moms with a constant scowl. That the pressure of parenting would eventually thwack my sense of humor and make me super-serious.

Before my title changed from single woman to stepmom, I often referred to my role with Hank's kids as the "Fun Monkey." The term comes from one of the best books I've read on the subject, *The Single Girl's Guide to Marrying a Man, His Kids and His Ex-Wife.* As I understood it, the job of the Fun Monkey comes down to keeping everyone happy, smiling, and kidding around. Fun Monkey is supposed to ignore uncomfortable realities (like war, homework, and divorce), at least for the afternoon, and keep the mood of the bio-parent elevated.

A smart Fun Monkey will pick encouraging environments, like the county fair (cold beer and funnel cake) to ensure enhanced moods for everyone. When the roller-coaster ride comes to a stop (usually after four or five hours) and everyone hits the wall, the Fun Monkey suddenly disappears. ("Hey, where did she go? We were having so much fun.") The Fun Monkey is a trickster.

When we were living in California and I was just the girlfriend, I was really good at the disappearing act. When things got heated or tedious, I'd just say, "Okay, see you guys later. I have errands to run." It was a fabulous setup.

It wasn't until the boys moved to Texas to live with us full-time that they began to learn the unavoidable truth: I'm just not fun every hour of the day. Talk about a buzzkill. But, I ask you, how does one maintain Fun Monkey status when dealing with things like toilets that won't flush? My new not-so-fun status was leaving a bad taste in my mouth, like two-percent milk in your coffee when you're used to half-and-half.

With Hank gone and me acting as guardian, I kept expecting one of them to say, "You really used to be more fun. You know, before you changed." *Daggers to my heart!* I dreaded such an accusation because I'd have to agree with them. Even I didn't recognize myself these days: Ruler of Cleanliness and Order. I asked my new girlfriends online, "Is this what it means to be a stepmom, obsessing over smudges on the counter and dishes in the sink?" I was annoying *myself*. One steplady offered me this encouragement: "Believe me, it could be worse. Try the twenty-four-hour flu and only one bathroom."

The more I thought about it, losing my Fun Monkey persona wasn't the worst that could happen. The boys rejecting my so-called authority would be a bigger crush. So far, I hadn't suffered this humiliating defeat. In fact, the boys were pretty agreeable and, dare I say, respectful of my new stepmom status. I had to think the early influence of their stepdad John was the reason for this. John had co-parented them from a young age and broken them in to twitchy newcomers. I thought about sending him a thank-you note. That is, until the next night, the one before Hank was scheduled to return, when The Young One and I had our first official squabble. The kid has a hard time sitting still. "His motor's always running," is how Patricia describes it. As it often does in school, his little engine frequently gets him into trouble at the dinner table. On this particular evening, The Young One was doing an aerobic routine (getting up, sitting down, getting up, and so on) toward the end of our un-Hank meal: meat lovers' extra-cheese pizza. The Tall One had already excused himself after complaining that he "felt sick" and needed to lie down. Hank has a rather strict rule that the guys aren't allowed to get up until the meal is over. This is a fair request, as far as I'm concerned. I've seen him enforce it hundreds of times, but Hank wasn't around.

So I had a choice to make: Let the kid get away with it and give up my power, or be a hard-ass and show him who's boss. I chose door number two.

I said to The Young One, "If you get up one more time, your meal is over."

He took another bite and, just when I thought he'd accepted my authority, he was up out of his chair. *Game on.*

"I mean it," I said.

But for him, this was just an invitation to taunt me. He smiled wide and gave me a look like *No, you don't—you're the Fun Monkey, remember?* He stood up again with a slice of pizza dangling out of his mouth and started to dance. The kid was going to make me prove it.

"That's it." I stood up. "The meal's over."

But he continued to gyrate and chortle, smacking on a piece of pepperoni. So really I had no other choice—I grabbed at the slobbery slice of pizza in his mouth and yanked, but he bit down harder and pulled back.

"Give it to me," I yelled. I jerked harder, but he wouldn't let go.

I can't believe this, I thought. *It's like I'm fighting a feral cat over a fish taco. Ridiculous!* I could pretty much guarantee that this approach was not in any parenting book. I tugged a minute longer, but finally had to give in. I worried I might break loose one of his front teeth, and how would I explain that? He smiled triumphantly, like he'd won, so I ordered him to his room.

What kind of terrible parent am I? I wondered. Two nights on my own and I resort to a physical assault. I sulked around the house for an hour, looking for the Fun Monkey. Where did she go? I could hear the boys down the hall snickering, no doubt gossiping about my lack of control and bipolar personality. When I got tired of sponging off countertops, sweeping up cat hair, and berating myself, the Fun Monkey suddenly appeared, as if nothing had changed. *She's back!* I ran down the hall and burst into the kids' rooms, saying, "Okay, boys. It's time for a vaudeville dance-off."

"Yay!" The Young One cheered and jumped on the bed. Then, "Wait," he said. "What's that?"

See what I mean? The Fun Monkey is a trickster.

Hank returned the next evening and announced he was taking me out. The guy's no dummy.

In his absence, I'd been planning to institute date night (where we get out once a week, fondle in public, and avoid discussing money or kids), so his timing for an adults-only evening was perfect.

I'd spotted a wine bar downtown that I wanted to check out for its big-city vibe: sidewalk tables in a busy shopping district. We sat outside in the warm autumn air and ordered from an extensive selection of wine flights.

The couple seated next to us said hello. Naturally, I was suspicious of their intentions, but decided I'd try to go with the Texan flow and assume the best. I desperately wanted to make at least one girlfriend in town whom I didn't have to hire first. I'd begun referring to myself as Cathy Cling-On, a lame joke about my not-actually-funny-at-all habit of flinging myself at Hank as soon as he walked through the front door at the end of the day. I'd wrap my tentacle-like arms and legs all around him and hold on until he'd have to say, "You're crushing me and I have to pee."

In other words, I was getting a little too needy.

I didn't want to admit this to those who used to know me in my old life. I'd gone so far as to avoid phone calls from some of my friends in San Francisco. What did I have to report? "My social life and career are in the shitter, but I'm perfecting the parent-teacher conference and how to dress like a beggar." I was certain that if any of my former colleagues engaged me in conversation, they'd be able to tell from the dreariness in my voice that I was in the same dirty warmup pants I'd worn yesterday and that I'd forgotten to put on underwear. Again. *Oh, no; was this how Gonorrhea Girl got started?*

But tonight I felt like my former self—clean, coiffed, and confident. After the first flight of "sexy reds" I let my guard down, and before I knew it Hank and I were carrying on like old friends with our wine-bar neighbors. When the subject of children came up, I confessed that I didn't belong to any mommy groups and that "my uterus is tight as a drum."

"But," I added as a consolation, "I'm a new stepmom! Two growing boys. One's five foot eleven."

She took a long drink of her wine, sizing me up.

I offered weakly, "It's going really great?"

She said, "Well, that's a great way to keep your body. You look nothing like a mom." It was meant to placate and it worked, although I knew plenty of moms whom I'd love to look like (my friend Ruby in particular, who's married to a hairdresser and looks like a supermodel).

"Thanks." I raised my glass to my new Texas pal. Sensing we'd just made fast friends, she went on to say, "Have you seen the Lifetime movie *My Stepson, My Lover?*"

I choked on my Malbec. "What?"

Did Lifetime really make a movie with that title? And: No. She. Didn't. She *did* just go there!

I secretly vowed that once we got home, I'd put on some very baggy mom jeans and ramp up my search for a new gal-pal who wouldn't lump *stepmother* and *deviant straight from a television drama* in the same category.

The very next week I decided to shed my shy self and make the first move. I started cruising Austin—trolling for girlfriends. *Mom would be so proud!* As long as I can remember, my mother's had intellectually curious, feisty, and solid women in her life. When I was blubbering my sad good-byes and heading off to the heart of Texas, where I didn't know a soul, my mother whispered to me . . .

Stepmom Rule Number Five: All you need is one good girlfriend.

"Once you meet another woman whom you can call in a pinch," she said, "for coffee or a walk, you'll be fine."

It was time for me to take her advice seriously. What did I have to lose? I psyched myself up before heading out for the day. "Hi." I smiled into the bathroom mirror. "I like your belt. Do you want to be my friend? And maybe my bridesmaid?" I felt a little like a stalker, but these were desperate times. I was in dire need of a good old-fashioned girls' night out.

Hank is a worthy girlfriend stand-in (he lets me dress him in seasonal colors, like hibiscus and lettuce green; he enjoys a good cry; and he gossips like a girl), but Hank alone is not enough. Our husbands can't be everything to us.

By the end of the week, I buddied up to the cashier at our neighborhood grocery, joined a ladies' book group, and signed up for bridal boot camp. The concept: Get fit for your big day, with an emphasis on reducing back fat and tightening flaccid arms. The idea of a group of neurotic brides-to-be getting together twice a week to squat and sweat sounded downright comical. I mean, technically I was already married, but I wouldn't tell them that. I hadn't squeezed into a white dress that cut off my circulation yet, so I signed right up.

On Friday night, Hank and I sat out back in bare feet and short sleeves. I told him about my ambitious plan to snare a girlfriend. "I can feel it—my new BFF is right around the corner." Hank, the constant Izzy enthusiast, smiled and said, "I'm happy for you, babe." But he looked a little hurt, like I was overlooking the obvious. It took me a minute, and then, *Ah—I get it.*

Hank. My husband. Doesn't he count?

"You know you're my best *boy*friend," I said.

But now that I'm a new stepmom, you better believe I need some supporting estrogen.

NOVEMBER

She's Come Undone

My new morning drill of pain goes like this: The alarm goes off at 5:15, and *don't even think about snoozing!* I fumble into my workout clothes, hurry out the door, and drive myself in a mad frenzy, praying all the while that I make it to the gym on time to line up with twelve other disheveled-looking women who have elected to work out with The Evil One.

Welcome to bridal boot camp.

I joined a group of professional women who, I imagine, wear lipstick and high heels and boss underlings around from nine to five, but you wouldn't know it at a quick glance, judging by our trembling assembly line of fear. *Oh no, oh no, what's it going to be? Inside or out?*

The general thinking was that if we worked out inside the gym, someone would likely vomit on the treadmill; on the other hand, if we were sentenced to outside training for an hour, we worried that someone would end up dead.

Because we learned the difference between torture (in) and extreme torture (out) pretty quick, our group often began a desperate muttering of "please not outside, please not outside" as soon as we got into line. The Evil One could smell our fear, and this sealed the deal.

"Get in formation. We're heading out. Leave your waters behind."

I'm going to die. And I will die thirsty.

Today's workout began with blindfolds, wet grass, and cupcakes.

"Get on the ground," The Evil One barked. We dropped to our knees (a word about shorts: a mistake in these circumstances).

She explained the obstacle course she'd devised for us: a maze of cupcakes (white sugar is bad, bad, bad) in tall grass that we were forced to navigate in total blindness, and on all fours. One false move—even a knuckle grazing the cup of a cake—and it's one mile, my pretty.

The miles add up fast, and The Evil One enjoys every minute of this frantic scene—twelve women crawling around on the ground with scraped-up hands and knees, begging for proper directions. *Which Way, Evil One? Left or right?*

Once we were completely covered in frosting, dirt, and blood, we found ourselves up off the ground, blindfolds ripped off, running for our lives.

"How do you feel?" she yelled.

Are you kidding me? I have scraped-up knees and frosting in my hair.

But actually, I felt good—disgustingly filthy and hideous, but good, and very much alive.

She yelled, "Let me hear you say, 'I'm selfish!' "

The Evil One explained that this sweaty, dirty, achy, humiliating, painful hour of suffering was all ours. It was ours to OWN. One hour to spend on our bodies and our minds, no one tugging, asking, talking, or needing us in any way. *Thank God, because I can barely take another step without peeing on myself.* An hour to be self-aware and self-consumed. An hour to take care of ourselves, because for the rest of the day we'd be taking care of everyone else.

AMEN!

She was right, and that's why I knew I'd come back in two days and do it all over again. This early morning hour of mine took me out of the stepmom routine just long enough to miss breakfast-table battles over milk, and endless searches for socks. If I stayed home for those, I would become The Evil One. I'd much rather reserve that title for someone else. And really, boot camp is a relative breeze compared to the stepmom drill. Both involve feeling desperately around in the dark, but the grueling physical challenge I can take. It's the mental demands of my home life that have me whipped.

Now that I was getting my body back in shape, and with the boys somewhat settled in Austin, I was ready to return to my career. Landing a job in Austin was turning out to be much harder than I expected, however. The local TV and advertising scene was smallish—even cliquey—and seemed to want to stay that way. I'd been so self-assured that I'd ride into cowgirl country and be elected Princess Bluebonnet, but oh, no, I was rebuffed! Austin was doing just fine, thank you very much, and didn't need another hotshot producer from Frisco stirring up dust. There were a lot of us, it turned out, who had moved to this booming town to grab up all the affordable real estate and flood the workforce. What I understood now (after about the tenth rejection—*You're totally qualified, but we're not interested. Stay in touch, 'kay?*) was that Texans were loyal to their own and chose their newbies carefully. I had to be patient and wait my turn. Austin had just hired an out-of-towner to make TV waves. Yes, it had. And he was my husband.

I worried that my struggle to secure work would eventually turn into resentment toward Hank. Plus, I couldn't help but think that if I was having trouble finding a job, this was not good news for June. At least I was already here and I could bang on office doors—*Give me a chance! Really, I'm a keeper!* But June was still in California, waiting for the right opportunity to present itself. What if it never did? I could be waiting a long time for relief.

After falling into a five-day funk during which I convinced myself that I'd be a full-time stay-at-home stepmom for the rest of my life, I concluded that I was in the midst of an identity crisis.

"This is not who I am," I told Sarah the shrink.

"What do you mean?"

"This washed-up producer. It's breaking my spirit. I'm losing my instinct to bathe."

Sarah sensed I was coming undone all over her Pottery Barn loveseat and leaned in a little closer—the universal posture of concern.

"I hate that I don't have to be anywhere tomorrow morning—or any morning. No one is counting on me to show up. This isn't who I was five months ago. I *was* somebody five months ago."

"And you *are* somebody now," she challenged me. "But, yes, I agree; professionally, you've given up a lot."

I thought of myself wandering around our quiet house during the day, trying to engage the cats in watercooler talk. She explained that losing my "external support systems" and my familiar routine would naturally make me feel like someone in mourning.

"You've also gained a lot," she ventured.

No way! I'm sweating my ass off in bridal boot camp!

"You've gained a family," she explained.

Oh, she was good. Without saying the words, Sarah was telling me to snap out of it, to get over myself and stop whining already! I'd gained a life I didn't think I ever wanted, and I had to admit that there were pieces of it that were sweet.

Sarah said gently, "Experiencing grief over the life you left behind is where you are right now. And you can't really skip over it, but instead of spending your time thinking about how to get yourself *out* of it, why don't you figure out how to be *in* it?"

In other words, *Stepmom Rule Number Six*: Accept what is.

I sat still and considered her proposal. *I did choose this,* I reminded myself. If I could endure this lousy feeling now, just long enough to get through it, then maybe when I wasn't looking the universe would shift, the sky would brighten, and I'd be able to flex my little wings and lift myself up off the ground. I was concentrating on this image—me swirling around in the air, an exuberant and pretty little bird—when she compared me to a slug.

"She called me a snail without a shell," I told Hank that evening. He was out in the garage looking for a box full of God knows what.

"So that's why you don't like margaritas with salt?" *Ba-dum-bum.*

"Exactly," I said. "Keep the salt away from me. It burns."

That night I lay in bed pondering the difference between identity and character. I knew there was one, but I was struggling with the distinction. The truth is, I woke up some mornings and I didn't know who Izzy Rose was. I felt stripped, exposed—a disoriented slug lost in Texas.

And then, later that week, the sky brightened. I got a call from a TV guy in Houston who wanted to hire me for a freelance gig.

I jumped at the chance: "When would you want me to start?"

"The day after tomorrow?" he sounded doubtful.

"That'll work."

Houston—home of big hair and big oil. Here I come.

I threw my shapeless clothes to the back of my closet and dusted off my designer boots. Houston is an uneventful three-hour drive from Austin. Pecan stands and warehouses peddling explosives are about the only sights along the way, but I decided that getting back in the game and producing for Big Tex news was worth the drive. They'd hired me for a month, so I packed up and hit the road with Hank's blessing. In fact, he practically pushed me out the door. He was thankful, I think, for anything that would restore my joie de vivre.

"Go kick some Houston ass," he said.

My first assignment was to write promo copy for a story about prostitution overrunning Houston. I was strongly encouraged to incorporate the phrase *tricks of the trade* into my script. "Write me something gritty," my new manager said. I snickered at this but diligently got to work. Later that morning, when I submitted my copy for review, I was promptly called into his office. He'd marked up my script with a red Sharpie, and I waited like a good schoolgirl for his critique. He had only one comment: "Don't you have any sound from a pimp?" *Was this playa for real?* I said, "No. Not from any ho, either."

He wasn't amused. He told me to go to lunch.

My Houston coworkers satisfied my old stereotype of Texans. They were big fans of fresh meat for their midday snack (Angus chopped steak ranked high on the list). But when they felt less carnivorous, they were at the Coffin Café, an understated market that sold a hodgepodge of sandwiches, chow mein, energy drinks, and gum, and made its home in the lobby of a huge mortuary company next door to the TV station. Sure, the market was *really* called the Sunshine Deli, but my new promo pals found their title more fitting. I had to agree.

As we stood in line to order, I had to ask: "Is this actually the building where the cold bodies are stored?"

"Who cares?" they said. "Just order egg salad on wheat. It's only two bucks."

It was a rush to be working again, to be part of a staff of unapologetic news junkies instead of shuffling braless around the house. And it was a thrill to be somewhat independent again. I'd accepted the company's offer to put me up in a hotel during the week and drive back to Austin on the weekends. I love hotels and I was treating my Houston assignment as a mini-vacation: king-sized bed, take-out meals, maid service, and all the fluffy white towels I could soil. I missed Hank and how he warmed up our bed (his backside alone generates a tremendous amount of heat; in the event of a natural disaster, I'm confident his rump could double as a hot plate), but I was thrilled to temporarily slip out of the newly married stepmom role and ride solo again. My first night alone in my room, I drank an entire bottle of red wine and watched the Home Shopping Network. It felt so wrong. *It felt so right.*

On day two I was assigned an associate producer, someone who would help me pull tape, log shots, that kind of thing. Lena reminded me of a typical Tom Robbins heroine: mid-twenties, fiery red hair, small-town sweetness, and old-soul wisdom. She was dressed in pinup couture and cowgirl boots. I fell in love with her right away.

Lena was an outstanding help. It was clear that she didn't know how valuable she was. In many ways, she reminded me of myself before I hit thirty and hardened around the edges. I wanted to put her in my pocket and take her home.

"Lena," I kidded her, "why are you doing my grunt work? You should be running this place."

"Not yet. I still have a lot to learn, so believe me when I say, I'm watching your every move. You better know what you're doing."

We immediately got each other's humor. This girl had potential—
to be my one good girlfriend, that is.

Work in Houston was going well in that I'd met a promising gal-
pal. The bad news was that the station had hired me to bump their
ratings, not to socialize, and I found the work hard to bump. After
a week of dining in the house of the dead and working for a man
with a fetish for over-the-top titillating news promotion, I realized
that perhaps my Bay Area colleagues had been right: Many of them
had encouraged me to take even more than a few months off from
work and dismissed any concerns I had about losing my mar-
ketability.

"You've got talent," my former boss said when I called him for an
emergency pep talk a week before Houston rang. "People will want
to hire you. Don't take a job just because it's available. Really think
about what you want to do next." But I'd panicked and jumped at
the first offer.

Alone in my hotel bed, I had to admit that in my haste to regrow
my shell, I'd accepted a job that didn't really fit. Sure, I liked the pay-
check and the much-needed ego boost, but exposing Houston's
seedy underground wasn't enough for me, and also, I was three hours
away from my husband. I'd made a mistake. On Friday, I confided in
Lena as we filled up on rotgut office coffee from the automatic machine.

"It's not like me to walk out on a job, but I think my days here are
numbered."

"Oh, no! Did we run you off already?" she said.

"*You* didn't," I said. "I wish I could take you back to Austin. Do
you want to quit today, too?"

"It's tempting, but if you're leaving, I'm in the perfect position to
make a run for your job."

"Smart and sneaky."

"Get out of here." She winked. "The next time I'm in Austin I'll give you a call. My parents live outside of town, and I just started dating a guy there."

"Perfect. I'll take you out for girly cocktails and write it off as a strategic team-building meeting."

"It's a date."

That afternoon I swallowed my last bite of an unimpressive two-dollar sandwich and turned in my first and last time sheet. My manager was furious, and I didn't blame him. I gave him my best apology, but what I wanted to say was, "Yo, this just ain't the right street corner for me."

I called Hank and gave him the news. "I'm coming home."

"Good. I miss you."

And I missed him, especially the Hank I used to have more to myself; I longed for the lazy stretches of uninterrupted time we had when he was only a part-time dad. The weekend I fell hopelessly in love with my Southern hunk, a thunder and lightning storm crashed down on the Bay Area, flooding streets and driving everyone inside. The boys were with June, so we took refuge at Hank's place, safe from the pounding downpour, snoozing throughout the dark afternoon, naked and entwined under a flannel sheet, waking only to make love to the dreamy vocals of Damien Rice.

Was it wrong of me to want moments like this back? Who wouldn't? But I recognized that in the wanting was the implication that I blamed the boys for making those passionate afternoons disappear. What an ugly confession! I sounded like a spoiled brat: "I WON'T SHARE HIM. HE'S MINE!" But it was true. Now that we had the boys 24/7, it was difficult finding alone time.

As a stepkid who had a greedy, needy stepmom, I knew that asking for solo time with my man was potentially dangerous. I didn't want the kids to feel like I was hijacking their time with Hank. It was important that the three of them continue to nurture their related-guy bond. At the same time, having some kid-free moments with Hank was essential for me. But how could we balance the two? I didn't marry Hank just so I'd have company in the grocery-store line. I need more from a husband. And a marriage.

One wise woman from my online community warned that a step-mom who competes with the kids for her husband's affection is sure to lose. I got that—I had no interest in a muddy tug-of-war. What we needed was a time-management professional—someone to sort this all out. I called my mom.

"Go ahead and say it. I'm a hideous person." I was on my cell phone, driving back from Houston.

"For not wanting the kids around all the time? Why don't you give yourself a break?" she said. "Remember when Stanton and I used to go outside and sit on the curb?"

"No."

"Yeah, you do. We used to go sit out on the front curb with a bottle of Safeway scotch."

"How often?" I snickered. This sounded tragically ghetto.

"Oh, shut up. Not that often, but every once in a while we just had to get away from you girls and be alone for a while where we could sit side by side and talk, and not be interrupted."

I tried to remember this, but couldn't call up the memory. This must have been during my junior-high years, characterized by heavy stage makeup (and I wasn't even in drama class) and my conscious decision to ignore anything that didn't have to do with me.

I liked the idea of making space for just Hank and me. But we were new to the zip code and hoping to make a good impression. I was pretty sure drinking from a paper bag out on the street would reduce our chances of joining the neighborhood BBQ alliance. Instead, I decided our front parlor, with its sage walls and cucumber couch, would make the perfect retreat for ensuring healthy matrimony.

After I returned from Houston, Hank and I began making a habit of retreating to the green room. We'd shut the French doors to the rest of the house and take twenty minutes to focus on each other, and unravel the details of the day. Sometimes we'd sip cocktails out of my grandmother's vintage tumblers. On these occasions, I was tempted to serve onion dip and put on a string of pearls.

I convinced Hank that the occasional visit to the green room was crucial to our relationship and our sanity, and he agreed, albeit a bit guiltily. He fretted that the boys would feel left out and wonder why he wasn't hunkered over the stove, or teaching them how to caulk tile. (Hank and the boys have always bonded over handyman home-improvement projects, rather than by playing ball.)

My best guess was that he'd spent so many years as a single, part-time dad that it was habit to give the guys his constant attention when they were in his care. Not only was it habit, but Hank believed it was his *duty* to be totally available. Was this to make up for the times when the boys were with June and Hank was no longer there? *Was he still beating himself up over the divorce?* I wasn't sure. But over the weeks I noticed him relaxing into a new role: Almost Always Available Daddy. And the boys seemed just fine with this; really, what kid wants Dad hanging around all the time?

A couple weeks or so after my return from Houston, we stretched out on the couch and I said, "Have you heard anything from June lately?"

"Like what?" said Hank. *Like what?* Had the man had a lobotomy?

"Like when is she moving here? It's been almost four months. I thought she'd be here by now."

Hank stiffened. "She can't find a job. Anchor positions just don't open up very often, and she's not going to move here without work."

But I did.

"Has she tried other markets outside of Austin, like Houston or Dallas?"

Hank was sitting up now, not at all relaxed. "Yes, and she can't find anything."

"In the whole state? Doesn't she know Texas is bigger than France?"

Talking to Hank about June was always a strain, no matter what the topic. I felt like Hank automatically defended his former wife when he should be sticking up for his current one. Hank felt like I pushed him into battle with her.

"I have to be careful," he said.

"Hank, you're not going to lose your kids just because you say something she doesn't want to hear. She's a reasonable woman."

In fact, according to the horror stories my stepladies had been sharing online, June was not only fair, but saner than most. Many stepmommy bloggers were waging holy wars with bio-moms, commonly identified as BMs.

I appreciated that Hank was in a sticky position—right in the middle of two headstrong women. I wouldn't want to be in his wingtips, either, but I wasn't going to back off. On the issue of June keeping her end of the bargain and moving to Texas, I had a right to ask questions. I wasn't the third-wheel girlfriend anymore. I was raising her kids.

Our conversation was cut short by a polite knock on the glass doors. The Young One understood the new rule of the green room (leave Daddy and Izzy alone for twenty minutes), but he interrupted anyway. Hank responded, *"Yessssss?"*

The Young One walked in like a lawyer prepared to make his case. "Daddy?" he began.

"Yeah," Hank said curtly, "what's up?" Instead of backing out quietly (which is what I would have done), The Young One moved to the center of the room with the question that could not wait. I had to admire the kid; he was a gutsy little guy.

"If you had to donate one of my body parts, what would it be?"

His question du jour caught Hank off guard. He sat motionless on the couch, drink in hand, ice cubes shifting, a line of disbelief stretching across his forehead. I suppressed a smile. A moment passed and no one said a word until Hank broke the silence.

"I really don't know, son. Can I get back to you in a minute?"

The Young One muttered, "Sure," and he didn't seem entirely surprised by Hank's dismissive answer. It was the green room, after all, and he had edged in when he shouldn't have. He turned and walked out. A moment later we heard him skipping through the house—a strong indicator he'd dropped the organ concern and moved on to a new subject. Hank turned to me with a grin.

"Body parts? Where does he come up with this stuff?" We both broke into laughter.

I had no idea where it had come from, but I was thankful for his curious ten-year-old mind and his ability to turn the tide when Hank got stuck. On this particular evening, I formulated

Stepmom Rule Number Seven: Keep laughing. Sometimes what you and your guy need is both your solitary time together and a meddlesome kid to remind you to laugh out loud.

November is a hard month to travel if you're in the TV news biz. Though the business is changing, November is still reserved as one of the bigger rating periods of the year, when stations go to war to command a lead. What does this mean? In simple terms, TV stations run stories they think viewers will find impossible to resist.

Here are some of my personal favorites:

Handbag Horrors
Toothbrush Tragedy
Organic Dumpster Divers

More viewers = higher advertising rates = bigger bucks = big-time bragging rights. If you're in TV news promotion, it's four weeks of chaotic deadlines that can trigger tearful fits, regretful language, skin disorders, and weight loss or gain. Usually, during this stressed month, Hank grows out his goatee and what's left on the top of his head. He claims it's for good luck, like painting your face orange to ensure your football team will win. I have discouraged this, for obvious reasons. The Tall One has likened the hair on his father's head to a rat, and has gone so far as to call him "rodent man." I'm glad he said it and not me.

Given Hank's job preoccupation, we invited his folks to join us for Thanksgiving, since leaving Austin for the annual carb fest wasn't an option. They accepted. And just like that, I shoved my work and ex-wife worries to the back of the stove so I could start planning for the mother of all meals.

What I needed was an apron.

Really, one must start with the basics. The first step to creating favorable conditions for holiday cheer is a beautifully appointed woman of the house. And according to the Sunday Styles Section, aprons were back in style. It seemed perfectly obvious to me that before I could shop for groceries, I had to purchase a suitable garment for smearing on smashed potatoes and gravy. I wanted something girly that said *I'm retro-chic and fun,* but also identified me as the authority in the kitchen. Controlled aesthetics come second only to promoting good spirits.

I found my perfect apron in one of those popular vintage boutiques where everything looks old and quaint (but let's face it; some little kid probably finished sewing on the buttons last week). The one I chose was crimson red with muted violet flowers, a white ruffled hem, and paisley embroidery. It had a small, worthless pocket, probably for lozenges or pistachios. Regardless, it was cute with a capital *C,* and sure to impress.

I was a little jittery about hosting the in-laws. Serving up fancy fare isn't my forte, and the pressure was on (even if it was only the self-inflicted variety). I could imagine the story coming out over the wires: *New daughter-in-law and first-year stepmom forgets to turn on oven, serves turkey raw.*

I imagined myself being called out in group therapy for lacking life skills: *Is there a woman in here who hasn't prepared a Thanksgiving spread?* I'd be the only one in her mid-thirties raising her hand.

It's not that I can't cook, but I lack experience with preparing big meat and elaborate meals. I blame it on my stepkid upbringing. I spent much of my life starting the grubfest in one house and then traveling across town to finish it at another (except for the time my stepsisters and I were dragged to a weird harvest party in Berkeley, where we had to dress up like pilgrims). The point is, I've never cooked the meal—I've always just shown up in time to sit down and eat it.

So it wasn't until now, after Hank and I moved away from family, that I had a chance to deviate from my childhood routine. I was excited and relieved to be free of the stepkid schlep, but that meant *I'd* be responsible for refilling the nut bowls and keeping everyone happy. If the conversation got stale, I wouldn't get to say, "Sorry, this was lovely, but I have to go. I'm late for my next dinner." No, ma'am, I had to stay put and keep the party going. Would it be possible to create the perfect Hallmark moment without drinking myself into unconsciousness?

My mother insisted I was being ridiculous. "You've watched too many of those stupid holiday movies where everything goes wrong."

Of course, as soon as she said it, she conceded that if there wasn't any truth to those tired plot lines, the studios wouldn't keep making them. Aha!

"I'm fine with a Hollywood ending," I said. "I just don't want the scary drama. Are you sure you don't want to come down here and hold my hand?"

"Next year, babe, I promise."

My family wasn't going to make it to Austin. Instead, they were staying put in northern California, where I imagined they'd dine on organic bird stuffed with homegrown herbs. If I failed miserably, who would be here to love me and my not-quite-pureed sweet potatoes unconditionally?

But I *did* have the apron, so I felt free to move on to larger issues, like what the menu would, in fact, be. Thanksgiving may be the most basic meal in the book, but I was entertaining people from the South. It wasn't until I started thumbing through Hank's cookbooks that I spotted two Southern favorites missing from my list: peach cobbler and macaroni and cheese. These people knew how to live! Pasta, potatoes, peaches, *and* pie. I felt bloated just thinking about it.

I made a master list of family dishes. I thought it was important that our collective tastes be represented—you know, honor our roots, that kind of thing. I asked the boys what foods were a "must."

The Young One said, of all things, "White dinner rolls."

"How unconventional," I teased.

The Tall One mumbled, "I know what I *don't* want. Pie. It's disgusting."

"You don't like pie?" I punched him in the arm. "Who doesn't like pie?"

He shrugged. "I hate cooked fruit."

I laughed. "Seriously, dude—who *raised* you?"

He gave me a typical teenage eye roll. "You're not funny, Izzy." The kid's quick; he got all my stepparenting cracks.

Reverting to hostess mode (just for Thanksgiving), I determined to make a bounty of desserts—chocolate gingerbread cupcakes to satisfy the oddball palate of The Tall One, in addition to my grandmother's pumpkin pie with pecan crust and a Southern peach cobbler.

Hank argued, "We don't need three desserts for six people."

"Hank, no one likes a stingy pilgrim. It's all about abundance."

But, in truth, I wasn't making the chocolate gingerbread *just* for The Tall One. I'd had these gourmet cakes before and they were, in fact, some of the most decadent, rich, and gooey morsels of pleasure I'd ever devoured (they call for nearly a cup of black molasses). I was tempted to take them to bed. And not regret it the next morning.

After soliciting some online advice, I was encouraged by other stepmoms to practice my signature dishes beforehand to avoid first-timer flops.

Izzy's Borrowed Cupcake Recipe

Find "Chocolate Gingerbread" on page 278 of *Feast: Food to Celebrate Life,* by the sultry Brit Nigella Lawson. Trust me, this gingerbread is as sexy as she is. You will notice that even *she* describes these treats as "very rich, very strong" and "not for children, but perfect for the rest of us." Proceed with caution. Enjoy thoroughly.

The Young One offered to help me, and I patted his curly head and applauded him for being reasonably useful. He took this as a compliment and an invitation to stick around and lick the counter. Generalization: Kids love sugar. I equate their insatiable appetite for the white stuff with my deep affection for red wine. Both raise our glucose levels and send us into dizzying states of bliss, so really, small ones and grown-ups are kindred addicts.

It turns out that The Young One had a few things to teach me; he has a distinctive baking style. It goes something like this: (1) Pack the powdered sugar; (2) Lick the fingers; (3) Whisk the batter; (4) Lick the whisk; (5) Dribble the mix; (6) Lick the pan. At one point, he dropped a saucy spoon and then licked the floor like a puppy. But he also cleaned as he worked, and that worked for me. We arranged the "rehearsal" cakes on an elegant platter and served them warm. The Young One and The Tall One declared them good, agreeing that they tasted like waffles.

Waffles?

Not exactly the compliment I'd hoped for, but since they do love waffles, I equated the comparison with a four-star review in the Special *Bon Appetit* edition of *Truck Stop Eatin':* This cupcake pairs exceptionally well with two eggs over medium and a side of bacon.

"Pass one over here," I said.

With that, I dipped a chocolate bite into my red wine and popped it into my mouth, declaring, "That's a damn good waffle."

With all the signature dishes practiced and approved, I was left with just a few days to go until the in-laws would be in my house. We had purchased the turkey, enough oysters to gag a horse, and a full rack of wine. Plus, I splurged on overpriced housecleaners. Seriously, who has time to clean the baseboards or dust the blinds? I had holiday charm to cultivate and green beans to prep.

And then a pre-Thanksgiving disaster struck: The Young One was sent home from school with a bad case of head lice.

Like I said before, Hank's boys favor what I call "homeless hair." I know that's not a nice thing to say, so I've been working on another descriptive phrase. Maverick hair? Summer of Locks? Anyway, they both have beautiful curls, but they resist brushing them. This results in an enormous, icky mane that, as I've been quick to point out, "will prevent you from entering caves or other crawl spaces with success."

Now, don't get me wrong; I've always liked crazy, wild, arty hair on guys who play bass and are totally wrong for me. My preference is eccentricity, not conformity, and I in no way wanted to screw with the kid's image, but when he came home with critters, I knew his trademark mop had to go.

"My hair is my *thang,*" the ten-year-old pleaded to his father, standing in front of the bathroom mirror with a towel draped over his slumping shoulders. The grinding of the electric clippers started up, drowning out his final cries. "Daddy, you dig?"

I had to look away. After all, it was gorgeous hair, and I *did* dig, but his tangled locks had been invaded. Those buggers knew a good head of hair when they saw one, and they'd been enjoying the high life until his teacher spotted one saunter out of hiding to take an arrogant look around—conceited louse!

The Young One was promptly sent home "to avoid public humiliation by the other children." I was sure the classroom banishment was really meant to protect The Young One from some of the more militant parents. "Off with his head!" I imagined them shrieking.

"Keep that unkempt child away from my innocent baby!" Your lamb of a child is probably where he got the lice in the first place. *Just saying.*

After Hank gave The Young One a home haircut, I tried to soothe him.

"I love your haircut," I told him. And I meant it. He looked so clean, so housebroken.

He leveled his eyes at me.

"Really," I said. "You look like a kid whose family doesn't sleep in an open field."

"You're hilarious, Izzy. And *not* in the good way." He was still mad at Hank, and probably at me, too, for not jumping in to save him.

"If it's any consolation," I said, "your brother's hair is also getting a trim."

"What?" demanded The Tall One. He'd walked up just as I'd broken the bad news.

"That's right," said Hank. "You might have lice, too."

As a necessary consequence of sharing a hairbrush, towels, and basic bathroom utensils with his brother, The Tall One was next in line for the clippers.

"I don't care if I have lice, just don't cut my hair!" he pleaded. To hairless Hank, this was not a convincing argument, and the kid's long-hair career was abruptly cut short.

The louse in the house was a stark reminder that I no longer had the freedom to retreat to a sterile apartment until all was clear. Accepting this, I started doing laundry, while considering,

Stepmom Rule Number Seven B (optional) : Hair is kept short until you're seventeen.

After what seemed like forty-seven loads of laundry and a couple of unhappy meals together ("I won't eat again until my hair grows back"), we emerged victorious . . . and squeaky clean.

The boys looked ready for company. But the house did not.

I hadn't planned on the time required to delouse the house prior to Margaret and Big Hank's arrival. I wanted to invite my in-laws into a clean space, but obsessively washing every sofa pillow and bedspread hadn't been on my to-do list. I went to visit Sarah for some mental realignment.

Sarah said, "So, what do you want to work on today?"

"I'm trying to let go of the perfection thing, but Hank's parents will be here tomorrow and I'm feeling a tad panicky about appearances."

She asked me to explain. I told her that I was worried that my new Southern relatives might have particular expectations based on their cultural tastes and that I ran the risk of disappointing them.

"Like what?" she asked.

"I don't know—like using the wrong linens or teacups or something."

"Are they really that uptight?"

"No."

Sarah gave me a smirk. "I think you can probably let anxiety over teacups go."

"Okay, how about this: What if the boys suddenly decide to ignore everything I say in front of their grandparents and, *you know,* undermine my authority? Or what if I try to be funny and say something like, 'Don't give your Grand-mom lice' and they don't get my weird humor? What if Margaret and Big Hank think *I'm* the big joke?"

"Who's critiquing Izzy?" she said. "Them or you?"

She had me there.

I walked out of our session excited to share with Hank my new, Thanksgiving-flavored

Stepmom Rule Number Eight: Relax. We're all imperfect, and let's be thankful for it!

I caught him as soon as he walked in the door and followed him into our bathroom.

I said, "Hank, the Thanksgiving meal is the perfect opportunity to celebrate imperfection, because everyone has a different way of preparing a very specific menu. Take potatoes, for example. Do you like yours whipped, smashed, made with buttermilk or skim? Do you put things in them, like garlic and seasoned salt, or are you more of a purist?"

"Uhhhh," he said. I'd caught him with his pants down. "Whipped?"

"Look, I've been obsessing about respecting all the family traditions, but why don't we just mix them all together and create new ones?"

"I can get into that." He gave me his amused smile. "But can you leave me alone for a minute so I can do my thing?"

After I gave him his privacy, here's what we did: We gave everyone an assignment.

Margaret: gravy and stuffing
Big Hank: sweet potatoes
Hank (as presiding man of the house): turkey
Boys: crack jokes, trash duty

The instructions for the cooks were very simple: Make it however you want to make it.

I assigned myself gingerbread cake, peach cobbler, cranberry-apricot relish, green beans with roasted garlic, and a wilted spinach salad. I may be trying to let go of my perfectionist ways, but I'm still an overachiever.

In the midst of all the midday cooking, I asked Big Hank to tell me about his upbringing in Missouri. Hank's dad is a great storyteller—detailed, calm, and eloquent. He talked about the cotton farm he grew up on, learning to raise crops alongside his daddy. He described the simple house they lived in and his hardworking mama's spirit. I listened intently while stirring fresh cranberries on the stove, thinking, *This is how an extended family does it.* We share our histories, and by doing so, we entwine our lives. In truth, I'd known this all along. If it hadn't been for my mother's remarriage, I wouldn't have gained two fantastic stepsisters whose ancestors crossed the Donner Summit, but luckily weren't in the party that ate one another.

At five o'clock we sat down to the antique dining table that Hank's grandmother had passed down to him. We piled our potatoes high on Royal Ironstone china that came from my side of the tracks. I'm pretty sure the boys, who were arguing over their equal share of sparkling apple cider, overlooked the significance of the moment, but it touched me. I untied my apron and relaxed into my chair. Our judgment-free approach to the holiday was a success; no one stormed out or threw a dish. I didn't end up in the bathroom crying. If I hadn't been self-conscious about sounding overly sappy, I would have given a toast about how grateful I was that this unlikely cast of characters had become a family.

Instead, I made a joke. "Has anyone tried the gravy martini? It's called the Dirty Bull. I read about it in the *New York Times* . . . vodka and beef stock."

"Ewwwwwww," choked The Tall One. "I need to go throw up somewhere."

* * *

The next day, after pie for breakfast and lunch, I plopped down on the couch and called my stepsister Gigi in California. She was already planning for Christmas and had hauled out her favorite hip-hop carols and blinking lights. She asked me how T-day went. I gave her a synopsis in list form:

"Number One," I said, "I am in love with cranberry sauce."

"I thought you hated cranberry sauce," she said.

"I did, but here's the thing—I've figured out the magic key. Serve it hot and use the following recipe: fresh cranberry, ginger, apricot preserves, and OJ. Boil it down and enjoy. It is porntastic."

"Since when did you start gourmet cooking for a crowd?" Gigi asked.

"I pledged fifty bucks to the local NPR station, and now I get *Bon Appetit*. Number Two: Sharing cooking duties with the in-laws makes the day of the feast almost completely stress-free. Everyone has a job, everyone's significant. And opening the first bottle of red wine at noon doesn't hurt."

"Of course," agreed Gigi, who has ended up with more than one set of in-laws.

"And Three: I now appreciate why Hank considers gravy a meal."

"That's revolting," Gigi laughed.

"No, it's delicious."

Margaret's Memphis Gravy

Boil turkey neck and giblets in saucepan for about an hour. Take neck bone out. Cool. Pick off all meat, pieces, and parts, and put meat back into the stock. As the stock continues to boil, make a roux—put 2 tbsp. of corn oil or grease on to heat, then add in 4 tbsp. of white flour, mixing the whole time. Keep it moving until it's the color you want it, like the beige of Nilla Wafers. Start adding your roux to the turkey stock, stirring and adding more and more roux until it's the thickness you like. Season with salt, pepper, poultry seasoning, and oregano. Then add chopped hard-boiled egg on top. Serve in a gravy boat.

Hank's folks left a few days later, and by that time I'd had my fill of family meals. I'd enjoyed their company, but I'd lost my enthusiasm for nonstop food and conversation. Too much eating. Too much talking. I needed some relief.

"I can't do another family dinner right now," I said to Hank the first night after they left. I feigned dry heaves for dramatic effect.

"I'm with ya," he said and closed the refrigerator door and walked out of the kitchen.

Really? He doesn't want to cook?

I decided not to question this glaring departure from normal Hank behavior and just go with it. The boys, on the other hand, were programmed. Around eight o'clock they shuffled into the living room with runt-of-the-litter looks. I guessed this was their way of saying we ought to serve them a meal.

"You guys can't honestly be hungry. You've been eating like royal hogs for days." I was thinking of all the rolls, potatoes, and sweets I'd seen them devour. The amount of carbs alone could keep them alive until Christmas.

They both gave me incredulous looks. Were they going to call Child Protective Services?

Let's recap: Since the boys moved in, Hank and I had served up a home-cooked meal six out of seven nights of the week, a menu that typically included huge amounts of meat and milk. As someone who, for years, dined primarily on cheese and crackers, it's been a lot for me to stomach. In fact, I considered billing June for intestinal distress: *A box of Prilosec for every week you stay in California!*

While I do subscribe to the belief that setting aside time every evening to connect as a family is important, there were nights when I thought I might gag before the meal was over. "Isn't there a pill we could just take?" my grandmother had often mused on days when she was reluctant to sit down to another family meal with *her* teenage daughters. A pill would be nice since dining with children is often stressful—not a radical idea, I know—but it's different when you're sitting across from kids who don't give you biological "props" and who developed their unique conversational style (bickering and interrupting) and quirky chewing habits long before you came along.

I'd become pretty good at lasting through the workweek, and then the slightest gripe, like, *This chicken smells like a flea collar,* or an explanation of a primal instinct, like *I always eat couscous with my hands,* would twist up my insides and send me away from the table with a stomachache. I have to say, this was happening less frequently, but when it did happen, I'd take an emergency evening off and be back at the table the following night, refreshed and ready to give it another go.

Hank was critical of my on-and-off schedule until Sarah the shrink—who'd begun making appointments for Hank, as well—explained it to him in running terms. She told Hank to think of himself as an accomplished athlete, a marathon runner, and to think of me as someone who was training for the first time. I was getting faster every day, but it would take me a while to catch up to Hank, since he'd been running for years.

Don't you just love therapy?

"I'm easing into it," I told Hank. "I'm running as fast as I can, but sometimes I need to slow down and take a water break."

"Exactly," said Sarah. She looked straight at Hank and added, "And sometimes you get to take a break, too."

So, *Stepmom Rule Number Nine*: Sometimes you both need a break.

But back to the boys . . .

They were staring me down, standing in the living room in the same clothes they'd worn since Thanksgiving.

Is that a green bean on The Tall One's shoulder?

I announced, "It's make-your-own-dinner night." Piper, Gigi, and I were delivered this line frequently as kids, which is how I learned how to fry bologna and boil ramen noodles. Sarah the shrink institutes a similar tradition in her own home, but she calls it "free dinner." Either way, it's just another way of saying *We're not cooking tonight.*

They huffed and looked at me like *We're hungry and we don't have patience for any more of your gimmicks.*

"What's that mean?" asked The Young One. "I don't know how to cook."

"You know how to make cereal," offered The Tall One. "And toast."

"*Arghhhh,*" growled The Young One. "That's not funny."

"Ignore him," I said. "He's just trying to get your goat."

"I don't have a goat."

"It's an *expression*—look it up," I teased. "I'll expect a full report tomorrow. In the meantime, here's how make-your-own-dinner night works: We, the parents, have the night off from cooking. We all fend for ourselves. You can eat whatever you want as long as you make it and you clean it up. If you want to eat an entire jar of jam, knock yourself out. Just wash the spoon."

They looked confused. I reiterated, "Like I said, if you want to eat an entire jar of jam . . ." Now suspicious, they left the room without saying a word.

I found The Tall One in the kitchen a little while later pouring himself a gigantic bowl of Special K and heating up a can of Ranch Beans.

"That's a good-looking combo meal," I said.

He smiled. It was the look of empowerment. He sat down to his two bowls of gruel and dug in.

You see—with free dinner, we're all liberated.

DECEMBER

The L Word

It had been several months since The Young One last saw his mother. He insisted he was suffering from "separation anxiety," and I had to agree; he did seem to be missing her with intensity—slumped shoulders, loss of appetite, and, most noticeably, a dramatic need to display affection. The kid was oozing emotion of the soap opera variety.

Earlier in the week, Hank walked outside to get the *Times* and The Young One treated it as a formal departure.

"Bye, Daddy. I love you."

"I'm not going anywhere. I'm just getting the paper."

"I know. I just love you, anyway."

Since then, he'd been throwing the L word around like he was afraid of losing it. Poor kid—I could tell his bravado was shot. He'd reached his limit. It had been too long. He needed his mom—not the step-, but the real one, June. Video chatting was not cutting it. He was tired of talking to her forehead, and who could blame him?

This morning, Hank shuffled into the bathroom and was about to shut the door when The Young One appeared in the hallway. "Bye, Daddy. I love you."

Hank also recognized that his little man was falling apart. "Love you," he indulged. "But I'm not going anywhere. I'll be right back."

"Okay," said The Young One. Hank slowly closed the door, leaving his son standing out in the hall, waving a tearful good-bye.

Even The Tall One was exhibiting signs of a heavy heart—he was listless and mopey, although he wouldn't admit it was from missing his mother. Unlike his brother, The Tall One keeps his feelings tucked away and his disappointments quiet. I understood this. I was just like him as a kid, and in moments like these I feel a strong bond with him.

"Are you okay?" I asked The Tall One over the kitchen table. I passed him the box of Glorious Grains.

"I'm tired," he said, his eyelids at half-mast. Then he closed them completely, like he was meditating or thanking the universe for the creation of oats.

I felt the boys' heartache and I wanted to comfort them, but I held back. I wasn't sure they'd accept consolation about their mother's absence from me. So I kept my distance, feeling a little left out of the maternal-love thing.

You know *that feeling* mothers talk about? Unconditional, unquestionable, and sometimes even irrational love? The feeling that comes with having a child of your own—absolute, instinctual love.

I knew how to love, but I didn't know what that maternal type of love felt like. I imagined it must be similar to how I felt about my own mother, my father, Gram. I gave my love to them freely, without thinking about it. And I never ran out. I always had more.

When Hank and I first got together, I guessed there were many who assumed—or, like Hank, *hoped*—that I'd instantly fall in love with his boys, too. But that wasn't the case. I was charmed by the boys right away, and most days, even now, living with them, I was tickled by the things they said and did. But that didn't mean I was going to be first in line to donate a kidney. I know this sounds pretty awful, but let's be honest—how many stepmoms love their stepkids at "hello"?

The truth was, I just didn't feel *that way* about The Tall One and The Young One yet, and I had to wonder, would I ever? I cared for them a great deal. I was very fond of them, but did I *love* them?

I've long felt that society expects women to feel exaggerated sweetness for anything with a heartbeat, especially children. Like we were all born with an indiscriminate gushing gene. How did this rumor get started? Children may be easier to love than, say, your office cube-mates, but it's not instant. I've always been quick to point out the obvious—children are just small people, and people aren't always easy to love.

But, Hank's kids were lovable. I just hadn't fallen yet.

Mom, in an effort to encourage me, said she remembered the moment when she started to feel motherly love for my two stepsisters. "It took years for me to have my moment. There were many times when our family was battling and I'd think *Why am I doing this? Am I nuts?*"

I asked myself the same question. Why was I doing this? Because I loved Hank—and because I knew that eventually I'd probably fall for his kids, too. If I hadn't thought my shaky heart would relax, I wouldn't have signed up for the job. Still . . .

"I don't think I've had my moment," I told Mom. And I felt terribly guilty admitting this. It seemed there were some feelings too raw to be expressed out loud.

I wanted to know how other stepmoms felt, so I asked some of my favorite online steps. Plenty of women said that I couldn't and *shouldn't* force feelings. Just because you adore the man, they said, doesn't mean you will feel the same way about his kids. Or that they will adore you. Love doesn't happen right away. *Of course it doesn't!* Many of my girlfriends painstakingly screened men for years before they found one to truly love. It took me thirty-five years to find Hank, and I didn't tell him I loved him until I knew I really meant it.

I supposed I was doing the same thing with his boys. I hadn't told them I loved them—or they me, for that matter. I felt kind of mean withholding the L word, but at least I was being real. I wanted to wait until it came naturally. Kids are smart, especially my little brainiacs—they would know if I was just feeding them a line.

Some of my online gals suggested I might not ever experience the type of love I was describing until I had a child of my own. Which was exactly what a lot of them had done.

When Margaret nudged me at Thanksgiving, saying, "So, when do I get more grandkids?" I thought, *More? I need to birth some, as well?*

I was able to knock her off topic by bringing up the wedding. "You know, we still have a big ol' Southern wedding to plan. There's just no time to be thinking about babies right now. Maybe afterward."

But the truth was, I wasn't sure I ever wanted my own. For now, stepkids were enough kids. I had my hands full. Seriously, what kind of masochist would add a newborn to this mix? And actually, I was thankful that my clock appeared to be on the fritz. I'd been warned, "Once you hear the tick, there's no turning the damn thing off." For years, birth control had been my trusted friend, and this disappointed some of my girlfriends, who couldn't understand why I'd let my eggs go to waste. "You should freeze them," my girlfriend Claire said, "just in case." *In case what? I decide to fulfill my womanly duty?*

My ovaries resented the peer pressure. These were some of the same women who hassled me for years to get married. And then, as soon as I got engaged, they started demanding more. *Mama wants more. Gimme some baby fat.*

In fact, it wasn't so long ago that I showed up at a holiday party alone, disappointing Claire, who took one look at my solitary self and snapped, "Where's Pete?"

Here we go again. "We broke up," I said easily, and handed her a bottle of wine.

She stood before me in her party dress and oven mitts and gave me the sad face. I hate the sad face. Her pretty pink cheeks creased and she started to cry. So I took the baked Brie out of her hand and held her. "Claire, it's okay. Don't be sad. It was my idea. I'm fine with this."

But she was not fine.

"I thought you were going to get married," she whined.

Wait a minute—had I just wrecked *her* plans? I thought this was about me. She had hopes, I guessed, that I'd move into her cul-de-sac, where we would end up planning barbeques and playdates. When Hank and I got engaged, she was the first girlfriend I called. She wept. A month later, she wanted to know when I was going to start having babies.

Well, this Christmas holiday was only a few weeks away, and the only baby in our house was lying in a manger, part of the nativity scene that Hank had pulled out of storage and set up on a prominent side table. I hoped I was hiding my dismay. It's not that I have anything against the baby Jesus or his swaddling clothes—I just didn't want Christmas kitsch taking over the house. It was our first holiday living together as a family and I was fairly certain Hank and I didn't see eye-to-eye regarding festive decor. I favored the Martha Stewart look: elegant trimmings and complementary colors, with a dash of sentiment and an overall sense of uniformity. You know, the secular approach. But I'd married the son of a preacher, so naturally I worried that the five large boxes marked CHRISTMAS now parked in the middle of the green room contained religious artifacts that I'd be forced to display. And possibly to genuflect to.

I'd resisted unpacking them all week, but I couldn't put it off any longer. A naked six-foot fir was standing in the front window begging to be dressed. We'd just brought her home, and as the self-appointed queen of holiday style, I felt it was my responsibility to cover her up.

The boys expected an artificial tree, the one Hank had carted around for nearly a decade—the one I'd secretly dumped in the trash before we left the Bay Area.

"Where's Daddy's tree?" asked The Young One.

"That tacky thing in the box?" I gibed.

"It's not tacky," insisted The Young One. "It's the best tree in the world. It looks *exactly* like a real tree . . . except for the hooks you hang the branches on," he added.

In the world? Wow, I thought. *This kid really needs to get out of the house more often.*

"I'm sorry," I said, "but the days of the fake tree are gone. From now on, in our house, we're getting the real deal."

If this sounded like a decree, it was, and my stern delivery surprised even me. But I meant it. I was putting my foot down. This was a battle worth picking. And I was sure my California family would agree.

We'd always had a live tree growing up. In fact, I don't think I ever even knew anyone who had a fake tree. I supposed this might have had more to do with geography than anything else. Sonoma County (and specifically the West County, where I'm from) is full of Christmas-tree farms. Why buy a plastic look-alike from Home Depot when you could enjoy a family jaunt into the neighboring woods and cut your own? Getting the annual tree was an event; it lasted, at the very least, an entire weekend morning, and calendars were marked for the occasion. And who wouldn't love wandering through a pine labyrinth, row after row of Douglas fir, Monterey pine, sugar pine, and Silvertip, searching for a timeless beauty with perfect stature and scent? Once we chose "the most beautiful tree in the forest," someone (usually the male attending) got down on all fours and started sawing away, muttering something festive like "s@n of a b!tch" that the women and children would traditionally ignore. I adored this ritual and felt the season wouldn't be the same without it.

Is it possible, I now wondered, *that some families reject this ritual? Inconceivable!*

When The Young One complained that "live trees drop needles, and why can't we just spray the tree with a pine scent?" I wanted to give him a time-out. Then I realized his flawed thinking was forgivable; it wasn't his fault. He was only following his own family tradition, and I supposed I ought to be respectful.

"Pine needles, you say? Since when do you care what gets on the floor?"

"They make a mess and jam up the vacuum."

This made me laugh. I was pretty sure the kid had never turned the vacuum on.

"Okay," I said. "How 'bout this . . . I'll make you a deal. We can set up the plastic tree for Christmas, but you have to keep it in your room the rest of the year."

"Fine, I'll store it in my closet," said the little smarty-pants.

"No," I corrected him. "You have to keep it *set up* in your room all year."

I knew I had him—he was speechless. I could see his ten-year-old mind turning, trying to work out a solution.

"It won't fit," he challenged, "unless I put it on top of my bed."

"Or just move your bed out," I offered, "and sleep under the tree."

He crossed his arms and puffed out his bony chest. I knew I'd won.

"What do you think?" I laughed. "Is it a deal?"

"She got you there," Hank chimed in. He'd hauled in another CHRISTMAS box.

So, I'd gotten my tree. We weren't able to cut our own, but we found a nursery with noble firs from Oregon, and even after the long haul to Texas they still smelled heavenly. By the time we got ours into the house and standing upright in the front window, The Young One was swooning from its sweet aroma. He gave an exaggerated whiff and said, "It smells just like the holidays, doesn't it?"

What a diplomat! "Now, that's the spirit!" I said.

So, here we were, in the holiday mood. Hank was hanging mistletoe, Ray Charles was singing about the spirit of the season, The Young One had embraced a new tradition, and if I was half the grown-up he was, I would do the same—and stop fantasizing about throwing Hank's ornaments out with the cat litter.

I opened the first box of ornaments and took a deep breath. *Jesus, Mary, and Joseph!*

Hank's decorations were of two categories: House of God and Baby Bear. For several years, Margaret had sent Hank the same ornament—a jumbo bulb with a picture of her church on it. I thought hanging just one would be an appropriate tribute to her life's work (hanging the collection might bring down the tree), but I knew better than to suggest this. Margaret knew when I'd been bad or good—*I better be good for goodness sake.*

So I hung the churches and then I sprinkled some of my nondenominational ornaments about and then considered what to do with all the baby bears. In my mind, bears—not grizzly, but teddy—were kind of like glitter-dipped carnations on Valentine's Day: a little trite for my taste. I'd made a frowny face as I unpacked teddy bears on sleds, in stockings, eating candy canes, ringing bells.

The Tall One emerged from his room and offered to help me decorate. I appreciated the assistance but every time he hung a cub I cringed. I felt irritability start to take hold, like I might turn into El Izzy Loco at any moment and throw ornaments at the wall. I told myself to calm down. *'Tis the season for acceptance and love.* I remembered that Mom and Stanton always drank hot brandy when they decorated the tree; perhaps that's what I needed. I took another deep breath and forced my shoulders to relax. I unwrapped another ornament—teddy holding a big present. The Tall One took it out of my hand and said with delight, "I remember this one!" I stiffened. What was my problem? Why was this making me so uptight?

I looked down at our decorations. I had unconsciously separated them into two piles: theirs and mine. I looked up at the tree. *My* ornaments were easy to find. They were up high, and in the front. I'd been careful not to hang any on the lower branches or in the back, where they might be missed. Hank and the boys had so many ornaments, and I had so few. When The Tall One wasn't paying attention, I hung my favorite ruby slipper on a prominent branch. I supposed it was kind of like how I felt in this family: There were three of them and only one of me, and if I didn't force myself to the front, I ran the risk of disappearing.

Dear Santa,

For Christmas this year, I'd like to be less territorial and insecure.

Yours truly, Izzy

Just as I was about to shamefully leave the room and search for some brandy, The Young One skipped into the room and handed me his typed Christmas list. He looked up at the tree and spotted the slipper. His eyes sparkled at the sight. "Where'd that come from?" He said. "That's awwwwesome." The kid has excellent timing.

The Young One's X-Mas List

1. 2 lb. of concord grapes
2. De-FIB-ulator
3. People counter
4. Chocolate fountain
5. Speed-sensing baseball
6. Electric folding bike
7. Portable beach cabana
8. Mini fridge
9. Memory-foam mattress (twin)
10. 12-hour voice recorder

The Young One has a tradition of preparing eccentric wish lists (most items courtesy of the *SkyMall* catalog—the kid flies a lot). Earlier I'd heard him banging away on his old Smith Corona manual typewriter and figured he was typing up something beyond his years, like an outline of the Industrial Age, but he'd been hard at work on something kid-appropriate—his Christmas list. All four of us crowded onto the green couch, surrounded by a wide assortment of holiday decor, and read through the items. I couldn't determine which he wanted more—the portable beach cabana or the grapes.

The Young One supplied Hank and me with two copies of his list—one for us, the other for June and John. We'd arranged for two separate celebrations this year, and he didn't want duplicate gifts. *Good thinking*. He reminded us to consider shipping costs and gave us the price breakdown for the big-ticket items. "I'll get right on it," I indulged him.

I was looking forward to having our own style of festivities this year, divorced from the patterns of the past. And I knew I wasn't the only woman with a ready-made family who was feeling this way.

A recent comment by one of my stepmom buddies had struck a nerve. It was about too much togetherness and it hit on a very touchy subject: What are the expectations of the new stepmom during the holidays? The woman who wrote it was struggling with how to play nice during the holiday with her husband's ex, who wanted to spend Christmas night—the whole night—at her house.

This scenario sounded very familiar.

Before I came along, Hank had a similar arrangement with June. In the interest of keeping children and parents together throughout the holidays, the traveling circus celebrated together. Most often, Hank would simply head over to June and John's and join the party in progress.

Hank said, "It's just how we've always done it."

The first Christmas Eve that Hank and I were dating, he spent the night on June's couch in order to wake up early Christmas morning, start the coffee, and wait for the rest of the gang to gather downstairs in pajamas to open gifts. I was not included (nor did I really want to be) in their cozy party, and who was I, the new girlfriend, to question it? Still, I wondered:

a) How does John, June's new husband, feel about spending all of his holidays with June's first husband? and

b) How are the boys interpreting this? Two men under the tree and one mom. *Is this what divorce looks like?*

I kept my opinions to myself until the next year, and then I raised my voice, and not very articulately: "So, Hank, how does this work?" (Of course, what I wanted to say was: "I know this seems 'normal' to you, but if you haven't noticed, another woman—that would be me, your girlfriend—has been added to the group, and I need to know how you see me fitting into this scene?")

I understood that many divorced couples make accommodations that may seem odd from the outside but work on the inside, and I thought it was kind of admirable of Hank to keep doing this, but now what? Was I supposed to start sleeping on the couch, too? There may be only one of me and seven of them, but if I'm going to join the family, don't I get a say?

I gave myself a shot of courage and requested a change of venue. I suggested that Hank get his own tree, spend the night in his own house, and have a separate celebration with the boys . . . one that I could be a part of without feeling like an outsider.

Hank furrowed his brow and got that look, the one that says *Woman, why do you have to go stirring things up?* I knew I was the first "serious girlfriend" to come along and challenge the routine since Hank's divorce, so I expected resistance. I wasn't surprised when he said, "It's just easier the other way. We're all together. We all get along. We don't have to drive across town . . ."

When you say "we," aren't you forgetting me?

I nodded like I understood and then I said, as clearly as I could speak the words, "It might be easier, but it doesn't really work— anymore."

Ladies, you meet the man of your dreams, but he has kids, an ex-wife, and a lifetime of habits. How do you squeeze in? Hank and I had become a unit, and as far as I was concerned, our unit didn't include his ex, or any of mine. I'm not an extension cord. You can't just plug me into the family power strip. Still, I felt a little selfish asking to be accommodated, like my "girlfriend" needs weren't significant enough to be raised, and I half expected June to set me straight: *Hey, lady, I had him first, and this is how we do it. Don't ruin Christmas!* With this in mind, I thought maybe I should just drink the hot grog and shut up.

I was familiar with the mainstream thinking that shuttling kids between Mom and Dad on a holiday causes sadness and unnecessary logistical challenges. However, from what I could tell, The Tall One and The Young One were trained pacifists. They'd been tossed around for many years now; they seemed to expect it without question. I doubted they would protest splitting the holiday between their parents. If I was wrong, I'd explain that two houses on Christmas morning meant twice the gifts. "Take it from me," I'd say. "It's a pretty good deal."

After my parents divorced, I spent every Christmas Day with both Mom and Dad separately, and, really, it wasn't all that traumatic. A bit of a hassle, yes, but never did I lament *If only Mommy and Daddy were gathered under the tree together like old times.* But maybe my reaction was atypical. I'd read that children of divorce secretly want their parents to reunite, even if the marriage wasn't a good one. In Hank and June's case, they got along famously, even exchanged gifts, but they didn't want to be married anymore. I was confused myself—if it was such a party, why did they split up?

Hank explained that his marriage to June had its share of problems, but after they separated, they both felt it important to grow their friendship—for the sake of the kids. "We wanted to be more than the average divorced couple," he told me.

Okay, I understand that every family does it differently, but here's what I think my parents did right: They sat me down and told me it was over. Dad moved out and Mom moved on. They used the old Band-Aid method: Rip the mofo off. I can't imagine my added grief had I spent years hoping and believing that maybe someday my parents would reunite. But that was just me.

The stepkid in me couldn't help but question Hank and June's method. I wondered—when divorced couples say they don't want to juggle their kids between houses on a holiday, is this really about the needs of the kids, or more about them and their guilt over dissolving a marriage and breaking up a family? The split becomes unmistakably clear when your kid has two stockings: one for Mom's house and the other for Dad's.

Now, with us in Texas and June and John still in California, there hadn't been much debate about whether we'd celebrate independently. Hank and I would have an early celebration with the boys in Austin and then we'd fly them to the Bay Area for the actual holiday. The boys seemed perfectly pleased to have back-to-back weekends of holiday cheer, mostly because it meant more eggnog, of which they are avid fans. They'd be gone a full luscious week, and Hank and I would have the house to ourselves for the first time since the boys moved in. I had big plans for hot, married sex. I prepared Hank for the inevitable, saying, "I'm going on an all-dick diet."

Our bedroom had gotten pretty quiet over the past few months, and I found myself suffering from the same sexual apathy that plagued many of my married-with-children girlfriends. Too tired. Not in the mood. Don't feel sexy. Although coming from them it was understandable—they were cleaning up newborn barf and chasing willful toddlers around the house. What was my excuse? *I'm a stepmom to a moody teen who stays in his room all day and to another who follows me around asking questions?* I couldn't believe how quickly this had happened. We hadn't even been married six months and already the newlywed excitement was gone. This was tragic! I thought about all those dumb jokes—Nothing spoils your sex life like a marriage— and how true they were.

At least our situation hadn't gotten to the point it had for my friend Mary. She was actually considering hypnotherapy to recapture her desire. She told me over the phone, "I used to love it, and ever since the second baby, I don't know what's happened to me. I'm just not interested. Ever."

Like Mary's husband, Hank, too, was discouraged by the limited access I was giving him to my lower half. I hadn't lost my interest, but I was repulsed by the presentation of my goods. Since I'd been out of work and spending more than I was making, I felt it only fair that I should cut back on certain expenses. My bimonthly bikini wax was one of them. As a result, my girl parts were overgrown and practically unreachable. I cautioned Hank, "Once you go in, you might never come out." I deserved my own show on Animal Planet.

Hank required no convincing that our sex life needed a pick-me-up. Why is it that men equate good sex with acrobatics? The closer we got to the Christmas break, the more frequent his fantasy descriptions of aerobic stunts became. He'd been browsing through a book that a buddy gave him called *Sex Every Day in Every Way* and had decided on two positions worth exploring—The Jaws of Life and The Heisman. I wasn't sure he had the balance or the upper body strength to pull either off without injury, but I encouraged him anyway. "That sounds hot, baby." Perhaps it was just a matter of having the right equipment, or at least a yoga mat on the floor?

I was looking forward to the break, not only for rekindling the passion, but also to rest and recover. For the first time in months I'd be able to let down my stepmom guard and breathe. Plus, my hope-to-be new BFF Lena had just called. She was coming to Austin, and we made a plan to play. And just in time. I was desperately missing my sisters and West Coast girlfriends—shopping and prepping for the holiday just weren't the same without them, and with all the Christmas music I was playing, my sentimentalism was raging. It's tradition for Gigi, Piper, Mom, and me to meet for holiday cocktails in San Francisco's finest hotels. Perhaps Lena and I could start our own tradition in downtown

Austin this year? Maybe in that boutique hotel on Congress Avenue with the antler chandeliers and cowhide sofas.

The holiday season was bringing out other emotions as well. There were certain feelings I hadn't been honest about, words I couldn't say to Hank without causing a fight, bitterness I wanted to keep hidden from the kids. I unloaded on Sarah the shrink.

"I'm a little upset with June." If I was going to refresh my spirit and start the year anew, I had to clear out the ugly gunk first.

She nodded and gave me the look. You know, the one that says, *Spill it.*

"I feel like I'm the only one brave enough to say it: Where *is* she? The Young One is having a mini-crisis and The Tall One acts like he doesn't remember who I'm talking about—*Oh, yeah, Mommy. Can I go back to my room now?*—and I don't know what to tell them. Don't get me wrong, I think it's been healthy for Hank and me to have distance from June and John to establish our own Texas foursome, but enough already. This was not the plan. I didn't leave my family, my job, my home, and my friends because I was dying to move to sagebrush country. This was the 'group' decision and we all agreed to it. If I'd known I was going to be raising her kids full-time, I never would have left the Bay Area. At least there I had a support system. Here I have no relief, and frankly, I'm overwhelmed."

"People do sometimes change their minds," said Sarah, "and if June decides to stay in California, are you prepared for what that might mean?"

"You mean not move here *at all*?"

Sarah nodded.

"You mean, I'd be expected to assume financial and emotional responsibility for her kids? *Just like that?*"

"Maybe," she said.

"No way. That's not fair."

Sarah seemed amused by this. *I pay this woman to be on my side, not so I can entertain her.* "You don't think it's unfair?"

She smiled wide now. "It might be, but you can't control what June is going to do. You just can't. She's going to make her own choices, and you might not like them, but they're her choices to make and all you can do is stand by the choices *you've* made. It may not be fair, but that's not the point."

Yeah, yeah—life ain't fair. But Sarah did have a point. Did I want to spend my energy battling with expectations, or just dealing with what was? I added another

Stepmom Rule to my list. Number Ten: Surrender your expectations.

Sarah said, "If it helps, you're doing a great job." But was I?

I'd been managing, sure, but it's not like I'd been given a WORLD'S BEST TEMPORARY MOM coffee mug. I guess I figured June was always on her way, that in no time she'd be knocking on our door with babes in hand and take back the mother role. So I never totally dug in. But here's the simple truth: June's not here—I am.

I left Sarah's office determined to give the boys the best pre-holiday they'd ever had. I found myself in the closest grocery store searching for Sara Lee Pecan Coffee Cake in the frozen foods section. This is Hank's Christmas must-have, and the man had been searching high and low for the dessert, but with no success. He was adamant: "It has to be Sara Lee, and it has to be pecan. Not crumb. Not streusel."

And then, a Christmas miracle! I stumbled upon the mother lode, hidden behind the reduced-fat pound cake. I threw six of them into my basket and headed over to the bakery and picked up the closest thing I could find to honor my taste buds. (My California family gorges on pizza bagels with lox, cream cheese, and red onion first thing Christmas morning. It's bizarre, I know, but aren't so many of our family traditions? And isn't that what makes them great?)

Back at the house, I switched on all our twinkling lights and put on my favorite holiday CD—*That Special Time of Year* by Gladys Knight and the Pips—and bebopped into the kitchen and pulled out my grandmother's cookie cookbook. Yum, Russian tea cakes—that's what I'll make.

I called out, "Hey, guys! Wanna make cookies?"

No answer. Where were they?

Determined to put the little elves to work, I headed back toward their rooms, cookie book in hand. I passed by the bathroom and, noticing the door was ajar, pushed it open. Turns out it was occupied.

The Young One looked up from the toilet and screamed, "CLOSE THE DOOR!!!!"

He was mortified. I'd intruded on a private moment. He was sitting on the can with his holey jeans down around his ankles, reading from the Book of Luke.

"Sorry!" I said and pulled the door shut. And then I added, "You want to make cookies?"

"Not NOW," he barked.

I wasn't surprised to discover him engrossed in a good story. He savors the written word, whenever and wherever he can get it. But the Bible? On the can? *The kid really is getting into the Christmas spirit this year.*

But then again, Hank and I had recently noticed that some of The Young One's favorites (*Swiss Family Robinson* and *Wiring 1-2-3*) had been cast aside. In his free time, he was burying himself in the Word. No doubt he inherited this spiritual fire from his grandmother, and I had no objection to the kid exploring his faith, but this wasn't the first time I'd found him in the bathroom reading for an extended amount of time. I felt awkward butting in, but his behavior just wasn't practical. The kid was denying others time in the sanctuary. Namely, his brother.

A week later I caught him at it again, but this time he'd locked himself in, leaving his brother with nowhere to go. (Yes, there are two bathrooms in the house, but *ours* is off-limits to kids and guests. What can I say—my confessional is not open to the public.) Hank wasn't home yet, so I knocked on the door, saying, "Can you please wrap it up with the Boss so your brother doesn't have to pee in the hall?"

No answer. So I taunted, "I have a key."

No response, just the faint sound of a page turning. The Tall One pounded on the door. "Open up!"

Nothing.

The Tall One looked at me with watery eyes; he was in desperate need of a solution. I said, "Dude, the Spirit is stirring in there. Can you relieve yourself on the hedge out front?"

"Izzy," he cried. "Can't I just use yours?"

That's when the front door swung open. Hank was home from work. "Hi, it's me," he called out. "Where is everyone?"

He found us huddled together outside the bathroom door, and before I could silence him, The Tall One gave me away: "Dad, make him come out. He's reading the Bible again, and Izzy wants me to pee on the bushes."

"Welcome home, babe," I chirped "Wanna make cookies?"

It was early evening and we'd had our first Texas Christmas with the boys. Never mind that we were the only ones in the neighborhood who opened gifts one week ahead of time; it felt right to us. The day began when Hank and I roused the boys from bed and lured them into the kitchen with smells of Sara Lee and salmon. After opening gifts and lounging in front of the tree until early afternoon, we started a new tradition when I announced, "Fancy imported cheese tasting." Hank and I drank wine and the boys gulped sparkling cider and we all spoke in phony French accents and smeared Brie on baguettes.

I was impressed with the boys' ability to adapt. We'd gone through the whole day and they hadn't asked questions or complained—they just rolled with it. I hoped their strength was sincere and that underneath their tough exteriors their hearts weren't heavy or their stomachs in knots. I knew it couldn't be easy having their parents so far apart. This was a first for them—Mom and Dad residing in different states for stocking exchange.

With the boys loaded on sugar and material treasures, Hank and I were officially off the clock. I was in the kitchen when the boys came in and wrapped their gangly arms around me. "Thanks for the gifts," they mumbled. They smelled like boys who hadn't showered in three days, but they were warm and I leaned right into them. I was pretty sure their father had put them up to this, but still, I was touched.

I felt my heart start to soften like the butter I'd packed into three dozen Russian tea cookies. *Uh-oh.* As soon as I realized what was happening, I willed myself to harden right back up. *Wait, why did I do that?* And then I had a Christmas epiphany: I'm afraid of letting go. And I was afraid to answer my own question—*Why?*

That night I had my first stepmom nightmare and woke up sweaty and scared. In it, The Young One turned bad. Meaning, he decided to hate me. And I hated him back.

My dream followed this basic plot line: The Young One returned from California after seeing June and set out to destroy my home. He scattered pieces of paper, erasers, pencils, gum, and toy parts all over the house. He began construction of an elaborate fifteen-story crane in the middle of the living room and invited a herd of ratty kids over who collectively pissed on my authority. They said spiteful things like "We can do whatever we want, Izzy. Get out of our way!" and The Young One gave me the look, the one that says, *I may be short, but I'm taking you down.*

That's when things got extra awful.

I said, "Bring it on! When your dad gets home you're busted!" Except he wasn't. Hank took The Young One's side and told me I was overreacting. "A metal crane would look just fine in our living room," he said.

Abandoned by Hank, rejected by The Young One, and ignored by The Tall One, I was stuck with my very lonely self.

And then I woke up and it was time to take the guys to the airport.

I was completely rattled. I couldn't shake the dream.

I'd read about women who battled so much with their stepchildren that their marriages eventually dissolved. As much as they tried, for whatever reason, they just couldn't get along. Every time I read one of these accounts I felt relief to not be that woman. But now I had the spooky feeling, as we drove to the airport and the boys bickered in the backseat, that I wasn't safe.

What if the boys come back from California and don't like me anymore? Or what if once they see their mother again, they don't want to come back at all? My stomach tightened. There was that panicky feeling again. Except this time, what was scaring me was not the fear of getting attached, but that I already had.

Hank looked over at me. "Are you okay, babe? You have a funky look on your face."

This made the boys crack up and, for some reason, it made me laugh, too. I snapped out of it and we made weird monster faces at one another the rest of the way to the airport.

When it was time to say good-bye I hung back, but The Young One wouldn't let me off that easy. After squeezing Hank hard and tight, he latched on to me—backpack and all. Even The Tall One, fourteen and put off by parental fawning, gave me a hug. If there was a perfect time to say the L word, this would have been it. I felt like I *should* say it—I think I even *wanted* to say it—but I just wasn't quite there. I stuffed the words back down my throat and hugged The Tall One until he pulled away and I said, "Hey, guys, maybe next year I'll lift my ban on artificial trees . . ."

The Young One threw his arms up in the air, saying, "Yay!"

"As long as it's cotton candy pink and covered in sparkles."

"Izzzzzyyyy," he groaned.

And then they were gone.

The Return
of the Stepkid Shuffle

Hank was sobbing into his pillow. Big, choking cries. It startled me awake. There was my brick of a man, completely disarmed and in distress.

"Babe?" I whispered. I rubbed his back. "Wake up . . ."

He rolled toward me with outstretched arms, grabbing for me with force and slipping into the space right underneath my chin—what I call the nook. I held Hank tight and cradled his head—one of the sweetest things I get to do in this life. Instant comfort, for both of us.

"That was awful, just awful," he cried. Whatever had him pulled him back under. He was shaking, tears soaking into my tank top.

Minutes later, he recounted the nightmare.

He was alone in our house when he heard something outside. He went out to the front yard with a flashlight (just like in your typical slasher flick) and found The Young One standing on the lawn.

"What are you doing here?" Hank said. "You're supposed to be at your mom's."

Hank explained that in the dream, he couldn't understand how The Young One had gotten back to Texas when we'd just put him on a plane to California. Hank walked him inside, only to discover The Tall One sitting alone on the kitchen counter.

"What are you guys doing here?" Hank said with alarm. "I don't understand—how did you get here?" Hank leaned in closer to The Tall One and touched his shirt. "Why are you soaking wet?"

The Tall One didn't answer. He sat on the counter without moving, a puddle forming underneath him on the kitchen floor.

As Hank told me this, my stomach did a somersault. His recollection was uncomfortably vivid, and creepy. I kept my interpretation to myself—that the boys were ghosts who'd been swept out to sea. Gone.

Instead, I offered in a neutral tone, "Why don't you call the boys and make sure they're okay? I'm sure they're fine, but you'll feel better when you hear their voices."

Hank got out of bed, wet and wounded, and dialed June's number.

Hank feels lost, crippled without his boys, but he keeps it hidden well—this paternal weakness. On the surface, Hank can appear indifferent, even cold—the stern father. He blames this on his deep-set eyes, says they make him look mean. It's a decent argument. Without his glasses on, he can look hard, but don't let this fool you.

Hank got June's voicemail and didn't bother to leave a message. He crawled back into bed and shrugged it off. "I'll call later. I'm sure they're fine."

Just like that his panic seemed to disappear, but I knew better. Hank was scared. What he was able to hide from most people, I saw in the dark. I'd seen him fall apart like this before, and I understood the complicated truth. He's afraid he'll lose his grip and the boys will be pulled back toward their mother, carried away like some Pacific riptide. I imagine this is a natural consequence of divorce, although I really didn't believe June would ever attempt to take the boys away from Hank. I'd never gotten that impression. But had something changed? Was there something he wasn't telling me?

I lay awake thinking about his nightmare. While I was indeed starting to have my own doubts that June would ever leave California and make it to Texas, I still trusted her original intentions—she wanted the boys to grow up with both her and Hank. And even though I thought packing up and moving around the country as a band of eight sounded like a ridiculous idea four months ago, I'd still bought in. I couldn't discount their efforts, and apparent success, at making it work for as long as it had. For nearly ten years the traveling circus had operated without a hitch, so I had to believe that June wasn't going to intentionally trash the tent now. But Hank seemed to be losing confidence, and I watched worry start to push him around like a schoolyard bully—a persistent little punk who showed up the next morning at our kitchen table ready to pick a fight.

Hank and I were drinking our first cup of coffee with a free Sunday to plan when I said, "What do you want to do today?" Of course I'd already planned a mental itinerary. We'd camp out all morning at Jo's on South Congress, watching a parade of tattooed hipsters sip espresso, then explore the latest museum collection at the Blanton on the UT campus, and then stroll around wintery Lady Bird Lake until

our bones froze. Finally, we'd find somewhere warm and cozy to retreat with a bottle of smoky red.

I waited for Hank to weigh in with a better plan, but he just sat at
the table, crunching his Flax 500 cereal, making no effort at conversation. After about seven sullen bites, I sighed. "So it's finally just you
and me again, and we don't have anything to talk about, is that right?"

He gave me a sad stare. "I miss the boys."

I really wanted to punch him. This was our vacation, our break.
For the first time in months, we had one precious week to relax, to
forget about parenting, to be newlyweds! I glared at Hank's cereal
bowl. Newlyweds, don't eat fiber-rich cereal in separate silences; they
feed each other mango, papaya, and other fashionable fruit, for fuck's
sake. I took a deep, calming breath but my tone remained impatient.
"I know you miss them, but they'll be back *very* soon, so I think we
should enjoy our time—you know, when it's just you and me."

Hank gave me a look like I was an abusive nurse at the orphanage.
I continued anyway. "You don't agree?"

Hank looked at me hard. "Why don't you just say it?" His tone
had taken a scary turn. "You don't want them to come back!"

Ouch. I admit I never seem to run out of snarky stepmom com-
ments, but that doesn't mean I want the boys to pack their suitcases for
good. My sarcasm is just my shtick. My entire family prides itself on
our jabbing humor. "Passed down for generations," my dad has always
said. Hank knew this. He'd married into it. Plus, he'd witnessed my
recent surge of sentiment at the airport. In the emotional-attachment
department, I was making real progress. But if he didn't see this—
if he thought I had secret hopes of breaking up their blood-bond
threesome—I might find myself on the losing end in a fight over loyal-
ties. Oh, no—my terrible nightmare was coming true! In fact, I'd just
read about this type of situation; one of my online gals confided that
her husband warned her to *never* make him choose between her and

the kids because there would be no question whom he would pick. *If push came to shove, would Hank shove me out of the front door?*

Fearing a stinker of a bomb might go off, I proceeded with caution. "That's not true. Yes, sometimes the stepparenting gig makes me crazy. Sometimes I need breathing room. But that doesn't mean I don't want them to come back."

I thought about adding, *and it doesn't make me (or you) a bad parent to enjoy a little kid-free time,* but decided to keep this nugget of wisdom to myself for the time being.

He gave me a long look. "Okay," he finally said. "But since you're speaking in double negatives, let me see if I've got this right—are you saying that you *want* them to come back?"

It was a direct question; I had to say yes and dissect any wavering feelings later.

This seemed to put Hank at ease. His shoulders relaxed and he said, "I had to ask. I'm sure every stepparent has been asked something like that at some point."

He had to ask? Did he really question whether I wanted his kids around? Hadn't I proven that? I was mad at him and I was mad at me, so I left the table and holed up in the bathroom. I stared at myself in the mirror to see if I looked as ugly as I felt. Not quite, but I put on some makeup anyway. After playing around with three different lipsticks and four shades of eye shadow, I remembered how I used to steal away in Dad's house as a preteen and play with stepmom Crystal's makeup. This was how I discovered liquid eyeliner and how to curl my eyelashes. Had Dad and Crystal ever had an argument like this? I knew that she was jealous of the private time I got with him, and they had ongoing spats that sounded like this:

Crystal: Why do you and Izzy have to spend so much time together, just the two of you?

Dad:	What are you talking about? All three of us watched a movie together last night. You and I went to dinner the night before.
Crystal:	Yeah, but then you guys always have to do your "father-daughter" thing.
Dad:	What's your point?
Crystal:	Well, I don't get it. I don't understand why you need separate time.
Dad:	Because we have our own relationship, just like you and I have our own relationship.
Crystal:	Well, I don't like it.

And then she'd stomp out of the room. Or maybe she didn't, but that's how I remember it.

The woman was insecure. She needed my dad's full attention, and that often left little for me. I didn't hold it against him. I knew Dad was wild about me and he was stuck playing referee between a jealous wife and a needy kid. He and Crystal stayed together for five years, until she nearly sabotaged all his relationships—not just with me, but also with his old fishing buddies and many of his colleagues. Not long after they split, Dad took me aside and choked out a tearful apology. "She never understood why our relationship was important. She didn't get it." It was probably the saddest I've ever seen him. I don't think there's anything more devastating than someone broken by regret. He held my hand and cried. I loved him so much in that moment, for standing up for his kid. And now Hank was standing up for his, and I admired him equally. *But I wasn't a selfish Crystal.*

I went out into the garden. Last night the temperature dipped into the low thirties, but now the chill was gone. I let the sun hit my face. I needed to thaw. I toured the yard. All of our ornamental trees were dormant, the passion vine along the back fence had died back to the ground, and the wisteria branches were bare. The only color in the yard came from the crimson berries on the holly tree. The sun felt good, but the yard looked bleak and I felt equally empty.

I walked in circles on the dead Bermuda grass. Hank didn't think I wanted his sons around? Was that how he saw me? As unloving? *How awful.* I made a point of avoiding my reflection as I passed the dining room windows. I knew I had a tendency to be self-absorbed, but I wasn't without warmth and compassion. I'd signed up for this job, and I wasn't trying to weasel out of my responsibility. And anyway, quitting the kids was unconscionable, plus I cared about them. But there was something that was keeping me from getting deeply attached. I kicked some rocks into a patch of faded Mexican feather grass.

If I keep some healthy distance, I won't get hurt. If they keep some distance, they won't get hurt. There it was, the old *no one wants to get hurt* argument. How predictable.

I'd have to come up with something more profound than that. No one ever wants to get hurt, and in my case, this was a really poor excuse, since I'd had a pretty pain-free life. Unless . . . had I forgotten something? I searched my mind for injustices. I wasn't forgotten at the hospital or left out in the snow. I'd never gotten lost in the wilderness or left behind at the mall. Yet I could hear Sarah the shrink whispering in my ear, *Abandonment issues.*

I sat down on the back steps and started picking at the dead geranium leaves. I looked around the yard, as if I were expecting to find some nosy reporter scribbling down my thoughts to publish in tomorrow's tabloid. What was I hiding from? Sarah had asked me to remember how I felt when my parents divorced. My mind drifted back more than twenty-five years to a typical little-kid day. I had returned home from school, excited to practice "Bad, Bad Leroy Brown," my upcoming alto number in the school chorus recital. I was jubilant as I came through the front door, singing "Badder than old King Kong . . .

meaner than a junkyard dog." I found Mom and Dad both home from work early, seated together on our old antique rose couch. Something was off. They asked me in calm, restrained voices to sit down, and then they told me they were splitting up. Just like that.

They used the D word—*divorce.* I'd heard it from my friend Laura in school. Her parents were divorced. When I told her mine were splitting up, too, she said, "Welcome to the divorce-kids club." I remember shrinking into my favorite overstuffed chair, staring down at my lap, the only safe place to look. They told me it wasn't my fault and that they loved me, that everything would be okay. I'm sure they said other meant-to-be-comforting things, but I don't remember because I stopped listening. I sat there with my sheet music in front of my face, doing my familiar cry—a short, choking, strangled sob. Dad stood up and slowly walked over to me, took the lyrics out of my hands, and led me over to the couch and positioned me in the middle. We sat together, the three of us, just like we had always done, except this would be the last time, and I think we all knew it. Dad packed his suitcases and left that night.

I never saw it coming. My life was happy, simple, and safe, and then suddenly it wasn't. Things were never that simple again.

It could have been a lot worse. I was shell-shocked, sure, but to my parents' credit, they spared me their unhappiness. They kept any hostility or discontent quiet in an effort to protect me, and when they parted, it was civil—a term I became very familiar with at the age of nine, along with *shared custody.* In fact, the only time I walked in on a fight between the two of them was after they split, when Dad came over to divvy up the furniture. They had a testy argument over the love seat. I was a B student in the fourth grade, and even I recognized the irony of that.

Has being a child of divorce made me less trusting? Over the years, I came to understand the complexity of my parents' marriage. Their divorce was the inevitable conclusion to buried hurts and betrayals that finally broke the surface. In other words, they didn't just decide on Tuesday morning to get a divorce; things had been rocky for a while. But I guess the little person in me has never fully recovered. On an emotional level, I'm always braced for surprise, which isn't necessarily a bad thing when you grow up along a fault line. But I've grown up suspicious of people; I expect hearts to shift, things to fall apart, and this isn't a good worldview.

"You're a heartbreaker," my stepsister Piper said to me a few years ago, after I broke it off with yet another perfectly acceptable man. I can't deny that I have a record for banging around a heart or two, but if someone's going to hit the road, I need to go first. Let someone else say *I never saw* that *coming*.

Yet I'd finally come around, hadn't I? I'd married Hank, and for reasons I still didn't understand, I'd suspended my distrust of the un-predictable heart. With Hank, it felt natural to slip off my protective armor and pull him in close, but I was still shielding myself from his kids. Was I afraid they were going to abandon me? And go where? To live with their mother?

I really didn't feel like I was in competition with June. It's not like I was trying to win a popularity contest, because let's face it—there was none. June was the real mother and I was the step. If anyone was dispensable, I was (*if both June and I get terribly sick at the same time, who do you think will be spoon-fed medicinal broth?*). Sure, I wanted the boys to like me, but I wasn't going for the favorite mother vote.

So why was I holding the boys at a distance? What would Sarah the shrink say? *Attachment . . . trust . . . more abandonment stuff.* I plucked off another crinkled geranium leaf.

And just like that, shock came like a punch to the gut and I caught my breath. *Is it me? Am I scared of my* own *fickle heart?*

Maybe I'd been looking at this whole thing backward. Was it less about trusting the boys, and more about how much they could trust *me*? Trust me in what way, I wasn't sure, but I knew that depending on people was scary stuff and they'd already had their share of disappointments.

"OUCH!" I screeched. I jumped up from the ground and began a frenzied dance just as Hank appeared in the doorway. "What are you doing?" he asked.

"Fire ants," I said, slapping my legs. "Help—I can't get them off."

Our morning had started out rough, but we were able to save the afternoon. We made it down to Lady Bird Lake just before the sun went down and transformed the tree-lined trail into a shadowy wonderland. When Hank asked me how I wanted to spend the evening, I said, "I think it's time."

"Time for what?"

"The Jaws of Life."

In case he'd forgotten, I reminded Hank that he and my girl parts had become distant friends and we'd made a pact to get reacquainted as soon as the boys were away.

"Tonight, you're mine." I winked. "Prepare to be violated. And possibly bruised." Hank smiled and barked like a puppy.

We walked back to the car hand in hand and I thought, *We can totally do this.* We're high-functioning people. A slacker sex life just wouldn't do anymore. Plus, I'd recently read about a couple who chronicled their marathon sex—365 days in a row! The article, I guessed, was written as a wake-up call to the rest of us suffering sex-starved marriages, a deprived circle I refused to be a part of.

"This story," I said to Hank as we got into the car, "says that the average married couple has sex sixty-six times a year." I paused for emphasis. "That's like three hundred days off."

Hank turned the key in the ignition. "I love it when you do math."

But later that night, after a bottle of Kenwood cabernet and smoked pork ribs that we devoured down to the marrow, we crawled into bed much larger, and not necessarily lust-filled, people.

"I'm so tuckered," I whimpered.

"I'm gassy," Hank moaned.

The idea of throwing each other about, rolling around, mounting, and dismounting sounded exhausting. The only position I craved was horizontal, unconscious with blankets on top. So I suggested we make a change to the lovemaking schedule.

I said, "If we don't have sex now, then we *have* to set the alarm for six A.M., and do it then. No questions."

"Fine," Hank said and passed out.

At 5:50 A.M., the alarm went off. I looked at the clock and mumbled my signature morning greeting: "Snooze it."

"We're supposed to wake up and have sex," Hank grumbled into his pillow.

"Not yet," I argued. "Ten more minutes. Snooze it."

"Oh, right." Hank laughed. "Sex promptly at six, and not a *minute* sooner."

Yes—we did the deed. I was proud of Hank and of myself for keeping our pact when it would have been so easy to slip back into our familiar slump—consensual abstinence.

"You and your new lover aren't the only ones doing *it,*" I said with an air of smugness when I called Lena later that morning to brag. "Hank and I had hot, nasty, married sex."

Lena gave her high-pitched squeal, which inevitably gets a laugh out of me. The woman is always appropriately enthusiastic.

"I want details," she said.

"Gross—no way."

Later that evening, we joined Lena and her Austin boyfriend at a downtown art gallery to partake in one of Austin's newest trends: the supper club.

I goosed Hank in the parking lot before we walked in the door.

"Hey!" he said. He snapped my hand away and gave me a disapproving frown.

"Babe," I drawled, "I'm just keeping you in the mood, is all. They say that couples who want to prevent their marriage from growing stale have to experience new things: restaurants, people . . ."

This got a chuckle out of Hank. "*They* say? What's with all the data lately? Are you going through a stack of sex manuals or something?"

"I won't reveal my sources," I said. And then I goosed him again.

According to the article (in a reputable newspaper, BTW), the unexpected sparks romantic brain chemicals, so sitting down with twenty-five strangers to eat outlandish food, I figured, would be just the right aphrodisiac to keep Hank and me going for at least one more night.

We sat at long candlelit tables where waiters served us an eight-course meal that took four hours to consume, including chestnut soup, scallops with caper-and-apricot relish, prime rib with yogurt, red wine, and a chocolate tart with pomegranate sorbet that nearly sent me over the edge.

It wasn't so much the intense ingredients I devoured, but the scene: Hank and I dressed up, out on a date with new friends, engaged in adult conversation, with no curfew to keep. We sat with our knees touching, looking at each other often. Laughter and low light framed the scene and I thought up

Stepmom Rule Number Eleven: Every woman needs impromptu moments alone with the man she fell in love with.

* * *

The kids were due back soon, which meant our sexy alone days were numbered. I'd read that many stepmoms dreaded the "handoff," when the little darlings return from BM's house after being gone for a day, a week, a month. One new stepmom found the transition so disconcerting that she hid for an hour before she had the confidence, and the will, to creep out of her bedroom and resume stepmom duties. I admit, I had a bit of the old anxiety. *Attack! Lock the doors!* I'd gotten quite comfortable in our hushed house with Hank all to myself. But after Hank's biting accusation that I didn't want the kids around, it was important that I make a point of welcoming them home.

Days later, The Tall One and The Young One were back in the house and I was at the stove stirring a rubbery pot of four-dollar ragu. I'd persuaded Hank to take the night off from cooking. I had this romantic vision of myself preparing a simple Italian meal for my men— penne with fresh mozzarella, basil, garlic, and vine-ripened tomatoes. But then I'd gotten lazy and pulled an old jar of pasty tomato sauce out of the cupboard. Plus, the kids had been complete drips—surly and distant—since they'd returned from California, so I reasoned that my Mamma Mia effort would have gone unappreciated by at least two of the three.

When The Young One walked into the kitchen, went straight to the fridge, and started pouring himself a pint of enriched vitamin D nothing-skim-about-it milk, I said, "Whoa, whoa, whoa. Water at dinner—you know the rules." (We try to limit their milk-guzzling to two meals a day or they go through eight gallons a week.)

"We get to drink as much milk as we want at Mommy's," he said coolly.

"Okay." I struggled to avoid the obvious retort; *We aren't at Mommy's, are we?* I took a breath and called on my inner peace child and said, "Well, that may be true, but when you're in our house, you're expected to follow our rules."

He gave me a long look, went over to the table and sat down with his big glass of lactose and took a defiant slug.

What happened to the little charmer who just one month ago helped me decorate the Christmas tree? I liked that kid better.

Then, as if they'd planned it, The Tall One slunk into the kitchen and flung open the refrigerator and went straight for the milk.

"Hey," I said, louder than I should. "No milk at dinner."

"Fine," he snarled back. He walked over to the table and slumped into his chair.

So this is what it feels like when your stepkids finally decide they hate you. I wanted to cry, I wanted to drink a bottle of wine, and I wanted to pack their bags and send them back to the land of milk and Mommy. Instead, I just left the room.

Hank found me in the bedroom thirty minutes later, freshly showered and smearing on anti-aging lotion.

"What are you doing?" he asked. "Do you need help with dinner?"

"No, it's all ready. You guys go ahead. I'll eat a little later."

Hank regarded me with suspicion. "Why?"

"I thought it would be nice if you had some boy time. They haven't seen you in a couple of weeks—let them have you all to themselves for a night."

"We'd love it if you joined us," he said.

"No, really. Go be with your boys."

Hank gave me a tentative smile and left the room. I stretched out on our bed and propped myself up with white fuzzy pillows I call the bunnies. I let out a long exhale. I was feeling a little guilty, but I was also relieved that I'd avoided what could only have been a bad stepmommy dinner.

The boys may not have been at the top of my favorite-people list at that moment, but I could understand their frayed nerves. I remembered all too well what a drag it was to traipse back and forth between my mom's house and my dad's when I was their age.

After my parents divorced and moved into separate houses, my new life looked dramatically different from my old one. First off, everything came in twos.

Izzy—Age 9

1 house
1 girly bedroom
1 set of parents
1 cat

Izzy—Age 10

2 houses
2 girly bedrooms
2 sets of parents
2 stepsisters
2 cats

Not to mention two house keys, two phone numbers, and two different routes to school—plus, the most confusing part: two new sets of rules. I went back and forth between the two houses—you guessed it—every two weeks.

I call this the stepkid shuffle. It's the schlep a child of divorce makes between parental homes, and take it from me—it's no fun, and goodbyes most definitely suck. Yes, the routine creates efficient packing skills, but at age ten, is this really necessary? Every couple weeks I'd pack up my loot in an orange duffel bag and haul it out to the curb and wait for pickup. I was always thrilled to be reunited with the parent I'd been away from, but the coming and going was unnerving, and the solitary trek back and forth was lonesome.

Yet, as far as divorce goes, I believe that I was one of the luckier kids. My parents never moved away from each other—they stayed in the same town, and while I felt at home in both of my girly rooms, it always took some time to get comfortable. If you ask me, settling in has to be one of the hardest things for stepkids—readjusting to a new set of walls and doors, a different set of faces down the hall. As soon as I relaxed into the routine at one house, it was time to pack up again and return to the other. What kid wants to split her world in half, even if she is getting two of everything?

Given my understanding of the schlep, I couldn't really blame Hank's kids for acting grumpy. After all, I was personally responsible— at least partially. The adults in their lives had created this complicated scenario. The boys had a five-hour plane ride between doors, not an easy backseat schlep across town.

As I relaxed into the mattress, I concocted

Stepmom Rule Number Twelve: When the kids have a 'tude, suck it up and don't take it personally.

Still, I wasn't going to let them act like professional punks forever. I'd give them seventy-two hours—a grace period, if you will—to shake off the routine at June's and settle back into this one. In the meantime, I'd make a concentrated effort to be agreeable and stay out of their way.

With that, I drifted off into bunny-land.

As it turned out, I didn't need to keep my distance. The very next morning The Young One was by my side. I was pouring a cup of coffee when the kid was suddenly leaning up against me in rumpled clothes and with sleepy eyes.

He said, "Why can't things be the way they used to be?"

I took a deep breath. *Oh, boy. How many hours you got, kid?*

I could tell him that things can't be the way they used to be because they *aren't* the way they used to be. I could tell him life is unpredictable. Families often split apart. Relationships change. Life doesn't always go the way you want it to. Your little world is sometimes hit with bigger forces. But I resisted.

Instead, I rubbed his bony shoulders as he stared out the window into the bright Texas morning.

"I miss Mommy and I miss California . . . and I miss doughnuts."

I felt his heartache, but I also felt helpless. The things he was nostalgic for, I was unable to provide.

The Colorado River, which runs through the middle of Austin, is indigo, gentle, and arresting, but it doesn't compare to the magnificence of the Pacific Ocean.

And we're not a doughnut-buying family. "I will not contribute to America's growing obesity problem," I'd preached early on when they'd beg me for a box of raised and glazed every time I made a grocery list.

And without question, I wasn't Mom.

There's just no replacement for the original. Moms are pure gold—like the ticket in the Willy Wonka chocolate bar—and every kid wants one. As the stepmom, I'm more like a Snickers—satisfying, good filler. But eventually you get hungry for more. I thought about sharing my candy bar analogy with The Young One in an effort to get a little laugh, but I could tell that he was uncharacteristically blue and not in the joking mood.

"I'm sorry," is all I said.

"I really like doughnuts," he said, almost misty-eyed.

"I know you do." I tentatively touched the top of his curly head. Was he trying to talk me into caving on the doughnut issue, or did he really think living here was a bad second?

The Young One had his own room full of books and robotic creatures; our house was within walking distance of the greenbelt, where he loved to swim and collect rocks; and he had his father's full attention.

But the grass is always greener in paradise. And right now, paradise is where Mom is, in the fog, with Krispy Kremes.

What I wanted to say was, *Your original idea of paradise may seem lost, but if you can stand still long enough to study the Saint Augustine in Austin and the Mello Jade in the Bay Area, you might find that the grass is green in both places. Give it some time to grow.*

I was back in Sarah's office, thinking that the woman would be able to retire soon on her earnings from my sessions alone.

She said enthusiastically, "So, how was your time alone, without the kids?"

"I think I had an epiphany."

She gave me that proud shrink look. "Do tell."

"Well, I'm still trying to sort it all out in my head, but basically, I can see that my parents' divorce has caused me to be guarded with people my whole life—because I'm afraid that either they'll leave me or I'll leave them."

"Hmm." Sarah raised her eyebrows.

"In relationships, I tend to be the one who leaves." I took a deep breath and caught Sarah looking at me like, *I didn't have you scheduled to leave your husband today.*

"With Hank I'm totally committed—don't worry. I have no intention of abandoning Hank. I wouldn't have married him if I wanted to leave myself an out. I actually don't believe in outs, which is one of the reasons I've never believed in marriage."

She looked concerned.

"I'm just kidding—stupid joke. I'm not going anywhere. I'm locked in with this man, but in terms of the kids, I'm not so sure—"

She interjected, "That you won't leave the boys?"

"No," I corrected her. "I don't think it's a matter of my leaving—although I understand if they're hesitant to trust me. For all they know, I *could* pack up and leave."

"But you're not going to do that?"

"No," I said with certainty. "I think it's more about how present I can be—how much I'm capable of giving."

"Can you say more?" asked Sarah.

"Well, what if I can't give enough?"

"You really can't control how much they need you. Or don't need you."

"I want them to depend on me, like for peanut butter sandwiches and getting them to school on time, but after that, how close can we afford to get?"

She eyed me. "What does that mean?"

"I don't know." I was frustrated by my own confusion. "Obviously, I lean on people for more than sandwiches. I depend on Hank, and on my family back home."

"But do you also depend on them?"

"The kids? What would I depend on them for?"

She shrugged her shoulders. She wasn't going to figure it out for me.

"At this point, all I know for sure is that I want the boys to see that marriage can work. I don't want to be another sad statistic." I recited the latest numbers: six out of ten second marriages end in divorce. "I want Hank and me to be the exception, an example for them, to show them that it doesn't always fall apart, that they don't have to be afraid to trust people."

"Do you trust people?" Sarah asked.

Good question.

Later that week I called my good friend George, the art director at my old TV station, for an update on big-city living.

"Ah, you know. It's foggy, windy. News is news. I miss you."

And I missed George, the news, and the *look* of the fog.

"We just lost Will, so now we're down a producer," he grumbled.

Will had taken my hotshot producer job after I'd left and become an even bigger hotshot himself.

"Really? Where did he go?"

"L.A.—some big studio job."

I couldn't help but feel jealous. After the Houston flop I'd started to work again, but it was far from Hollywood. I'd accepted a position at an environmental ad agency in Austin, which sounded like a conscientious and superbly trendy way to spend my days when I first applied, but after a few weeks into the job it was clear I wasn't meshing with the culture—emphasis on cult. There were Monday-morning sharing circles and a list of company core values that we were strongly encouraged to recite on demand, and "with passion." My favorite value was WILLINGNESS—classic company-speak for "Work hard, be underpaid, and don't complain." We were graded on our level of willingness, and the big players at Whales That Smoke, my nickname for the agency, were super-competitive. Recently we'd been separated into teams for Pay It Forward Day. *Who's more giving?* And now the planning committee had asked all employees to create a company scrapbook to honor the principles of the agency. *"Include photos and memorable moments . . ."*

Let me be clear—I'm all for eating local, not wasting water, and recycling my own cans. But the vibe at this place went against one of *my* core values: to avoid forced chumminess.

I told George about the scrapbook project. He laughed. "Wow. And I thought I had things to complain about. You just made my day. Thanks, Izzy."

"Sure," I mumbled.

"Well, you know, you could always come back here."

I sighed, resigned to spending the next few weeks embracing January's "value of the month"—FUN!

"Really. We could use a freelancer for February sweeps."

"Whaaaaat?" I said, my voice thick with skepticism.

"I'm just saying, you already know everyone in the newsroom, you put out a good product, and"—George paused—"I'd love to have you around again."

This was a crazy idea. Go back to San Francisco? To my old job?

"Really?" I said. But my mind began to race, trying to figure out if this made any sense, if it was something I'd even want to do.

"Think about it," George said, "and buzz me later."

I hung up the phone. Was this something I wanted to seriously consider? My analytical mind said no—everyone says you can never go back—but my heart said *Yes, I want to go home.*

Three hours later, sitting in traffic on the Congress Street Bridge, I found that my earlier excitement about leaving Whales That Smoke and returning to San Francisco had started to wane. I couldn't leave Austin. Hadn't I just told Sarah the shrink that I wanted the boys to learn to trust and depend on people? What kind of example would I be setting if I left them? Plus, Hank would never go for it.

When Hank came home from work, I was waiting for him in the green room with two glasses of wine.

"I'm so glad to be home," Hank said and kissed me hello.

I smiled at my handsome man. Did I really want to ruin this sweet moment?

"I talked to George today," I began.

"Oh, yeah? How's he doing?" Hank sat down and kicked off his shoes.

"He's doing all right, but Will left, so everyone's scrambling a bit."

"Will left?"

"Yeah. Some L.A. job, but here's the thing . . ." I wanted to keep the conversation going, moving along, before I lost my nerve to suggest how I could fit into this picture. "George asked me to think about coming back, just for sweeps."

"To San Francisco?" Hank looked confused.

I'd been right. Hank didn't like it. "Yeah, I know—it's a stupid idea. But earlier today it sounded like such a dream to make a decent bundle of money again doing something I love to do—something I'm good at." I wavered. "But you're right—I can't go back."

"Now wait a minute." Hank reached over and took my hand. I stopped talking and nervously took a sip of wine. "How long would you be gone?" Was he actually considering this?

"Six weeks?"

"Hmm . . . That is a long time." Hank pulled at the copper hairs on his chin. "How much would they pay you?"

"We'd have to negotiate, but at least twice what I'm making with the Whales."

"Do you want to do it?" Hank said.

This is one of the reasons I love this man. He is not a me-first guy—ever.

"I think I do," I finally squeaked out. "But on the other hand, I don't like the idea of being away from you for that long, and I worry about leaving the boys. They just got back, and The Young One is tragically heartsick . . ."

"I don't like being away from you, either." Hank rubbed my hand. "I miss you as soon as I walk out the door and leave for work every morning. It breaks my heart."

That settles it, I thought. *I'm not leaving my adoring husband.* But before I could jump into his arms and call it off, he said, "I think you should do it."

He pulled me in close and focused his gray-green eyes on mine. "You need this. The boys and I will be fine. Just don't forget to come back."

I Left My Identity
in San Francisco

"Sir, here it is," I spoke up from the backseat. "Pacific and Steiner. It's the Victorian on the right."

"This is the one?" he said, slowing down. "The blue house?"

I smiled to myself. Sure, I'd love to say this multimillion-dollar piece of Pacific Heights real estate was mine, but I was only borrowing it for a month and a half. As George had predicted, the TV station I'd worked for before moving to Austin was delighted to bring me back on board for February sweeps, but housing wasn't part of the deal. To stay in a hotel in high-priced San Francisco would cost the bulk of my salary; their offer wasn't going to be worth it unless I could find a place to stay for little to nothing.

As the driver hauled my oversized suitcase out of his trunk, I gazed up at my lofty new digs: a turn-of-the-century, four-story home planted firmly in one of the most coveted neighborhoods in San Francisco. "This is unbelievable," I whispered to myself.

"Welcome home," my driver said.

I made it to the top of the stately brick staircase, but before I opened the front door (of what I would soon be calling "my mansion") I turned around to take in the view, just as a lavish sedan came up and over the hill. I caught the eye of the country club–type woman behind the wheel and said under my breath, "Take a good look, ladies—I'm back."

The house belonged to Sara and Peter, friends of Mom's. They'd lived on this block for many years until they moved north, where they could stretch out on a bigger piece of land. They kept their PacHeights property for weekend retreats, holiday parties, and fund-raisers. Most of the time the house was uninhabited, save for a caretaker couple who watered the plants and lived on the third floor. They graciously made room for me.

The place was downright elegant: chandeliers hanging from ornate ceiling tiles, chocolate-colored hardwood floors, vintage stained glass windows, a grand piano, and original art dressing up one white wall after another.

The vibrancy of the turbulent northern California coastline, the soothing hillsides of Sonoma County, and the meandering Russian River were Peter's great loves. He was a big-time art collector. Huge, brilliant canvases hung throughout the house. It was like getting a private gallery tour, except I got to unpack and sleep over. I was completely dazzled, and touched by their generosity. I'd never even met these people. I felt a little ashamed, actually, to have accepted such a handsome gift. But did I dial Sara and Peter's number and say, "Really, guys, this is too much. I'd feel better camping out in the nearest BART station"? No. I made myself right at home.

I hauled my suitcase up another grand staircase, this one covered in cabernet-colored carpet. If you've ever lived in San Francisco—or any major city, for that matter—you can appreciate the amount of space I'm describing here. It's unheard of—at least it is in my thirtysomething circles. We just don't live like this. When, at thirty, I finally moved into my very own one-bedroom apartment after sharing flats and living with roommates for years, I boasted, "I have a living room *and* a separate bedroom. I have arrived, girlfriends." So when I opened the door to the guestroom, which was actually two rooms with a balcony and a black-tiled deco bathroom with Hollywood lighting, I gasped. *This is insane!* From my second-floor perch I could look down upon the lush and landscaped back courtyards of my richy-rich neighbors. *So this is how the wealthy live. So civilized!* I stood there for a few minutes, wondering who lived to the left and right of me. It was very *Rear Window,* and indeed, I was beginning to feel just as glamorous as Grace Kelly.

I decided to do a full look-see of the house later. The sun was setting and before the light disappeared there was something I had to do. I left my suitcase in the middle of the floor, creaked downstairs, and headed out into the wind and fog. I had to walk only two blocks to get where I needed to be: the corner of Fillmore and Broadway. A perfect bird's-eye view of the Bay, blue and bright, right there—just how I remembered it. It took only a few deep breaths of Pacific air to confirm that I was home. I let my long winter jacket blow out around me and whip in the wind. I stood high above the city for a long time, looking down at the marina, out to the Golden Gate Bridge and the Marin Headlands beyond. The floodgates opened and I began to cry. After struggling for the past six months with a new identity—wife, stepmom, *Texan*—I finally remembered who else I was.

That first night I wrapped myself in expensive silk sheets and slept like a princess. Who wouldn't? After eight luxurious hours, I woke up to the old familiar voices of KQED, the NPR station in San Francisco. It was Monday morning, and *what am I doing here again?*

I was returning to work. But it wasn't just the job. Going back meant recovering my former self—the person I was before I left my home, my friends, my family; the before Izzy who hadn't turned into a mother. The old me, who, I was convinced, was more interesting than the new one.

I was excited. I was nervous. I talked to myself in the shower, on the toilet, as I got dressed. I needed to calm down. A line of sweat was developing on my upper lip and along my hairline—not a good look. In an effort to settle my jitters and clear my mind, I decided to walk to the TV station. It was a long haul, but I estimated I could make it in under an hour with enough time to reacquaint myself with the scents and sounds of the city, and even pick up a Peet's coffee (*oh, how I love thee*) along the way. My route would take me through my borrowed neighborhood, across busy Van Ness Avenue, up and over the cable car lines that zigzagged through Russian Hill, down into Chinatown, across Columbus Avenue into the Financial District, and up Battery Street to the TV station's front doors.

Ahhhhh. It felt great to be out on the streets again. I missed the mobility of my strong, stocky legs (they might not showcase well in a swimsuit, but they do get me up and over San Francisco hills quite nicely). I'd been warned before I left the Bay Area by my snooty jock friends that I was moving to a state where people sat more than they walked. "Keep an eye on your butt," they said. And it was true—some of the fattest cities in the country are in the Lone Star State, although Austin averages pretty well in the fit department.

Back in Austin, I had been going to bridal boot camp, but I was also loading up on chips and *queso* and driving everywhere I needed to go—including the 7-11, which was just around the corner from our house (how much lazier does it get?). When I pulled on my jeans this morning, I noticed a bundt cake where my butt used to be. I stretched my legs out in front of me and picked up the pace. San Francisco was experiencing an early spring and the sky matched the coolness of the air. Camellia and antique rose bushes bloomed up and down Pacific Avenue and cherry blossoms decorated the side-walks in pink. I could see the Bay: a calm, washed-out blue.

"Well, hello," the security guard at the front desk said with surprise. "What are you doing back here?"

If it hadn't been completely inappropriate, I would have hopped the desk, wrapped my arms around his protective vest, and sobbed into his beard. I was that happy to see him.

It's hard to describe my first day back. I compare it to those final scenes in the holiday classic *It's a Wonderful Life.* Remember how George Bailey, played by Jimmy Stewart, returns to his life after throwing it away (that is, jumping off a bridge into an icy river), and how overjoyed he is when he's reunited with friends he thought he'd never see again? I wasn't throwing colleagues into the air and kissing them frantically, *per se,* but I felt very fortunate to be given this rare opportunity to go back to my past—and pretty wonderful—life.

It didn't take long for me to snap back into the routine. I spent the majority of the morning in my director's office getting caught up on the biz. At noon I went to lunch with an old promo pal and by early afternoon I'd received my first news assignment. By the end of the day, my professional confidence was back, and Austin felt like a distant land.

On the hike back to the mansion I called Hank.

"Hey, where you been?" he said. In Austin, we'd gotten into the habit of calling each other at least twice a day to check in. I relied on those calls more than Hank probably knew. Usually by midweek—

what I termed Weepy Wednesdays, when I'd be crying into my cereal after everyone left the house—his soothing Southern drawl was the only tranquilizer that calmed my feelings of isolation and self-doubt. He'd give me his best motivational speech—*Babe, you're fucking great*—and it often rallied me when, like George Bailey, I wanted to jump.

But today had been different. I hadn't needed the extra encouragement. "I meant to call, but the hours just flew by," I explained lightly.

Earlier in the afternoon, after the soundproof door to the edit bay swung shut and I sat down with my old friends—two flat-screen monitors, an audio mixing board, and a tape deck—I realized what I'd been missing: my passion. Sure, I'd had my share of lackluster jobs—such as lead wrapper in a holiday gift basket assembly line when I was twenty—but in terms of choosing a profession, I'd been blessed. I'd fallen into a line of work that inspired me creatively and challenged me personally to study the intricacies of the larger world. I loved being a TV producer. I was never, as they say, "working for the weekend." I was working for the work. When I fired up the machines in the editing room, I was hit with the reality of what I'd done: I'd sacrificed my career—I'd given up my dream job to be with the man I loved.

"Well, how did it go?" Hank said, bringing me back to the moment.

"As soon as the elevator doors opened on the third floor, it was like I'd never left. It was all so familiar; comforting, even."

"Well, don't get too comfortable," Hank teased. "I miss you already. You sure you want to stay for the full six weeks?"

I did, but I didn't say so. For the first time in months, I felt strong, capable, and valuable—qualities that often came up missing in my new stepmom role. I was grateful to have a man, a husband, who loved me, but today I didn't need his love to love myself—that was the difference.

"I'll be home before you know it," I said to Hank.

With no family dinner to prepare or show up for, I decided to explore my snazzy neighborhood on the hill. My mansion was an easy walk to Fillmore Street, an upscale shopping haven dotted with cafes, an independent movie theater, and at least a dozen gastronomically enticing restaurants that I vowed to review before my stay was over.

I wandered into The Grove, a cozy bistro that looked part hunting shack and part ski lodge. I was immediately taken and declared it my new favorite place. It was crammed with sturdy wooden tables and a mix of people like me, dining out with their laptops, plus several young urban couples, an older man with his dog, and an all-women's discussion group. I ordered the tuna melt and a glass of cabernet and grabbed a table in the corner. I sat there for two hours, savoring the best sandwich I'd had in recent memory.

Unlike some restaurants, where a woman dining alone seems to draw the pitiful glances of everyone in the room, including the busboy (who pushes three baskets of bread on her in an effort to satiate her loneliness), The Grove was the perfect retreat for the solo diner. A welcoming space to be alone, without feeling lonely. And anyway, I wasn't by myself. In addition to all my West Coast friends and family just north of the city, I had my online stepladies at my disposal, and I started checking in with them daily.

In San Francisco, I was conscious that I was enjoying a decadent slice of Izzy-centric pie, and while I didn't want to rub it in to the less fortunate, I also wanted to know if other stepmoms craved family-free time like I did. Well, of course they did, although they didn't necessarily want six weeks off from duty. Usually all they needed was a night off, or an hour in the bathtub. One woman explained that it wasn't that she didn't like her home life; it was just that sometimes she didn't want to be

there. I totally got that. Sometimes we just need to get away. I pledged
to look at the next six weeks as my opportunity to care for and indulge
myself. I had to do this, I rationalized, for all the other harried stepmoms who weren't able to land such a sweet deal. Over the next few
days, whenever I found myself in a delicious setting. I'd jot down the
reasons why it was a perfect stepmom getaway, like A-16, on Chestnut
Street, where, I believed, a bottle of wine paired with the *mozzarella
burrata* would help any woman forget about her blended-family woes.
And what about H & M, off Union Square, where for a couple hundred
bucks any stepmom, feeling like she had put herself last on the list,
could update her tired wardrobe with something off the European runway? I encouraged all my online gals to follow suit should they find
themselves boarding a plane to San Francisco for a solo weekend away.
And then I had an even better idea: What about organized stepmom
trips all over the country? You know, like they do for senior citizens and
international bike riders. Can you imagine—a busload of stressed-out
stepmoms touring cities best known for inspiring rest and recovery?
Stop this bus right now, I fantasized screaming at the driver. *You just
passed a happy-hour special: Manicures and Martinis!*

After nearly a week of playing virtual tour guide, I called June and
asked her to lunch. Hank's first wife and I had never spent a minute
alone, sans circus, and I thought it was time we try to connect. I mean,
we had at least two things in common: Hank and the kids. Okay, three
in total.

I'd been conversing online with other stepmoms about their relationships with the BM—bio-mom, remember? There were some, although they were in the charmed minority, who behaved like champs
and encouraged the rest of us to put down the gloves and just get
along, already. These women spoke about the advantages of having a
relationship with the ex-wife, if for no other reason than they could

stop using their husbands as go-betweens. I could appreciate this. Relying on Hank to be June's translator had been the source of much frustration for me. I never felt satisfied with the information he provided; I wanted details, and Hank liked to keep it vague. On the topic of June and John's moving to Texas, Hank and I had been having the same tense conversation for months, with no resolution. Hank would say things like, "She says she's working on it." And I'd fire back with, "What does that mean—working on it? Does she have any job offers? Does she still plan on moving here? Is their house on the market?" And Hank would say, "I don't have any of those answers. I just know she's working on it." I'd clench my teeth and talk myself out of shoving my head through the wall. It was in one of these clenched-teeth moments that I conceived

Stepmom Rule Number Thirteen: Relinquish all grand ideas of gaining control.

With this in mind, I didn't plan to interrogate June over a Cobb salad—*I want answers, damn it!* I was just hoping she might enlighten me about the future, our collective future. Surely she had it all figured out, or maybe together we could come up with a plan. I was a big believer of Tina Fey's maxim that "bitches get stuff done." I was inviting June to lunch to establish a friendly partnership, not to foster a friendship. This is a distinction worth exploring; shall we?

When Hank and I first got together, he and June were what I'd call, quite chummy. They had mutual friends, chatted frequently on the phone, and even referred to each other as "best friends." This, I thought, gave both John and me awkward second-place positions, but I stepped aside. I was new to the crowd and just trying to fit in. Eventually, I expected, they'd finally break up. Either that or Hank and I would.

In those early days, and to Hank's credit, he encouraged his two women to get friendly by taking me along to assist in the schlep. We'd go over to June and John's house and hang out in their living room while June rallied the kids. It wasn't the best of times to get acquainted, with two small ones clinging to June's legs and the older two ignoring her pleas of "Boys, get your shoes and socks on. Your father's here." I'd usually stand quietly off to the side while Hank and June discussed homework assignments and the next week's schedule. I often felt like the village mute nobody talks to, but really, what did I have to contribute? Science projects and doctor's appointments were not my topics. Eventually, June would call out to the boys, "For the last time—I mean it," and I'd watch as they tumbled downstairs and gave her lingering hugs and "I'm going to miss you, Mommy" kisses and then the four of us would walk out the front door.

After about the fifth visit, I said to Hank, "I can't do this anymore."

"Do what?" he said with alarm. He thought I was ending our relationship.

"Go with you to pick up or drop off the kids," I said with trepidation.

"Okay," he said slowly. But I knew he didn't mean it and I could sense irritation under the surface.

"Hank, it's so awkward. I feel like a complete outsider."

"You're not," he said with an edge to his voice.

"Yes," I shot back, "I am. There are the two of you, and then there's me. I feel like a shadow on the wall when I'm there. You guys are divorced, but you're palsy-walsies, and then there's me—the new girlfriend. How does this work?" *Seriously, we need some boundaries here!*

"Well, I don't know what to do," Hank said. "I'm trying to make it easy for you two to get to know each other."

I appreciated Hank's effort to encourage a sisterhood, but I argued that it wasn't his job, but our work to do—hers and mine—if establishing a relationship was important to us. And early on, given my understanding of their nomadic lifestyle, I believed it was. I didn't want a sister-wife or a new best girlfriend, but I thought it was necessary that we try to like each other. I knew that if Hank and I stayed together, I might eventually be asked to board the *Big Love* caravan, a ride that could prove cramped and uncomfortable if June and I weren't amicable.

So June and I tried, but the truth is, we didn't try very hard. We attempted to get together a few times, but something always interfered and one of us would cancel. After a while we just gave up. As a result, June and I were no more familiar with each other now that Hank and I were married than we had been in the early dating days, when I was the new girl and Hank and June were still acting like best buddies. Except now I was no longer the newcomer, but the new wife and Hank's new best friend—a shift in roles that left June on the outside. At first, I blamed myself for busting up their cozy friendship until I realized that Hank and June's relationship was compromised long before I came along—starting with the day they decided to divorce. Still, my presence seemed to accelerate their eventual split and because of this, I was fairly certain June and I would never braid each other's hair or shop together at the outlet mall, but at the very least we could have a friendly lunch and discuss our similar interests: The Tall One and The Young One.

June agreed to meet me the following week.

In addition to scheduling a parental powwow with June, I booked myself solid for the rest of the month. In the social department, I had some major making up to do. In Austin, I was still a virtual no-name, but back in my 'hood, I had a gang of gals I was eager to roam around with.

But not yet.

It was my first Friday night in town, and I was free. When my friend and colleague Beth and I walked out of the office at six, she teased, "So, single in the city again. Got any big plans?"

I said I did—and they involved a lot of cheese.

After a brisk walk back to Pacific Heights, I strolled into a market on Fillmore and Jackson Street where I'd been picking up staples throughout the week: vanilla yogurt, Q-tips, and a cork screw, for example. I just adore a corner neighborhood market. I love the narrow aisles cramped with canned foods, crackers, and toiletries. I swoon over a deli case stuffed with hunks of meat and cabbage slaw. I'm even amused by the predictable grump at the cash register. I find security in the neighborhood market, with its bright lights, essential items, and late-night hours, so I was naturally thrilled to discover that my mansion was within blocks of one. My market serviced an upper-crust crowd, so it was more spacious than most. After investigating the dim sum in the center aisle, I parked myself along the side wall in front of an impressive selection of California wines. I purchased a bottle of La Crema pinot and a hoggish selection of cheese. Gene at the front packed it all up, and I sashayed out the front door with my lovers— havarti, pecorino, and fontina.

I nudged the French doors open and spread out on the custard-colored chaise in my second-floor room. I poured myself a glass of wine and served myself a platter of cheese. *Now this is what I call a fantastic Friday night!* I giggled at how simply scrumptious this was—all alone in the quiet, surrounded by magnificent art, with a sparkling city outside and no one to please but myself. I poured glass after glass, curled up with my Alice Adams novel, thinking, *Sorry, Hank, but this is almost better than hot, married sex.*

I woke up hours later to the sound of rain. I'd fallen into a cheese coma on the chaise. I dragged myself over to my feather bed and crawled in.

* * *

The next morning I met Mom and Gigi at the Ferry Building just as they strolled off the boat from Larkspur. We were all hugs and kisses. I didn't want to let either of them go—I'd missed them terribly. If only briefly, my stomach tensed up from regret. *Why did I move away from these women of mine?* I thought about the boys and related . . . There really is no substitute for the comfort of a mommy, is there?

Before I could slip into a reunion meltdown, Mom snapped me out of it. "So, where are we going first?" she chirped. "And what time is lunch?" When the three of us get together to shop, this is her usual line of questioning. Who's got the agenda, and when are we eating? Today was no exception, although this outing was to be devoted to bridal shopping. That's right—Hank and I had finally decided on a time and a place for our post–City Hall wedding—the Peabody Hotel in Memphis, where Hank had proposed. If I was going to be the quintessential June bride, I figured it was time I start acting like one.

"We have an appointment at the Bridal Galleria at ten," I said. "It has a huge selection of couture designers, so I think we should check it out."

"Couture designers?" Gigi mocked. "Who are you?"

I laughed because she was absolutely right to question me. I, too, was surprised to hear bridal terminology spilling out of my mouth. In the past I'd always maintained that *if* I ever got married, "I will never wear one of those gimmicky Cinderella gowns. They're all so overpriced and predictable." But over the past few months my cynicism had waned. After thumbing through *Southern Bride, Modern Bride,* and *In Style Weddings,* I'd become as insatiable as the next girl. Monique Lhuillier, Vera Wang, Ines Di Santo, Melissa Sweet, Jenny Lee—I loved them all. So it seemed foolish to pass up the opportunity to shop for a dress while I was in high-fashion San Francisco.

Surely a city this chic would have something hanging on one of its designer racks that suited me.

I smiled at Gigi. "I've changed."

"Clearly," she said.

Judy, my personal assistant at the Galleria, led me to a dressing room and handed me a push-up bra and a pair of pumps. "Take off everything and put these on," she instructed. "I'll start bringing in the gowns." She was gone before I could protest.

I looked around my dressing room. There was an elevated stage in the center, surrounded by concert-style lighting and wraparound mirrors.

"You've got to be kidding me," I muttered. "I am not standing up there half-naked."

"Can we come in?" Mom and Gigi twittered from the other side of the curtain.

"NO!" I barked. "You two stay out there until I'm ready. I have nothing on except for a pair of hooker heels."

"Oh," Mom teased. "Slutty bride." She and Gigi howled.

The first dress I slipped on was an ivory silk duchess satin fluted gown with a ruched waist. "Oh, my God," I gasped when I saw my reflection in the mirror. "I look fucking amazing. *I want to marry me.*"

"Girls," I hollered through the curtain to mom and Gigi, "get in here."

Gigi pulled back the curtain. "Wow."

"I know, right? If only I could find jeans that fit this good."

"She has the perfect body for this type of wedding gown," Judy said with authority. "Tall and curvy." She turned me around gently and smoothed the fabric over my derriere. She cinched the waistline tighter with pins she pulled out of the air, and then regarded my silhouette with reverence. *The saleslady at Macy's never treats me this well.* "Yes," she continued, "this dress is made for you. Very beautiful."

That's all it took. I was hooked. I wanted to eat, sleep, and strut around in a wedding gown for the rest of my life. And possibly run off with Judy.

"What's next?" I demanded with the wild eyes of a crack addict.

"Next," Judy said, "I will bring you a satin organza trumpet gown with a sweetheart neckline."

"Yes, yes—bring it now."

Not only did I try on nearly thirty dresses that day, but I would also continue to visit the fitting rooms of San Francisco's finest bridal boutiques for the next month, even after I'd purchased "the one."

After shopping, Gigi, Mom, and I grabbed a late lunch at Ferry Plaza Seafood: crab cakes with sourdough, clam chowder, and chardonnay. We sat in high-top chairs at a marble counter that faced the Bay. I held my glass up for a toast: "To us. And to being back home."

The following week June and I sat across from each other at a restaurant in the Financial District. I'd forgotten how much the boys looked like her, especially The Young One. He has her heart-shaped lips and long lashes. And like her son, June is an animated woman who keeps the conversation going.

I didn't want to be obvious about pushing my agenda, so I sat waiting for the right opportunity to ask her about moving to Texas. But time was ticking—we'd already gotten halfway through our salads and I hadn't had the nerve to bring it up, and she hadn't gone there, either. She talked about everything else—her morning anchor job, her sleeping schedule with the new baby, and the crappy housing market in the Bay Area.

And then she said, "I really miss my boys. Are they doing okay?"

There it was: my in. *Be cool, Izzy.* I didn't want to say anything to give June the impression that her kids were miserable and that somehow it was my fault, i.e., I was a terrible stepmom. I also didn't want her to think that everything was fine and that she wasn't needed nearby.

"Well," I began slowly, "I think they're doing pretty well, but . . . it's not easy." I tried to keep brightness in my voice. "For them, or for me."

She smiled empathetically. "I know they can be tough sometimes. John feels for you. He's been saying things like, 'Poor Izzy. She got more than she bargained for.'" She crunched a crouton and grinned generously. "Have you thought about having your own?"

Pardon? And raise all three with my superhuman powers?

I forced a smile. "I really don't think I can take on anything else right now."

She stopped crunching and said gently, "I'll take them back. Seriously. Just say the word."

I was speechless. *What happened to moving to Texas? What happened to co-parenting? What happened to all for one and one for all?* She looked at her watch. "Shoot, I have to go. Thanks for looking after my babies." She paid the bill and, before she left, she said it again: "Think about it. You can send them back." And then she was gone.

"So, what does *that* all that mean?" Beth asked.

It was later that evening and we were sharing the signature chicken dish at Zuni Café on Market Street. The saucy bird takes an hour to cook, so by the time it arrived we'd already finished a full bottle of wine.

"That's the thing—I have no idea. I admit I'm a little neurotic about having a plan, but I feel like I never know what's going on and I don't want to push—June especially—but my life is being affected, too. I get to ask questions, right?"

"Absolutely," she scolded and waved the waiter over. "Can we see the wine list again, please?"

I appreciated Beth's perspective and lifestyle—an outspoken woman, a pro in her field, unmarried and childless in her late forties, and completely unapologetic about her sizable disposable income— a lifestyle that might have been mine had I never met Hank.

I continued unprompted. "I thought if I cut out Hank as the middle man and June and I sat down one-on-one, we'd get some things figured out, but now I'm more confused than ever."

"Well, what's the deal? Is she moving to Texas or not?" Beth asked.

"She didn't say she was, and she didn't say she wasn't."

Beth rolled her eyes and took a swig of wine. "What do you think about her offer to take them back?"

That's what had paralyzed me, caused me to lose my nerve and let June leave the restaurant before nailing down a plan. What was she saying to me? *If you can't handle my boys, give them back?*

I took a sip of wine and said to Beth, "Sure, it's not always easy having them, but it's not that I don't *want* them. It's that I want some help. Those kids need a mommy, and I'm a questionable alternative."

"Why don't you just hire a nanny?" Beth offered. "It seems like everyone has one."

I smiled at Beth and said, "I'm not sure that really solves the problem."

The next week I caught up with all my old girlfriends. On Tuesday I dined with Casey, the special-events director who, like Beth, is an independent woman, but not as thrilled about her single-lady lifestyle. Casey is gorgeous, a world traveler, and has no problem meeting men, but most of them never make it past the first date—she has a critical eye and refuses to settle.

"You're so lucky that you and Hank found each other," she said. "Believe me. I've dated a lot of idiots."

I laughed at her cynicism. "Well, it took me a long time to find him. And I wasn't looking for a husband."

"Or stepkids," she added.

"Or an ex-wife."

On Wednesday I grabbed a quick drink with Jane, the Web consultant, who has the big-city career, a successful marriage, and two beautiful girls of her own, but every day is a logistical struggle for her. Jane spends nearly four hours a day commuting by train into San Francisco and back home, which leaves her only a small slice of time for her family, and barely a sliver for herself.

"I wish we had never moved to the suburbs," she lamented. "We have a big house, but I'm never there."

"Do you ever think about moving back to the city?"

"Yeah." She sighed. "But we'd never get back in. It's too expensive."

I knew that one—affordable housing—from my pro and con list for moving to Austin. "I do miss the big city, too," I confessed. "Although having free parking in front of my house almost makes up for it."

On Friday I sat across from Kate, who would soon become a step-mom like me. *Unlike me,* she's more of a snuggly kid person, so the idea of marrying a man who came with two of his own didn't unnerve her. On the other hand, she was battling endlessly with her fiancé over their different parenting styles and when they would start having children of their own. "I always wanted a big family," she said. "I don't want to lose my chance."

"Babies are not at the top of my list right now."

"You'd better hope you don't change your mind. It's hard to persuade a man with nearly full-grown kids to start all over again."

"What will happen if you can't persuade him?"

"I'll probably end up resenting him the rest of my life."

It's all relative, isn't it? I'd spent the last several months in Austin coveting what I'd lost, but no one had it all, did they? And what had I lost? My single life? I laughed at this. Most women want to lose their single lives.

Many of my girlfriends had started families soon after college or early in their careers. I was a late bloomer. I had had years on my own that they hadn't enjoyed—to travel, to live alone, to fall in love with more than a few men. Naturally, the transition to family life at thirty-five was a challenge. I was an expert at taking care of only myself. It had been that way for so long, I'd started to believe I wouldn't be as happy any other way.

After a long day at the TV station, I stretched out on the chaise in my mansion, gazing up at a painting of a romantic purple mountain and a yellow sky. It had become my favorite image in the house.

Was it really that wonderful being all on my own?

My automatic response was yes. But upon further reflection, maybe that wasn't the whole truth. Sure, I had my freedom and independence, but I spent many years drifting in and out of a state of disconnection and emptiness.

A memory came to mind from a couple of years ago; I was alone on a Sunday morning in my neighborhood city Laundromat. Sipping coffee, I watched my clothes tumble and dry—an activity I find calming. I felt unhurried and unburdened. I had the awareness that I was free to do whatever I wanted to that day. I had no obligations, no prior commitments, nowhere I had to be. I remember thinking I should be elated, but I wasn't. I felt empty.

The next night George and I grabbed a late dinner at Vivande on Fillmore. We ordered grilled salmon over garlicky cannellini beans and spent the entire meal gossiping about the TV biz and exchanging playful banter. George jabbed me endlessly for abandoning his good friend Hank and for "escaping my mothering duties." To that, I threatened to appoint him maid of honor and put him in a horrific dress if he dared tell Hank about all the fancy meals I was expensing.

With full bellies and dizzy heads, we said good-bye and I walked alone toward the mansion. As I huffed up Fillmore I caught a reflection of myself in the window of Shabby Chic. I stopped and looked at thirty-five-year-old me with sudden clarity. I'd gotten caught up in my own romanticized version of my single self, hadn't I? Moment of truth—I did not always love being alone. My new life was better.

The next two weeks passed quickly, and then abruptly, I was over it. I mean, really over it. I missed Hank, and I even longed for the boys and their random factoids. Producing for the TV station was still a nine-to-five high, but San Francisco was losing its charm. A couple of specific instances finally pushed me over the edge.

I'd been putting a lot of miles on my feet and my toes looked like they belonged to a troll, so one day after work I took a detour and wandered down to the marina for a pedicure. As soon as I turned onto Chestnut Street, I found myself pushed around by rude people who were too hurried to make room for anyone else—trolls included. I was tired and hungry and not in the mood, so I put on my mean-girl face until I could duck into one of those closet-size, walk-in salons called something like The Most Glamorous Nails Ever. I relaxed into a massage chair and was quickly attended to, my feet propped up, scrubbed, and rubbed. Unlike how I'd just been treated out on the street, inside this sterile salon with its tinny music and congenial attendants, I felt respected—even if I was paying them to hold my haggish toes in their pretty little hands. But then, well before my glamorous nails were dry, the owner pointed me to the door.

"Up, up, up," she said to me and escorted another woman over to my massage chair.

I argued, "But my toes are not dry."

She threw her arms up in the air and shouted something at me in Cantonese, which must have been "dry enough to give up your chair right now." I quickly gathered my things and left in a huff.

Standing out on the street like the Little Match Girl, I whined, "What's wrong with these people?"

From the nail salon, I shuffled with wet toes down to Walgreens. I mistakenly went in through the out door and was verbally assaulted by a man with a tight face, "Hey, lady. You used the wrong door."

"Sorry," I whimpered and backed out onto the street. A year ago I might have told that jerk to "suck it"; now I was cowering out in the cold. Had I lost my big-city-girl edge? *No—say it isn't so!*

I considered that my time in friendly Texas had saddled me with that thing Hank called "manners." *Oh, dear.* I couldn't bear to suffer another identity crisis within the same year. I was Izzy—the sassy sometimes-snob who felt right at home in an urban jungle, right? I wasn't soft; I was a hard-core city mouse!

I pushed my shoulders back and turned up my nose, determined to act tough the rest of the way back to the mansion. I put on my best "don't eff with me" face and started walking again, but it was hard to strut confidently in my flimsy nail-salon flip-flops. Before I made it to the end of the next block, I stubbed my toe and screwed up my pedicure. While I was bent over assessing the damage, someone ran into me from behind and practically knocked me down on the sidewalk. *Goddamnit—how about a little consideration for a girl who's lost her way?* I really wanted to cry. And I wanted my husband to scoop me up in his strong arms and carry me home. I found myself thinking something I never thought I'd say: Get me back to Texas, to good ol' Southern hospitality.

* * *

It was my last weekend on the West Coast, so I went up north to Sonoma County to visit my family. The only defector from California, I had many rounds to make before I returned to Austin, but I was lingering on Mom's couch and boring her with my new theory on the importance of common courtesy and neighborly love.

I concluded my diatribe by saying, "Now that I think about it, I don't think I've ever felt entirely rooted here. The bedrock—and by that, I mean *the people*—is too hard."

"Oh, for God's sake," she gibed. "You are so full of it. You *are* rooted here, you lamebrain." Mom likes to call me names when she thinks I'm exaggerating. "You've been living out of a suitcase for six weeks," she continued. "Maybe you just miss living like a normal person? And maybe you miss your husband?"

I was smiling at her now. "Lamebrain?"

I fell asleep on her couch that afternoon, wrapped in a blanket, wearing knee socks and one of Mom's sweatshirts. I woke up to kitchen sounds. Stanton was baking a ham. In late middle age, he had discovered a belated love for the other-white-meat and prepared it, Mom explained, every chance he got. I let the heat from the wood-burning stove warm me, feeling very much like a kid. But it was time to go home. To the one in Texas.

Stanton's Ham Recipe

Drive to the grocery store. Park the car. Ask the guy at the meat counter, "Do you have one of those big goddamn hams wrapped in heavy plastic?" Buy it. Put in a baking pan. Bake it. Take it out of the oven, and because it's already precut and seasoned, serve immediately.

*   *   *

"Why don't you just call Hank and tell him you're moving back to San Francisco?" my news director said with a smirk. He was kidding, but I sensed an honest invitation to come back to my old job should I so desire.

It was my last day at the TV station and I stopped by his office to say farewell. I admit, it was tempting to stick around town for the work. I missed the rush of the newsroom already. I had no idea what career opportunities I'd find when I returned to Austin. Maybe I'd become a professional wedding planner—if only to coordinate my own.

"I don't know about moving back," I said. "Texas is starting to grow on me."

I packed up six weeks worth of promo scripts and slipped out at five o'clock. I trudged through the long Broadway tunnel, traffic rushing past me, thankful for the time I'd had in San Francisco. Truly, how many women get to go back and revisit the single life they've left behind?

That night I walked to the corner of Fillmore and Broadway for one final look. I stood in the cold, looking out at my city, draped in fog. Maybe she was tough and sometimes mean, but who was I kidding? She was magical, too, and I would miss her. But this time, I was ready to say good-bye.

Stuck in the Middle

I'd read my depraved celebrity rag from cover to cover well before my plane landed in Austin, so I studied the older couple in the aisle across from me for a good portion of the flight. They were a handsome pair, sitting easily with each other, both quiet and consumed by their respective paperback bestsellers. Without taking their eyes off a single page, they slowly took turns reaching into a supersize Fritos bag. I watched their little dance, waiting for one of them to go in for a handful before the other vacated the bag, but it never happened. No collisions—not even a near miss. It was like watching synchronized swimming: fluid, practiced, mesmerizing. How many trips together had it taken them to get this routine right?

I smiled and closed my eyes. As I drifted off I thought about Hank and me. Is this what marriage would look like years down the road? These simple moments of sharing chips while sailing through the sky?

Hank was waiting for me at the airport in khakis and his bright orange TENNESSEE STUD T-shirt. He'd gotten it as a novelty gift for Christmas from his sister-in-law—you know, the kind of thing you might wear to bed or to clean the bathtub in. Hank didn't see the need to keep this item hidden from others. He frequently wore it out in public, and with pride. I can't help but applaud the man's take-me-as-I-am approach to life.

"Welcome back, baby doll," Hank purred as I slipped into his arms. He smelled delicious—salty, slightly musky, and one hundred percent Hank. I took a deep breath of my seasoned stud and hung in his arms until I realized what was missing.

"Hey, where are the boys?"

"They're back at the house tidying up."

"How much are we paying the help these days?"

"Not enough, according to them."

When we arrived at the house, helpers one and two, and their cleaning supplies, were nowhere to be seen. What did I expect? That they'd be waiting for me at the front door with steaming hand towels? Come to think of it, after a day of using a funky airplane lavatory, warm towelettes would have been a nice touch.

"Boys!" Hank hollered as he lugged my suitcase into the green room. I pulled the front door shut and took a look around. The house was clean, calm, and quiet—until Hank barked even louder, "Boys!"

"Babe," I said. "It's no big deal. They don't have to greet me at the front door."

"Yes, they do."

I appreciated what Hank was trying to do. He wanted me to feel received, like my homecoming was a celebrated event, but his sons (not big fans of formality) were late to the party.

"Boys!"

Finally I heard The Young One holler from somewhere at the back of the house, "We're coming!" They both appeared in the doorway, just as I'd last seen them—in wrinkled T-shirts and with messy hair.

"Yes?" The Young One asked, as if I'd been standing at the front door for the past six weeks and my appearance was nothing to note.

"Say hello to Izzy," Hank instructed. "She just got back."

Ah. Nothing says awkward like pleasantries by demand.

I quickly jumped in instead of waiting for a clumsy response. "Hi, guys. Come here—give me hugs."

"Hi, Izzy," they returned in monotone and draped their limp arms around me.

Hank huffed at their sloppy behavior, but I laughed it off. Social refinement and chivalry would probably come with age. For now, I was content to wait. I was so elated to be back home that their weak hellos were charming enough and it was way too soon for me to become the focus of a "be nice to your stepmother" lesson. Sensing that they were excused, the boys turned back toward their rooms, mumbling "good night," and Hank and I headed toward ours.

There's something so satisfying about climbing into your own bed when you've been away from it for a while—especially when there's a man in it you adore.

After a passionate reunion, we lay facing each other with our light spring sheets pulled up around our chins.

"Can I turn out the light now?" Hank asked.

"One more minute."

He smirked self-consciously. "What are you looking at?"

"You."

I wanted to study his face—something I hadn't been able to do for six weeks. I never tire of looking into his gray-green eyes. Like Hank's overall character, his eyes reflect intensity and depth—a combination I find incredibly sexy. There were truths below the surface I knew I hadn't uncovered yet, and I could stare into his eyes for long stretches.

"Are you done now?" He smiled. "I'm turning it out." He reached over to the bedside table, where I noticed his tower of migraine medicine.

"How cute. We're already growing old together. You're that elderly guy with all the pill bottles next to his bed."

"And you're the one with her face covered in Oil of Olay. That's what my *grandmother* used to wear."

His playful grin was the last thing I saw before he turned out the light.

Spring in Austin hadn't quite sprung, but it was on the verge. Early the next morning, I sauntered out back to inhale the early scents of the day and discovered itty-bitty buds on the Carolina Jessamine and the Tangerine Beauty Crossvine. The Scarlet Wisteria and the Peppermint Peach were also waking up. Ever since I'd moved out of my city apartment and acquired a yard, I'd gotten friendly with what came out of the ground. Central Texas plants and I were on a first-name basis.

Hank quietly crept up from behind me and kissed my neck.

"I want to show you something," he whispered.

He led me to the back corner of the yard, to the dismal section I'd deemed "the dead zone" because of its complete lack of life and aesthetics. But where rocks and weeds had lived together before, neat and tidy rows of little green seedlings now grew in their place.

"We planted you a garden."

We? All three of them? I couldn't ignore the obvious symbolism. Spring—the season of growth and change. I took Hank's hand and kissed it.

"Well, that sure was sweet of you guys."

"It's your basic vegetable and herb garden," Hank explained. "Basil, mint, rosemary, tomatoes, peppers, and summer squash."

Hank was proud. I was flattered. "It's beautiful."

I mean, excluding the unenthusiastic reception of the night before, could my welcome home be any sweeter? A garden planted in my absence by the man-cubs?

Like anyone would, I saw the garden as a sign of good things to come. Hope for the future. Fertile ground for me to dig into my stepmom role—that kind of schmaltzy thing.

Hank took the sentiment further. "You know, boys usually show their love by making things—not by saying it. I read that in a book once."

Ahhh shucks. Ah, spring.

But ladies, come on—we've all read the fairy tales. When flowers bloom underneath your feet and blue jays start serenading you, things are often about to get ugly. If only I'd been aware of

Stepmom Rule Number Fourteen: Don't be shocked when your little garden party gets dumped on by a shit storm . . .

I might have been better prepared for what came next.

In the next few days after my return, I became aware of an elevated level of tension between Hank and the boys. During meals, for example, the brothers were bickering incessantly, and Hank was drinking a lot of Jamaican rum on the rocks. I figured they'd all just had enough of one another. For the past six weeks, Hank had been on single-dad duty, they'd been dining regularly on a do-it-yourself creation called "Meat Plate," and the closed-up house reeked of testosterone. Who wouldn't be on edge?

Additionally, The Tall One was demonstrating narcoleptic tendencies. When he wasn't debating heady issues like evolution versus the creation theory with his brother, he was passed out on his bed, reclined on the couch, or sleeping upright in a nearby chair. This display of debilitating fatigue drove hardworking Hank absolutely crazy. And because The Tall One also had a history of lackluster grades, Hank instituted a new house rule—Wake Up Or Else. Every time the kid drifted off into his comfortable zone of horizontal inactivity, he lost a privilege: computer, phone, TV. I suggested we add his *bed* to the list—perhaps that would help solve the problem.

We were aware of the studies about teenagers needing more sleep than a hibernating bear, so on the weekends, The Tall One was allowed to snore until he woke up to feed. But as far as I was concerned, the argument about teens needing more sleep was trumped by a newer study that exposed how overly sluggish teens had become in recent years. This new info maintained that less than three percent of kids his age exercise. (Exercise, I'm pretty sure, means achieving a heart rate just above coma.) With that in mind, Hank and I dismissed The Tall One's pleas for rest during the week. "Study now. Sleep later," was quickly becoming a hackneyed household phrase.

The afternoon the mailman delivered The Tall One's school progress report, I tore open the envelope and said to myself, *Oh, dear, this can only go one way. Not good.* Hank, I knew from past experience, would not respond well to another disappointing scholastic update. I walked straight into our bedroom and hid the grades in my top dresser drawer. It was instinct: Conceal the truth until I figured out what to do.

The situation reminded me of some made-for-TV drama where the trusting wife discovers the murder weapon and realizes her loving husband committed the crime and part of her wants to protect him (from his stupid self) and the other part of her wants to call the fuzz and have him hauled in.

I wanted to give The Tall One, who I always argued was smart and capable, the benefit of the doubt. Given the chance, perhaps he could explain this hideous blunder from the student records office. On the other hand, I knew the kid was probably guilty as charged; he hadn't performed well, and it was his own fault if he faced the wrath of his father.

I took the grades out of hiding, placed them on the kitchen counter, and poured myself a sizable glass of wine. Then I waited.

The Tall One returned home from school first, shuffled into the kitchen, glanced at the report with little interest, inhaled a bowl of cereal, and retreated to his room.

When Hank got home from work, the house exploded.

Hank exploding? *Isn't that a little out of character for him?* He's a reasonable man who can, on occasion, exhibit chafed nerves, but he's not someone who goes ballistic—*right?*

The truth is that my Southern gentleman has a low boiling point, a fact I've worked hard at hiding from others. Hank has a tendency to go from zero to one hundred degrees in a matter of seconds. The first time he lost his cool with the boys, I was stunned. My parents raised me with quiet and controlled discipline; no one ever yelled—at me, anyway.

It was early on in our dating when, seemingly from out of nowhere, Hank erupted in a rage. It was one of our first dinners together, and The Young One violated a mealtime law: He got up from the table without being excused. Before I even noticed the transgression, Hank transformed into a man I hadn't seen before. "Sit down RIGHT NOW!" he demanded. "You DO NOT get up without asking, you understand me?" Yikes. His bark had a ferocious bite.

Hank's words silenced the room. The Young One took his seat at the table and The Tall One looked down at his food. *What the hell just happened?* Was this the routine? I certainly hoped not. How could anyone be expected to swallow the teeniest bite of tenderloin with tension this thick? More meals like this and I could drop a good ten pounds.

Later, once Hank and I were alone, I struggled with what I felt I had to say. "Maybe it's not my business, but Hank, that scene during dinner was a little disturbing."

He let out a big sigh. "I was worried that my fussing at the kids would freak you out."

Fussing? That must be the Southern way of saying *scaring the shit out of everyone at the table.*

Hank and I hadn't been dating long, but I'd already fallen hard for the man. That he was volatile wasn't necessarily a deal-breaker, but it was definitely a red flag. This new insight into his character was disappointing. I could accept that Hank was flawed (who isn't?), but using combative language with his kids was difficult for me to justify—let alone stand witness to. At the same time, I knew that Hank was a good man with a conscience, a man who loved his boys, a man who didn't want to lose me. Given the last item on the list, I felt like I could be honest with him.

"It was your tone more than anything else. It was . . . mean."

His forehead wrinkled with concern. He nodded in agreement. "I know. I'm working on it."

"And . . ." I hesitated before dropping the always-popular ultimatum: "I expect you to never speak to me the way you spoke to those boys tonight."

He faced me straight on and said, "I won't."

I could have walked away. But no, I decided to take a chance. I continued to not only date but also marry a man prone to outbursts because I adored everything else about him and because he made a promise to "work on it"—a promise he has kept. Does he slip? Sure, but less and less, and with decreased intensity. Do I expect him to lose his edge and make a full recovery? No. Hank is what Hank is—a guy with a temper. All I can do is encourage him to be more temperate and run interference for the boys when he's not. I guess you could say that I have learned to function within dysfunction by appointing myself the middle man, or middle woman or middle mother, which is exactly the position I found myself in the day the grades arrived.

After Hank took in the full devastation of his son's educational progress, he stormed out of the kitchen and headed straight for The Tall One's room.

Oh, shit!

Hank threw open his son's bedroom door and yelled, "Get up!" confirming my fear that The Tall One was once again fast asleep.

The Young One, not understanding the cause for the loud boom, came out of his bedroom. "Daddy?"

"Not NOW," Hank bellowed. "GO BACK IN YOUR ROOM."

I stood at the end of the hallway watching this unhappy scene unfold, struck with complete helplessness. *Oh shit, oh shit, oh shit.*

Do I or do I not get involved? These are Hank's kids. He's the primary disciplinarian, and he has every reason to be upset with The Tall One. But what if it goes too far? What if he says something unforgivable, something he can't take back? I was afraid that Hank didn't see what I saw, that his temper could eventually jeopardize his relationship with his boys. Because I loved Hank and because I knew losing the love of his kids would destroy him, I felt like I should step in.

"I said GET UP!" he screamed at The Tall One again. "You're failing out of school, all you do is sleep . . ." And then he went on to describe a bleak professional future where The Tall One's only likely career would be as a Target stockboy. Hank had lost control.

All right, that's it. "HANK!" I raised my voice.

He turned around and shot me a look. The Tall One appeared in the doorway and did the same.

"THAT'S ENOUGH!" Suddenly *I'd* turned into a barker.

I could not stand by and let hurtful words take over my house. *Good God! Am I here to save this bloody family from one another?* I wanted to shield Hank from himself, stop him from saying regrettable words, but I also had to defend the boys. In an instant, my loyalty shifted away from Hank to his son. The Tall One had screwed up, yes, but he's a kid, and kids screw up. Hank needed to back off. I thought, *Can't we just sit down like civilized people and handle this in our quiet voices?*

I walked down the hall and said to Hank, "Enough. Let's talk about this later, when we've all calmed down." For better or for worse, I seem to be the only person in Hank's life who can calm his fury. He's always trusted my judgment, listened to my version of reason, and, thankfully, he did so again. Without saying another word, he turned and walked away.

I'd heard much griping about discipline from my online sisterhood. How are we supposed to keep a distance, not meddle, and still exercise control over our own households? *I may not be the mother, but this is where I live.* I have been invited into this family, but how far do I go in?

As we lay in bed later that night, disconnected and avoiding words, I wondered the same thing: Had I gone too far?

Many stepmoms, I'd come to understand, were frustrated with their new husbands for not exercising *enough* control over their kids. They complained that their husbands were pushovers, too soft—indulgent and afraid to lift a heavy hand. With Hank, graduate of the School of Tough Love, I often had the opposite dilemma. What was the difference between my situation and theirs? The only thing I could come up with was that many of them were battling with their step*daughters*. Maybe the dynamics were completely different when it came to a divorced dad and his girls versus a divorced dad with boys. I couldn't say for sure; all I knew was that my situation had its own special set of defects that needed adjusting.

I took a deep breath and dove in. "Hank, you scare me when you get angry. I don't want to feel like if I'm not here, you guys are going to kill each other."

"We're not going to *kill* each other," he said irritably.

"You know what I mean." I paused before I began again. "I realize that I'm fairly new to the scene; you guys obviously managed before I came along, but now I'm here and I'm stuck in the middle—feeling like I have to play peacemaker."

"You don't have to play the peacemaker. The boys and I will be fine."

This annoyed me—like they could have their own family dynamic apart from me. "But it's not just the three of you anymore. You're not a separate unit. I'm here, too. And I don't like the yelling."

Hank exhaled deliberately. I knew I was dangerously close to being accused of mothering him, giving him a dreaded lecture.

I softened my tone. "I worry that one day you'll push too hard and the boys will decide to stop taking it." *And leave you for good,* I thought, although I didn't dare say this.

Hank was quiet, and then he choked up. I tugged on him to move closer and wrapped him in my arms.

"I don't want to lose my boys," he cried.

"I know."

"And I don't want to scare you. I hate that I scare you."

"Well, you don't really *scare* me. It's just that sometimes you're scary."

"Same thing." He rubbed his eyes. "I love my boys and I know that I get angry and sometimes I lose control, but I'm not a bad person."

"No, you're not a bad person. You're a real person . . . one who struggles with anger." Hank tensed up. He resented labels—the guy with the "anger issue."

"Look," I said, "you're not the first parent in the history of the world to get mad at his kids."

He took a deep breath. "I know," he relented. "Still, I don't like it. I wish there were a switch I could just turn off."

"That would be handy."

He elbowed me. "You're not funny."

I held Hank against my chest until his breathing slowed down and the house felt calm again.

"Thank you," Hank whispered into the dark.

"For what?"

"For loving me. You help me be a better father. You are important to this family. We need you—we really do."

And with that, I fell asleep with a sense of peace. Hank was imperfect, but so was I. Our little stepfamily had flaws and quirks and moments of heartache, yet Hank and I would get up tomorrow and give it another go. He'd try to be a better father and I'd try to be a patient stepmom. We were working on it, and maybe in a blended family, that's as good as it gets. That said, the Tall One had better get his algebra together. *Or else.*

The next morning the house was quiet. Hank and The Young One had already left for the day. I sat across from The Tall One at the kitchen table, watching him despondently eat toast. I wanted to reach out to him, ease the sad look in his eyes, but he had his impenetrable teenage armor on. If he craved affection, he certainly wasn't showing it.

"Are you okay?" I finally asked.

He took a bite of toast and slurred something that sounded like "sure" or "yeah" or "leave me the fuck alone."

Honestly, I didn't expect much more than that.

On a regular day, the kid's no speaker of the house. He's a deep thinker, but he seldom shares his thoughts. I've learned not to press him. He'll talk when he wants to talk, but after last night's blowup, I hoped he'd give just a little. I wanted proof of his resiliency—that he hadn't drafted a suicide note or a plan to blow up his father's car.

Another crunch was all I got.

Fine. I knew the drill. Unless I engaged the kid in one-way lip flap, we wouldn't talk at all. Here's the problem: Monologues peppered with worldly adult wisdom aren't my thing. I run out of words fast when I'm the only one doing the talking, so I kept it short and sweet: "I'm sorry about last night. If you want to talk about it—or anything else—I'm here." Not exactly what I'd call an award-winning speech. I'd turned into just another clueless parent delivering the generic sound bite.

He mumbled "okay," although I'm sure what he meant was *Get ready for a slow death, lady. This stepmom gig will drive you to your grave.*

Toward the end of the week, the mood in the house lifted. Hank apologized to The Tall One for yelling. He explained that a woman named Sarah the shrink was helping him tame his temper. The Tall One agreed to try harder in school and brought out a stack of homework papers he'd completed. I stood in the kitchen watching their calm exchange. I'd continue to orbit around them, watch over them, and jump in when they needed a mediator, but Hank was right—it wasn't my duty to play peacemaker. I took a step back and left the room. They'd have to learn to work it out on their own.

On Friday night we ordered pepperoni and sausage pizza from the guy down the street who dishes pie out of his twelve-foot trailer. Mobile food vendors are the new big thing in Austin. Some of the best food in the city is served out of walk-up windows you stand in long and hot lines for. In fact, I knew some locals who refused to order tacos anywhere but from the popular taco stand with the memorable motto "Show Me Your Taco."

As we sat out on the back patio inhaling our weight in cheese, I watched my three men laugh and joke around. The tension from the previous week was gone, although *my* shoulders were still in knots.

"Daddy," said The Young One, "did you know that if you wear socks to bed, you live longer?"

Hank finished swallowing and said, "No, son. I did not know that."

"What if there's a hole in your sock?" The Tall One baited him. "If you only wear one sock, will you live half as long?"

"Shut up," The Young One said. He returned his focus to Hank.

"Daddy, did you know that it's illegal to have ice cream in your pants in Minnesota?"

"What?" said Hank, incredulous. He was laughing now, and playing along. "So I'd be arrested if I had a hot-fudge sundae in my pocket?"

I thought, *Now this is more like it.* Anger I'm not so good with; nonsense I can handle. With the coast clear, I took a turn.

"Hey, guys, would you rather use egg salad for deodorant or rancid relish for toothpaste?"

"Not *this* again," said The Tall One. "Neither."

"You know the rules," I said. "You have to pick one."

The Tall One smiled and rolled his eyes. "How much relish?"

"A huge glob, and you have to brush your teeth with it for a full five minutes, and you can't rinse it out," I said

"Relish," piped The Young One.

"Ewwww," I said.

"Izzy," he defended himself, "you'd put *eggs* in your armpits."

"You're right. That is pretty sick."

"Another one," he demanded.

"Okay . . . Would you rather have a small bird beak for a nose or a lobster claw as one of your front teeth?"

"Definitely the bird beak," Hank said.

We all cracked up at this.

With our household back to normal, I could turn my attention to my own troubled behavior. I'd been back from San Francisco for nearly a month and I was still avoiding the inevitable—employment. I'd burned my bridges in Houston, I'd failed at saving the environment, and I wasn't allowed to compete against my own husband in the same market. *Where do I go from here?* I spent an hour searching for jobs on craigslist until I came across the following position: *Private Satanist church seeks voice actor(s) for promotional videos, radio spots, etc. Specifically, we need two main voices for our products: Jesus Christ and our Lord Satan.*

Wow. The job market was grim. Even Lucifer had to apply. I figured shopping would serve as a good distraction. I drove over to South First Street and wandered through an artisan shop filled with a handpicked selection of watercolor paintings of the Hill Country, garden art made from scrap metal, and revamped vintage jewelry. As I scanned the walls, my eyes settled on a royal blue ceramic bird. I flew right over to her.

"Isn't she lovely?" the woman behind the counter gushed.

"Yes, I *loooooovvvvve* her." Indeed, Little Miss Bird looked just like one of the pack that followed Snow White around. "I must have her."

She reminded me of something a woman in my all-ladies book group had advised: "You have to build a nest. You can't just fly into one."

And yet that's exactly what I'd done. I'd flown right into a partially closed window with a crash.

The little bird also reminded me of *Are You My Mother?* a children's book I'd had as a kid. In the story, a baby bird is hatched while his mother is away looking for food. The baby bird goes on an extensive search for his mother, asking a cow and a hen and a dog, "Are you my mother?" This story always gave me a lump in my throat—this vulnerable little bird wandering around, lost without his mother. Thankfully, Mama returns in the end and happiness is restored.

I purchased the bird and took her right home where she could fly with ease and grace across my bedroom wall. She would be my reminder on self-conscious days that even though I wasn't the mom, we were building our own nest and, eventually, we'd settle in just fine.

And then Hank broke the news. "June isn't moving to Texas." According to Hank, she'd given up the job search. The circus was not coming to town.

Lena and I were looking down from the pedestrian bridge above Barton Springs at the early spring swimmers. Much to my delight, Lena had recently moved into the Barton Hills neighborhood, a ten-minute stroll from where we lived. We quickly established a regular routine of walking together around the lake. Over the past two miles, I'd given her the superabridged version of my stepmom saga.

"So, now that June won't be moving here, what does that mean for the boys, longterm?" Lena asked.

"Well, the boys will finish out the school year and go back to California for the summer, and then I guess we have to ask the kids who they want to live with next year."

"Really? You're going to leave it up to them?"

"No. The decision will ultimately be up to the collective parent network—Hank, June, John, and me—but the kids will get to weigh in." We walked in silence for a few minutes, the gravel crunching beneath our feet. "What do you think? I go back and forth. Maybe it's not a good idea to give the kids a say."

Lena shrugged. "Yeah, I don't know. That's a tough one."

"Yep. Asking kids to choose between parents is pretty awful."

When I was the boys' age, I didn't have to make a choice because my parents stayed in the same town. My stepsisters, Piper and Gigi, on the other hand, *did* have a choice to make. Their mother lived in Michigan and our little posse lived in California. I remember this being especially hard on Gigi. I have a vivid memory of her crying into her pillow, afraid to make a choice.

"I didn't want to hurt anyone's feelings," Gigi said when I called her after my walk with Lena. I wanted to confirm if my recollection of those times was accurate.

"Like, if you chose to live with your mom, then you'd be hurting Stanton?" I asked her.

"Exactly. That's why I traded off years, remember? One year with Daddy, and then the next year I'd live with Mom. I felt like that was the fair thing to do."

"Fair to them, you mean?"

"Yeah."

"So you were taking care of them? Your decision had nothing to do with what you wanted?"

"Not really. I wanted to be with both of them."

I called Piper next. She, too, had dreaded the annual decision.

"I didn't compromise like Gigi did by going back and forth. I knew where I wanted to be—in California with Daddy—but I was wracked with guilt every time I chose him over Mom. It was awful, but I can't imagine *not* being able to choose."

Hank and I sat on the June news for about a week. And in that time, I realized a couple of things. One: I didn't want to lose the boys. Two: I didn't want to be picked last. It had been close to thirty years since I'd stood on the elementary-school blacktop waiting to hear my name called by the dodgeball captain. I remember it like it was yesterday, the horror of being chosen last. Of course I knew that going up against June was a losing battle, no question. The only trick up my sleeve was Hank. He could very well increase my odds of winning.

Wait a minute—winning? I had to stop and check myself. Was this just an ego thing?

Well, yes. I was thinking about myself. I was thinking competitively. I was indulging in some stepmom lunacy.

I recognized that my meddlesome ego was wreaking havoc with my ability to think reasonably, but I couldn't help going there. I conjured up seventeenth-century New England, and there I was, the scourged stepmom in the town square, wearing a fat scarlet *F* (for failure, i.e., fuck-up) on my fleece vest. "Look at the pitiful woman!" the critical townsfolk cried. "She was abandoned by her man-cubs because of all her selfish grumbling." After creating a gross picture in my mind of the town drunk hurling a raw haddock fillet at my head, I snapped out of it.

Jesus, Izzy, get real.

What was underneath the vanity? Threatened with the idea of the kids leaving, I had to admit I felt sad. Their absence would leave an emptiness in the house. Given the choice, I'd rather have them than not. Even if that meant—and I couldn't believe I was thinking this—having them all the time. However, I realized there were some victories that their mom—the real one—was entitled to. Preferential status over the stepmom was one. After all, I'd always chosen my mom over my dad's second wife—even when she pulled out all the stops to win me over.

"There was that one birthday, you remember?" Mom asked. We were on the phone discussing the mom-stepmom pecking order. "Crystal threw you a birthday party and made you a cat cake?"

"Oh, yeah. That was pretty cool."

Mom said, "I remember dropping Piper and Gigi off at the party and coming in to say hello and seeing this elaborate cake she'd baked in the shape of a cat and thinking, *I never made you a cat cake. I never even* thought *to make you a cat cake.*"

"Oh, Mom," I sympathized.

She laughed. "I know—it was silly, but I remember driving away feeling like this awful mother, worried that you were going to decide to like her better than me."

"Impossible," I said.

"Well, you see? That's just it. There's something about a kid's relationship with his mother—the original, as you like to call her—that can't be touched. And I think, Izzy, that's the way it should be. The blood mother has earned the right to be number one. If only by default."

"You're right. I get it."

While I'd been working toward an understanding of my maternal ranking, Hank had been acting aloof, trying to disguise his own wounded ego. But I knew he was distressed by June's decision. His family was being pulled farther apart, and he blamed himself. After a week of adjusting to our new set of circumstances, Hank said, "I shouldn't have taken this job. I took you away from your family and your career, and the boys away from their mother . . ."

"Hank, *come on*—you know that's ridiculous. We all decided to move to Austin. All of us. And it hasn't played out the way we thought it would, but that's just the way it goes." (I was proud of myself for exercising Stepmom Rule Number Six: Accept what is.)

Hank sighed.

"It was an ambitious plan," I said. "Four professional adults trying to relocate somewhere that would serve us all, financially and personally?"

Hank tugged the hairs on his chin, looking pensively out the front window. And then he stood up with an air of resignation. "Okay, let's tell the boys."

"Now?"

"Yep. It's time we tell them what's going on. Plus, they already know something's up."

"Okay." I opened the French doors to the green room and called out in a chipper Carol Brady voice, "Hey guys—your favorite: a family meeting!" I wasn't looking forward to it, either, but I'd do my best to fake it.

They reported in and, thankfully, Hank took charge of delivering the news.

"Boys," he began. "Your mommy and John have decided not to move to Austin."

The Tall One and The Young One stared at Hank, defenseless.

"She's tried really hard to find a job here, but it hasn't worked out. We thought we'd all be living together, but they're going to stay in the Bay Area."

"So are we all going to move back to California?" The Young One asked softly.

"No, baby," Hank said. "Izzy and I are going to stay here, and so are you—at least until the end of the school year. Then the four adults will figure out what happens next year."

The Young One stared down into his lap. The Tall One mumbled,

"Well, I think I should stay here, because then I don't have to change schools again, and I've already made friends and stuff."

Hank smiled tenderly. "Well, I want you to stay here, too, but we need to talk it out and decide what's best."

The Tall One just sat in his chair. The Young One picked at a hole in his jeans.

"I know this makes it hard on you guys, having us here and your mommy and John so far away, but we'll work it out, okay?"

They didn't respond.

"Okay?" Hank repeated.

"Okay," they both said with heavy sighs.

Later that night The Young One wandered into the kitchen where Hank and I were putting away dishes. His eyes were red and weepy.

Hank said, "Come here." He held his arms out to The Young One, who pressed himself hard into his father's chest. They stood still like that for about a minute, until The Young One looked up and said, "Daddy?"

"Yes?" Hank stroked his head.

"Maybe I want to go live with Mommy."

Hank didn't say a word. He looked down at his son with a mix of compassion and regret. I felt devastated for both of them. The Young One needed his mother. And Hank needed his boy.

Over the next few weeks, I watched Hank demonstrate an amazing amount of humility and patience. Not only was The Young One on his usual fact-finding mission (Daddy, who invented the paper airplane?), he was also hell-bent on communicating his needs. He was demonstrating the quality many women say they want from their men: Feelings. Emotion. The kid has no hang-up with verbal intimacy, and in this respect, he may be the most eligible ten-year-old bachelor in the world. Except his focus was on one woman only: his mother.

As soon as The Young One got it in his head that he wanted to move back to California, we didn't hear much of anything else: "I need Mommy. I want Mommy." But Hank didn't cave, and this threw The Young One into dramatic fits. His flair for playing the tragic hero reached Oscar-worthy heights the evening he staggered out of his room with a puffy red face, clenching the phone to his chest. He held out the phone to his brother.

"It's Mommy," he croaked. "You might need to wipe it off because it's covered in my tears."

Okay, enough already. We know you miss your mom, but what about me? Don't I count for anything? That's what I expected Hank to say, but he didn't go there. He kept his cool.

I was back in Sarah's office. I'd just caught her up on the latest developments.

"So, how do you feel about The Young One's pleas to move back with his mother?"

"A little resentful." I could be honest with Sarah about things I wouldn't dare admit to anyone else. Seriously, what kind of woman holds a grudge against a ten-year-old for wanting his mother?

"Are you sure it's resentment? Could it be anything else?"

"Hostility?" I smirked.

She smiled. "The last time you were in here we talked about your plan to put some distance between you and the boys—to protect them from depending on you. How's that working out for you?"

Sarah the shrink was making a funny. *So, the joke's on me, eh?*

Her recollection was correct. I thought I'd put a buffer between the boys and myself, but they'd gotten under my skin anyway. And now at least one of them was threatening to walk out the door, which is exactly what I've spent my adult life trying to avoid: abandonment by men, big and small. So after convincing myself that I was trying to guard the boys from my own shifty heart, I realized the truth was I'd been really trying to protect myself. I was scared to invest in people I might eventually lose.

After Sarah and I shared a little *Izzy-so-silly* laugh over my failed attempts to remain unaffected, she revealed

Stepmom Rule Number Fifteen: Protecting yourself is an illusion.

Despite all my tough talk, I couldn't escape my vulnerability. I'd tried to put up a wall, but it had some major cracks in it. Something that felt like love had slipped through. I stretched out on our bed that evening, listening to the trains coming from the south and gazing at my little blue bird. "Miss Bird," I said aloud, "what can you tell me about empty-nest syndrome?"

To take my mind off the possibility that The Young One might fly off into the sunset, and also in an attempt to practice Southern hospitality, Hank and I decided to host our own supper club. With a gaggle of fresh faces in the house, perhaps I'd forget that The Young One could soon be absent. Since we were still newbies, our plan for a successful turnout included inviting everyone we'd met since moving to town—and yes, that meant the ad-company guy who'd interviewed me and *hadn't* given me the job, my hairdresser, and our shrink. Oh, and our new prospective best friends from across the street.

The house across from ours had been empty for months, affording Hank and me many hours to imagine what our new neighbors would be like. We were beyond hopeful—we expected that our new best friends would soon move in. We'd love them. They'd love us. We'd share decades of memorable meals together that would be documented in photo albums we'd refer to throughout the years. "Remember taco night," we'd say, laughing. "Look at Hank—hogging all the shredded lettuce. What a kidder!"

After months of thanking the universe in advance for bringing us our closest friends in years, the house had sold. *Thank you Rhonda Byrne!* But before we could plan our first magical cookout together, another secret was revealed—our new neighbors were assholes.

Soon after the FOR SALE sign was removed, a herd of construction workers invaded the house. Hank and I watched in disgust as they ripped mahogany cabinets off the walls, jackhammered the stone fireplace, and dug up years' worth of landscaping, including the lawn—only to replace it with a newer one! *Who are these new best friends of ours? Why are they yanking up the drought-tolerant plants? Don't they know a green lawn is passé?*

For several days, Hank and I had been watching the demolition from our front window. Hank was especially disappointed. Any premature man-crush he had developed on his new neighbor had vanished. "They're replacing all that perfectly good wood with cheap cabinetry," Hank scoffed. "What idiots!" I had to agree that our new neighbors seemed to lack the type of good judgment we'd expected from them, but since we hadn't met or even seen them yet, I still held out some hope.

Until today.

When I went out to retrieve the mail I noticed a flashy BMW 5 series zoom up to the house. The door flew open and out popped our new neighbor: Tony Danza. Well, his look-alike, anyway. Unlike the real Tony, who I think of as your typical nice guy next door, *this* Tony strutted around his ripped-up yard with an air of control-freakishness. He wore a white tank and what looked like three-hundred-dollar jeans, and he walked around sweating and barking very specific orders.

Who's the boss? There was no question.

I planted myself on the front porch and watched. His crew had just finished painting the front door a beautiful crimson. It was striking—it gave the battered house a much-needed lift. Tony stood with his arms crossed and sneered. "It doesn't, ya know, pop," he said.

His guys just looked at him.

"You understand, *POP?*" he said impatiently. "It's just nothing special."

I couldn't believe it. Who does he think he is? Not my new best friend—that's who. He most certainly was not going to be invited over for taco night. I called Hank.

"Our new neighbors are not invited to supper club. I just met—okay, assessed—the man of the house, and I fear the influence he may have on the boys."

"Whatever you say, babe." Hank was distracted, consumed by work, and had already divorced himself from Tony sight unseen, anyway.

"Who else can we invite?"

"Well, did you notice that the house on the corner just went on the market? Maybe our new best friends will move in there."

The theme of our first supper club was Yer Grandma's Cookin'. Hank and I invited everyone to make one of their grandmother's signature dishes. Twenty people showed up to our house on the last Saturday of the month, crowding into our kitchen with casserole dishes, beer coolers, and cake carriers. Lena walked over from her house carrying

a piping hot, five-gallon pot full of her grandma's seafood gumbo.
There was a savory noodle kugel, a chocolate Coca-Cola cake, fried
Mississippi corn, and Skyline chili. Hank made Trailer Park Pie—the
white-trash version of shepherd's pie, made with tater tots and smothered in American cheese. I made Gram's famous rum cake covered in
pecans. An ex-colleague from Whales That Smoke walked in with a
skinny brown bag and said, "My grandmother didn't cook, but she
drank a lot of sherry." I placed the bottle of Christian Brothers in the
middle of our dining room table.

Gram's Rum Cake

1 cup chopped pecans
1 pkg. yellow cake mix
1 pkg. Jell-O Instant Vanilla Pudding
4 eggs
½ cup cold water
½ cup Wesson oil
½ cup dark rum (80 proof)

Preheat oven to 325°F. Grease and flour 12-cup bundt pan.
Sprinkle nuts over bottom of pan. Mix all cake ingredients together. Pour batter over nuts. Bake one hour. Cool. Invert on
serving plate. Prick top and drizzle and smooth glaze evenly.
Allow cake to absorb glaze until all glaze is used up.

Glaze:

¼ lb. butter
¼ cup water

1 cup granulated sugar
½ cup rum

Melt butter in sauce pan. Stir in water and sugar. Boil 5 minutes, stirring constantly. Remove from heat and stir in rum.

Before we piled our plates high, we each presented our dish with a little family history. In some cases we revealed the "secret" in the sauce (typically, whole milk and real butter). We lifted our wineglasses and toasted our grandmothers—Miriam, Lorraine, Helen, Katherine, Phoebe, Edna, and Dorothy. I looked into the faces of all my new friends and knew that Gram would be proud. She'd successfully passed on her party-giving gene. Not to mention that, my guests were already raving about her alcohol-soaked cake.

Well into the feasting, The Tall One emerged from the kitchen with an antique glass dish crowded with dark chocolate hazelnut truffles, which he had made from scratch. All the women in the room swooned at the sight.

"You *made* these?" Lena said as she bit into one. "Oh. My. God." I thought she might tear his shirt off. "Where did you learn how to do this?"

The Tall One could not hide his delight. He was beaming.

Earlier in the day he'd told Hank and me that he wanted to make truffles for the party. *The overpriced bonbons?* Creating the perfectly rich and round bite-sized desserts seemed like an impossibility to manage, but he really wanted to give it a go, so we bought him all the ingredients. He slouched over the stovetop all afternoon, measuring, mixing, heating, and cooling chocolate. When the first of the guests arrived for the evening, he was still at it, and I worried that he'd set his sights too high.

But there he stood now, triumphant and dazzling all the women in the room.

So maybe algebra wasn't his thing. And maybe that was okay. If tonight was any indication, we had a budding chocolatier on our hands, and you don't have to be a math genius to use a measuring cup.

Hope springs in the strangest places.

APRIL

Marrying the Ex-Wife

My Alvina Valenta bridal gown arrived from San Francisco in an oversized box the next week. My dilemma: I had to try it on to make sure no future alterations were needed, but if I took the dress out of the box, how would I get it back in without wrinkling it beyond repair? My satin-silk number still had to be transported to Memphis for the ceremony in June. For a second, I wished I hadn't quit my college job at The Limited before mastering the retail chain folding technique. I stared at the box for a good ten minutes until I determined that hands-on Hank would be sure to figure something out.

Very carefully, I slid the sumptuous creation out of its cozy container and slipped it on, which was much harder to do without help from Judy at Bridal Galleria. I lifted the bottom hem high above my knees and walked into my bathroom, where I could assess the fit. I threw down a beach towel and stood on my tiptoes, so as not to pick up any cat hair from the floor. I could just see it now—the wedding announcement in the *Memphis Commercial Appeal* would read: "The bride floated down the aisle, her elegant train shimmering with tabby fur."

I studied my image in the toothpaste-smudged mirror. *Hot damn!* I filled it out perfectly. Not only did I look like a formidable bride, the dress elevated my sense of matriarchal stature. *I might be the second wife and the stepmom,* I thought, *but I'm the female head of* this *household. The woman in charge.* I straightened up with newfound confidence. No matter where the traveling circus ends up down the road, we still have a wedding ceremony to plan—one that honors our current little family of four.

I wiggled out of my fine-looking frock, hung her on the bedroom door, skipped into my office, and opened up the wedding file.

Despite what I'd always heard about wedding planning being the nightmare of all jobs, I found it to be a relative cinch.

Back in January I'd made several calls, written a few checks, and voilà!—the arrangements were in place. Planning a wedding is not unlike organizing a TV shoot: Choose a location, hire a photographer, order food for the crew, and show up on time. Maybe wedding coordination really was my next career move? I made a mental note to tell my remaining single girlfriends to hire me (or any other semi-retired TV producer) should they ever decide to walk down the aisle. I'd also mention the number one advantage of the destination wedding: The bride can't be totally in control (i.e., naggy and neurotic), which can work in her favor. In the long run, you end up with fewer stress headaches and exasperated family members. Because of Austin's geographical distance to west Tennessee, I'd been forced to put some emotional space between my daily life and some of the fluffier details of the impending "big day." I didn't have the luxury, for example, to set up appointments with ten different pastry chefs all over Memphis to sample thirty-five cakes before picking one. Rather, I made my decision based on the selections described in a brochure. I figured, *It's cake! People will eat shoes if they're covered in frosting.*

James, my wedding planner at the Peabody Hotel, confirmed my out-of-state theory. He confided in hushed tones over the phone, "My female clients who live in town just can't help themselves." He dropped his voice even lower and said, "I have some brides who are down here every week with their mothers—sometimes more than that—going over every little detail." I couldn't help thinking, *These are the women who give brides a bad name.* Not me. I would not waver. I'd be decisive and efficient. That's not to say I would be easy. I had a strong vision of my bridal bash, including who'd be attending.

In my mind, the perfect wedding looked like this: (1) My guests would dine on authentic Southern fare, specifically cheese grits and jalapeño hush puppies; (2) A gospel choir would bring down the house; and (3) The ex-wife would not be included in the festivities.

These were all reasonable requests, weren't they? I thought so. June thought differently.

I knew that with every wedding the bride suffers at least one complication. This was going to be mine. But what was the proper etiquette for handling the ex-wife? I searched through all my bridal magazines and came across an article titled "Treating Your Guests with Grace," but the focus was on appeasing bossy bridesmaids, uppity mothers, and forgotten friends. The ex-wife wasn't mentioned anywhere, and this omission spoke volumes to me, but maybe I'd skipped over something. There had to be some guidelines, a list of second wives' do's and don'ts? Based on June's reaction—she'd complained to Hank—I'd committed a big no-no, so I did a quick search on Amazon.com using the keywords *idiot's guide + second wife*, but the only title that came close was *World War II for Dummies*. Uh-oh. This was probably not a good indicator of things to come.

Weddings are tricky. When organizing hordes of friends and family, there's bound to be someone in the crowd who doesn't get his or her way. I just didn't figure that I'd be worrying about the hurt feelings of Hank's ex. I turned another page of *Today's Bride*. The featured article was "Things Not to Worry About." The first item on the list was "Trying to please everybody." *Amen, sister!* I wanted to embrace this advice—it got me off the hook. But now that the issue had been raised, I started to second-guess myself. Was excluding June the wrong thing to do?

I needed to know what other women in my situation had done, so I consulted my online stepladies. As usual, any topic having to do with the ex generated much debate. The more mild-mannered of the bunch explained that it was proper etiquette to invite the ex-wife and, conversely, it was proper etiquette for her to respectfully decline. Hmm. I wasn't sure I wanted to take the risk. The idea of having June there made me uncomfortable. For starters, where was she going to sit? With her ex-in-laws? With the boys? But they would be sitting with us.

It would be one thing if June and I were gal-pals, but aside from the one-on-one lunch in San Francisco, ours was more of a drive-by relationship (we waved from car windows when exchanging the kids). Shouldn't we share a few more salads before I invite her to something as personal as my wedding? I understood that June shared a closeness with Hank based on their baby-making days, but *my* father didn't go to my mother's wedding, and my mother didn't go to my father's wedding, even though they, too, had remained friends after splitting up. Could I just assume she would decline and not ask in the first place?

My more outspoken stepladies said yes. In fact, many of them screamed *HELL YES!* According to many, inviting the ex to their own weddings never crossed their minds, or if it had, they'd quickly scratched the idea. They reminded me that there's room for only one wife at the altar, and "it ain't the ex." Sure, weddings were about bringing families together, they said, but this marriage was between Hank and me. June should respect that this was our day and back off. Still, I struggled with the possibility that a firm decision not to invite her might earn me an unbecoming title ("the bitch Daddy married," for example). It wasn't my intention to offend June, and I appreciated the warning from other stepladies that a happy ex-wife is not a vengeful ex-wife, but what about *my* happiness? And it was my wedding, wasn't it? I'd seen nearly all my girlfriends get married, and I knew how it worked—the bride rules. If pushed, I was fairly certain I'd have to play the queen.

I dialed mom's number and dropped the problem on her. "Hank says that June's upset she's not invited to the wedding. I really don't want to go out of my way to disturb the peace, but can't I have one day all to myself? Don't we share enough already?"

There was silence on the other end of the line.

"Hello?"

"No comment," she finally replied.

"You're kidding," I said, shocked. "You're not going to tell me what to do?"

"No way—are you crazy? Not on this one."

"Since when did you start playing it safe?"

"Since I became the mother of the bride. My job at your wedding is to smile, look gorgeous, and get along with everybody."

"Wimp."

I hung up and sat motionless, staring at the wall. *Why does June want to be part of our wedding, anyway?* I didn't get it.

Perhaps I had overlooked an important piece of Traveling Circus Code: We move together, we marry together. I sat with this for a minute. Was it possible that June was worried about the boys? Did she fear that if she wasn't present the boys would finally be forced to confront the hard fact that Mommy and Daddy weren't getting back together again? Surely that was clear by now. From my perspective as a stepkid, I thought it was time the boys understood that, in some shape or form, divorce does indeed forever divide the unit. It often *expands* the meaning of family, but we're not all swimming in the same pool anymore.

When Hank got home from work, I grudgingly asked him for clarification. Poor guy. Here he was again—in between wives.

"Did she say why she was upset that she wasn't invited?"

I could tell immediately that Hank did not want to spend his evening justifying June's reaction or placating me. He tried to brush it off by walking out of the room and mumbling, "I don't know. She's probably just feeling left out."

Did he just say "left out"?

"Of what?" I snipped and followed him into the kitchen. "Our marriage?" My tone was a dead giveaway. I'd spent hours beating myself up over this. Now I was defensive. I was on the verge of throwing a fit. Okay, I was already there.

Hank regarded me with tired eyes. The man was exhausted—he was working long days to keep us financially afloat, The Young One had unwittingly broken his heart, and his ex-wife and I were busting his balls. I knew that if I wanted to start a nasty fight with him, all I had to do was fire off one more snarky comment and he would break, and then I'd have one more person mad at me. I inhaled deeply·and said, "I'm going to take a walk. I'll be back. I just need to breathe."

I walked down our long driveway and into the street. I could detect the first sweet hint of Texas Mountain Laurel in the air. I took a deep breath and exhaled. I was tired, too. The fight in me was weakening. For all my bravado, I really didn't want conflict with anyone. Not Hank. Not the boys. Not June. I am, it turns out, like nearly every woman I've ever met—underneath it all, I'm a people-pleaser, a caregiver to the universe. But that means taking care of myself, too.

If waiting to marry and start a family until my mid-thirties had afforded me any insight, it was this—

Stepmom Rule Number Sixteen: Compromise, but don't sacrifice yourself.

There were some things I was willing to do for the collective (like give up my great job and move to Austin), and then there were other sacrifices I was unable to make. Sharing my wedding with Hank's first wife—feeling awkward and uneasy—was one of them. For me it was an issue of boundaries, and I hoped that June would give me space on this.

I was back at our front door. I found Hank in the kitchen tossing together a stir-fry.

"I'm sorry I snapped at you," I said.

Hank gave me a shy smile and threw a handful of red peppers into the sizzling pan.

"Let me explain," I said. "I'm doing something I was pretty certain was never going to happen."

Hank looked confused.

"I'm going to put on a white gown and a floor-length veil and march down a gardenia-scented wedding aisle. For this occasion, I insist on being the belle of the ball."

"I understand." He grinned. "You don't have to convince me."

"So we're still in agreement on this one? Just you and me in Memphis? Even though it might challenge our popularity with June and John? We may never exchange Christmas gifts after this. We most definitely won't be joining the same bowling league."

"So be it."

And with that, I put four plates around the kitchen table and formulated

Stepmom Rule Number Seventeen: No one gets it all.

No one in this traveling circus was going to get exactly what he or she wanted. At best, everyone would take a turn in the center ring. And I had to believe this was the reality for every stepfamily.

For the next few days, I thought a lot about The Tall One. What was it that *he* wanted? He was such a quiet, accommodating kid who frequently took a backseat to his younger brother. I often worried that his needs weren't being met, although he seemed lighter since Hank announced that June was staying in California, I guessed because he could finally stop wondering what was going to happen next. The Tall One, I'd come to learn, liked having a plan (not unlike his stepmom). The kid wanted to know what was up ahead, and he got snippy when he thought the parental unit was making decisions about him without him. I'd overheard him muttering on several occasions, "No one tells me anything. I never know what's going on."

"Then ask," I'd say. "Tell us what you want."

"Never mind" was his typical response. (The passive-aggressive stepkid trick. I knew that one.)

Given his tendency to withdraw and let others control his future, I was proud of him for speaking up and voicing his preference to stay in Texas. He was very clear; he didn't want to move around anymore, and who could blame him? Still, I was kind of surprised that, given the choice, he would choose our house over his mother's.

Until I heard a knock on the door. That's when it made a little more sense. A young woman was standing at the front door with polished black hair and black lines around her eyes, wearing something long and black. So this was the girl. I'd been kidding The Tall One about the "friend" he sometimes dropped into conversation and then regretted mentioning.

"Soooooo, who's the girl? What's she like?"

"Not much to say." He'd shrug and and then quickly change the subject.

Since I'd been back from California, Hank and I had dropped him off at his friend's house several times, but before I could ever get a good look at the girl and confidently declare, "She's not in drag or in her forties," he'd disappear inside.

After retrieving him the last time I'd asked, "Why don't you ever invite her over to our house? Do we embarrass you? Do you think we'll interrogate her?"

The Tall One rolled his eyes. "Izzy, of course *you'll* interrogate her."

"Am I that predictable?" I grinned.

Since the kid was determined to deny me information (i.e., torture me), I decided to give his friend an appropriate nickname. I'd started calling her Snuffleupagus, or Snuffy for short. (Remember Snuffy? Big Bird's pal, the woolly mammoth who nobody believed existed—except for Big Bird, that is.)

The Tall One told me I was acting childish, and I said he'd given me no other choice. So there!

Then, just when I thought I'd never see the mystery woman, The Tall One made the following overture: He was going to a school dance Friday night, Snuffy was taking him, and we could "look" at her when she came to pick him up. The meet-and-greet package did not include speaking, but here we were—I had just opened the front door, and she was standing on the porch.

"Hi," I said, looking her up and down like the real mother of a real teenager.

"Hey."

I stood in the doorway with my head cocked to the side, much like Big Bird, as I couldn't quite see her eyes through all the dark makeup. *Was she looking at me? Was she* a *figment of my imagination?* I was about to reach out and touch her when The Tall One brushed past me and mumbled, "Bye, Izzy."

Before I could say anything more to Snuffy, The Tall One ushered his friend away from the house and they quickly piled into the getaway car.

"Okay, then." I waved. "See you later."

I watched them haul ass down the street, and that's when the simple truth dawned on me: She's why The Tall One doesn't want to move away from Texas. News flash: Being with parents isn't a teenage boy's only priority.

When I was fourteen, I wore heaps of black—layers of lace, ripped leggings, tattered skirts, and gloves with the fingers chopped off. For me, wearing black was a fashion statement, and it was also my way of surviving the socially awkward teen years. On some days, black was my way to get noticed (tough girl), and on others it was my attempt to be ignored (invisible girl). Some psychologists associate the color black with authority and power. *Ha!* At fourteen, I was hardly powerful or an authority on anything, although at the time, I suppose I believed otherwise. Looking back, dressing like Siouxsie (without her Banshees) was the armor I wore to hide my insecurity—I thought black could somehow protect me from a world I didn't yet understand, and cover up my changing body, which was an even bigger mystery. Maybe I was naïve, but my death-angel look gave me much-needed courage—something every kid requires. I thought about Snuffy, with her long black cloak dragging on the sidewalk. I couldn't help but like the girl. I felt like I already knew her.

Hank walked up behind me while I was standing on the front porch. He took one look at the empty driveway and threw his hands up. "Did they leave already?"

"Oh, no!" I burst out laughing. "You didn't get to see her!"

"Well, what did she look like?" He was totally in on the Snuffy joke.

I grinned. "Me."

Hank looked me up and down. I was wearing baggy orange pants and a CBS ball cap. "That's weird," he said.

The weekend came and went, and on Monday I returned home from the gym at the peak of morning madness. As much as I tried to time my arrival just past the routine insanity, I never missed it entirely.

"Let's go, let's go, let's go," Hank bellowed down the hall. "Shoes, socks, backpacks, lunches—let's go! We're already late."

The Young One charged out of his room in mismatched socks, carrying his dirty sneakers in one hand and dragging his unzipped backpack with the other. "I'm COMING," he whined.

"Get your lunch," Hank instructed, car keys in hand. "I'm walking out the door right now."

"Daddy!" The Young One growled. "You're rushing me."

I ignored their famous father-and-son act and headed straight for the kitchen. *Please let there be coffee. Lots of coffee.* Before I could reach the pot, The Young One flew past me, cut me off, and threw open the refrigerator.

"Whoa," I said. "Can I help you with something?"

"LUNCH!" He was rummaging through the fridge like some hungry Dumpster diver. "I can't find it!"

"Okay, calm down. I'm sure it's there." I peered in, but I didn't see it, either. "Are you sure you made it last night?"

"YES!"

I looked around and spotted it on the counter. "There it is."

"Oh, thank heavens." He sighed with relief.

I picked it up and handed it over. As usual, he'd written his first and hyphenated last name on the brown paper bag, except this time he'd added mine to the list. *How cute is that?*

"You put *Rose* on here," I said, pointing to the bag.

"Yep." He smiled quickly before dashing out the front door—like a bat out of hell.

All morning long I held on to the image of my name on The Young One's lunch bag. I wondered, *What motivated that?* I pictured him sitting in the school cafeteria later that afternoon explaining to the kids around him why he had three last names. What's in a name, anyway? I'd been contemplating this for a while, and I really needed to figure out, once and for all, how I was going to refer to Hank's boys in the real deal wedding ceremony. Would I call them my sons? My stepsons? We'd been living together for nearly a year now and I still got caught off guard every time I was put in the position of introducing them. And toward the end of the week, it happened again.

The boys and I were in Whole Foods when we ran into Lisa, an ex-colleague of mine from Whales That Smoke. She walked up to me in a company T-shirt as the boys and I stood in line for specialty sandwiches.

"Hey," I pretended to care. "How's it going?"

"Great," she enthused. "We just finished another trash pickup along the highway, and I need to grab a sandwich before heading back to the office."

"It's Saturday. You're working today?" Just another reason why I was never right for that job—picking up trash on my day off was never something I was willing to do.

"Yeah." She shrugged. "It's fine. Actually, it's kind of fun."

Fun? Did Lisa understand the meaning of the word? I determined right then to start referring to the agency as Droids That Smoke or The Stepford Whales.

"So," she said, glancing at the boys, who had their hands pressed up against the deli case, ogling the prosciutto. "Who do we have here?"

I froze. The following went through my head:

A) I could introduce them as my sons, but what if they loudly corrected me—"No, we're not!"—and everyone in Whole Foods turned to look at me like I was a child abductor? That would be awkward for me, and for Lisa, who still worked as a social advocate.

B) I could introduce them as my stepsons, which was accurate, but ran the risk of sounding cold—like I was making a point to separate myself from them, like they only partially belonged to me.

I stalled for another five seconds and then I did neither. I simply introduced them by their first names. They shook Lisa's hand, then we gathered our sandwiches and hightailed it out of there.

For me, putting the *step* in front of the name is a hard call. It's such an obvious label that more often than not attracts negative attention: *Hey, everybody, look at us. We're not a "real" family. We're the cheap knockoff version.* But that wasn't true. We were a whole and true family.

On the drive back I asked the guys, "How do you want me to introduce you?"

"Introduce us where?" The Tall One said.

"Like just now—at the store. Do you want me to introduce you as my stepsons?"

The Young One said, "Well, you're basically my mom because you married Daddy."

I was so stunned I practically ran into a parked car. Did he just use the word *mom* in reference to *me*? If June heard this, surely she'd throw up. Since she wasn't sitting in the backseat, I asked for further instructions. "So you'd like me to introduce you as . . . my son?"

"Well, basically," he said.

I let this sink in. "Okay. Well, how about I introduce you as 'basically my son.' Would that work?"

"Sure," he agreed.

When I was growing up with two sets of parents, I called my stepmom by her name, Crystal, and my stepsisters, Piper and Gigi, called my mom (their stepmom) by her name, Susan. I call my stepdad Stanton and my dad, Dad, and my stepsisters my sisters. Confused? That's the point—it absolutely *is* confusing, and my online stepladies confirmed that in every family name-calling is handled differently.

As I had, many women left it up to their stepkids to label them however they wished and, depending on the circumstances, those labels often changed. Donna, who is called Donna by her stepkids, said it's all about what makes the kids comfortable. Others were "mom" in the house and "stepmom" at school functions. Some were "mom" all the time because bio-mom wasn't around; and others were called by their first names in every situation. Several preferred the term "bonus mom," and others had nicknames that sounded nothing like mom *or* stepmom. One woman said, "I don't care what they call me as long as it's not derogatory."

As I read through their accounts, I was impressed with how elastic children of divorce often are, and by their capacity to make sense of things in their own way. It's the mothers—the bios and the steps—who get hung up on titles and defining roles. Stepmoms often feel like the word *step* puts them in second place. "There's this look you get," one said, "like you don't count." Bio-moms often feel threatened and insulted when wife number two is called "mom." Even I could appreciate this. If I shot a tiny human out of my birth canal, I think I'd want the kid to get my name right.

For the rest of the ride home I thought about my title, "basically the mom." I liked it. It was original and catchy and it made me laugh; yet I wasn't sure it would equally amuse or satisfy my contemporaries. We needed a better handle to define our collective role—something altogether different. "Stepmom" has too much bad mojo attached to it.

Naturally I turned to the French. If anyone was going to infuse some class and romance into an otherwise drab title, it would be them. After thumbing through my high school French-English dictionary, I found it: *La Belle Mere*. It's the French equivalent for *stepmother,* and I immediately took a liking to it. To me, *La Belle Mere* fills the void. It's feminine, it commands reverence, and, most important, it has style. (It also means "mother-in-law." Don't those French know how to flatter a woman? But let's move on.) I wrote it down on a Post-it and stuck it on my computer screen.

The Phone rang. It was Gigi. "Do you want a traditional bridal shower?" I'd appointed her and Piper my maids of honor, and Gigi was taking the job seriously.

I sneered. "You mean, where we sit around in a cramped living room with our legs crossed and open gifts? And play games? Ew!"

I could hear Gigi rolling her eyes. "We don't have to do any of that if you don't want to," she said.

"Hmm. Let me think about it. You know," I added, "there's never enough to eat at those things."

Gigi took a sharp breath.

"Although I suppose we could mix it up and serve whatever we wanted, like huge roast beef sandwiches and Pabst Blue Ribbon. It's *my* shower."

"Call me back," Gigi said.

I pulled out my trusty notebook to scribble down a few ideas. The thing was, Hank and I had been living together for a while now, and between the two of us we had at least five of everything (which was due in large part to Hank's insisting to hold on to everything he's ever purchased, as well as to our mutual need to keep our respective grandmothers' china—all forty-eight place settings). In terms of housewares, we were more than covered. In fact, we were cluttered. And let's be honest—isn't that the point of a shower, to get gifts and have an excuse to wear a bright floral sundress? I've been to many showers over the years, baby and bridal, and I didn't seem to be a natural recipient for either. What does a mid-thirties woman, an instant mother to half-grown boys and wife to a divorced man, require? Casserole dishes and baby-bum ointment were not necessities for me. Yet the more I thought about how I didn't really need my own shower, the more I convinced myself I wanted one. Who more deserves a kick-ass party with spiked punch than the stepmom, who gets no instruction or gestation period at all?

I stood up and started pacing around the room. What we stepmothers of the universe needed was our own tradition—an event that celebrates our female friendships, our good humor, and the courage required to raise children who aren't our own. I stopped and shot my fist up in the air. "By God," I said aloud. "We need a *stepmom* shower." And I had the perfect name for it, one that reflected the spirit and sentiment of the celebration: *La Belle Mere!*

I collapsed on the couch and let the image form in my mind. Picture this: The stepmom shower honoree arrives at the location of her choosing—shooting range, ice arena, poolside cabana—dressed to the nines (rhinestone-studded camouflage, say, or a skinny slut suit that would make Paris Hilton blush). Stepmother's Milk or other signature cocktails are offered in abundance. Fat-free dip is strictly forbidden. Instead of sitting around in a circle watching one woman open gifts, all attending ladies receive a little something from the *LBM* gift registry. Here are a few suggestions:

A case of wine

5 pounds of French cheese (crackers included)

A day spa retreat

Lipstick for a year

Scones for a month

New bras

I was sure this new tradition would catch fire as soon as I put it out in cyberspace. I wrote, "Ladies, I think I'm on to something. A movement. A revolution. A breakthrough. The stepmom shower: a modern-day celebration where new and seasoned stepmoms gather for an afternoon of girlfriend gaiety and adoration. Unlike the traditional baby shower, where the mama-to-be receives gifts for the arrival of the blessed babe, the stepmom shower honors the adult woman thrust into a scary and unknown world, infant-like in her naïveté and in need of care. We may have more years on the planet than a new baby, but when it comes to stepmothering, many of us were born yesterday."

Just like I expected, stepmoms from all over the country jumped onboard and contributed suggestions of their own. One called for a martini fountain, another for complimentary pedicures. The most cagey of the bunch suggested a Xanax sampler pack for every woman in attendance. What's more, they encouraged me to start planning it *tout de suite;* but I had to say, Hold on, girls! Clearly it was a good idea, but it wasn't the kind of thing I could pull off with the Memphis nuptials looming. First things first, I had to get back to Gigi and my bridal shower. I called her back.

"What do you think about this: I'll fly into San Francisco for a girls' night out. Instead of sitting around a punch bowl in someone's living room, we'll meet for cocktails, dinner, and maybe a little karaoke. Absolutely no gifts, and by that, I mean no corncob holders or monogrammed towels."

"Deal! When can you come to California?"

"Not until next month, after we get the boys off to their mother's."

"Oh, that's right. I forgot they were leaving. What about the wedding?"

"They'll be there. Their mother will put them on a plane and we'll meet them at the Memphis airport."

"Hectic."

"Welcome to my world."

That night, we took the boys to a trendy comfort-food restaurant in the SoCo neighborhood. As they inhaled their meatloaf and mashed potatoes, I said, "Let's talk a minute about the wedding plans. You guys know you're meeting us in Memphis, right?"

"Uh-huh." They nodded, their mouths too stuffed to speak.

"And you know your mother and John will not be there?" I had to put it out on the table. If the boys told me I was an ugly bridezilla for not inviting their mother to my wedding, *maybe* I'd have to reconsider.

"Yep," they mumbled.

"And that's okay with you?" I crossed my fingers under my napkin.

"Yep."

"Well, okay then. How about banana cream pie all around!" I said, and Hank shot me a look like, *Try to hide your delight.*

"Boys." Hank directed their attention away from me. "I've been meaning to ask you—would you like to be my best men?"

"Is that the guy with the ring?" asked The Young One.

"No," corrected The Tall One. "That's the ring bearer."

"We're not having one of those," I said. "As best men, all you have to do is wear suits and dress socks, and look handsome."

"Dress socks feel like leeches," said The Tall One.

"And I'm allergic to collared shirts," The Young One grumbled.

"Then you can be the flower girls," Hank offered.

"Daddddddddyyyyy!"

Right then the waitress appeared on my left and slid my empty plate off the table. As she did so, she leaned in close and whispered in my ear, "Your boys are beautiful."

I turned to her and said, "Thank you."

MAY

Season of Love

With the Memphis wedding no longer a distant fantasy, I renewed my commitment to bridal boot camp. I was suffering at the hands of The Evil One three mornings a week, and although my waistline was shrinking I was in a constant state of muscle fatigue and pain. In a rare moment of compassion, The Evil One gave me the number of her masseuse. She said, "Go get a deep-tissue sports massage," and because I don't dare defy her, I found myself lying facedown on a massage table with my white ass up in the air.

"On a scale of one to ten, ten being almost unbearable, how would you describe the amount of pressure I'm applying?" my masseuse asked as she shoved her knuckles into my shoulder blades. "Tell me if it's too much and I need to back it off."

"I'd say we're at ten and you can back it off," I whimpered.

"How 'bout now?"

"Nine and a half. You can back it off some more."

"Wow—you're really tight. You said you're doing weight training and a lot of anaerobic exercise. Is there anything else in your life causing you stress?"

"I'm a stepmom?"

"Ah—that'll do it."

I get this type of reaction almost every time I mention my step-status. *You're a stepmom. Here's a Valium.* There's this universal opinion (I admit, I've contributed to it) that stepmoms are a beat-up, pathetic bunch. Sure, I've felt my share of abuse, but I can think of more contemptuous positions. As I lay on the massage table con-torting my face and tensing my buttocks from the physical pain, I thought, *Like this one, for example.* While my masseuse tried to dig the knots out of my spinal column, I created a mental list of stepmom pros: no labor, no diapers, and if your stepkid ends up in prison, you get to blame the bio-parents. Criminal genes aren't your fault.

For all my griping, living with Hank's kids had turned out better than I'd expected. It had taken us awhile to get into a comfortable groove, but we'd finally done it. How?

Stepmom Rule Number Eighteen: Relax and be willing to bend your own rules. And realize that sometimes you can even break them.

Project Runway was the unlikely impetus for this breakthrough. After nearly a year, I'd finally gotten the boys on board with reality TV, although their interest was still tepid. It hasn't been easy convinc-ing them that pop culture is worth their time, or at least something you need to be aware of if you're going to be a contemporary person. As far as they're concerned, everything they need to know can be found on the History, Discovery, and Weather channels. That I've been able to expand their world to include *Project Runway* is indeed something of an accomplishment.

Last night, with remote in hand, I screamed, "Boys—guess what time it is!"

"Time for *Project Runway*!" enthused The Young One, doing his best runway walk into the living room.

"Dad," The Tall One called out, "Izzy's trying to turn us into girls again."

"No," I corrected, "I'm just trying to make you well-rounded men. Besides, you know you *love it*."

He smiled and sat down on the couch. "Fine. I'll watch for a few minutes."

"Okay, designers," The Young One intoned like Tim Gunn, co-host of the series. "Show me what you got."

As the three of us watched the flashy opening sequence, Hank called out from the kitchen, "Dinner time!"

"Babe, let's just eat out here. We're watching *Project Runway*."

The Tall One looked at me in shock. "Wait a minute—we can eat in the living room?" *Good catch.* Was I suspending House Rule Number Seven, which was posted on the refrigerator? We do not eat ANY-WHERE other than the dining room and kitchen.

"Yeah, why not," I said. "I'll make an exception."

"Really?" said Hank. He'd walked into the living room and was regarding me with disbelief. In fact, all three of my men looked at me suspiciously.

I laughed. "Jeez—you're looking at me like I've lost my mind. Rules are meant to be broken."

"WOO-HOO!" yelped The Young One. The Tall One did a little hip-hop gyration in his chair.

"From time to time," I added quickly. "Now hear this: One crumb on the couch," I said in my best Heidi Klum accent, "and you're OUT."

"Auf Wiedersehen!" sang The Young One. The Tall One cocked his head and, just like Heidi, waved a flirty good-bye.

Now, after an hour of clenching my jaw and gluteus, I got up from the massage table, dressed, and staggered out to the parking lot. I was so sore; I could have saved my money had I just asked the receptionist to take me out back and beat me with a lead pipe. I crawled into the car and headed across town, but my drive came to an annoying halt—someone had run head-on into the Snow Cone Airstream parked at the intersection of South Lamar and Barton Springs. Traffic was jammed. The car was nearly totaled, and the Airstream was a mess, but the late afternoon shaved ice–aholics were still in line. (Snow cones are serious business in Austin, and I've been criticized for my lack of appreciation for the summer treat.) "I'm going to be late," I groaned. The Young One was waiting for me at school.

When I finally got there, Patricia was in no mood for snow-cone excuses. She jumped all over me.

"We need to talk." I was not prepared for another one of her verbal warnings. I gave her bitchy attitude but she was not deterred.

"There was an incident today involving spitballs."

"Spitballs?"

Patricia explained that The Young One recruited a team of predelinquents to assault the boys' bathroom with a barrage of spitballs.

I looked over at The Young One, who was playing innocently with a pile of Legos. He didn't look like a schoolyard criminal. "We'll be sure to address this at home," I said as I waved at the kid to pack it up and go.

Once in the car, I turned to The Young One. "Dude, what's with defacing school property?"

He shrugged and looked out the window.

"Well, you must have a reason. You know better than that."

He continued to sit in silence.

"Are you okay? Did something happen in class today?"

He turned toward me and asked, "Is Daddy going to let me live with Mommy?"

Oh, I get it. The kid feels like he has no control over his life, and it's starting to really piss him off.

I reached over and squeezed his arm. "I know you want to move back to California, but it's not that simple."

He let out a deep sigh.

"It's a big decision," I said gently, "and your dad and your mom and all of us are trying to figure out what's best for you."

He sat with this. I pulled away from the school.

"Izzy?" he finally said.

"Yes."

"What's your favorite bird of prey?" The kid switches gears faster than anyone I've ever met. *His way of coping?*

"Um, I'm not sure I have one."

"My favorite is the golden eagle. Did you know their average wingspan is more than six feet?"

"Wow. That's one impressive bird."

After The Young One and I got home, I found Hank out back firing up the grill. The central Texas rains were upon us, but tonight the sky was clear. Indeed, it was a perfect evening to barbeque.

I stood close to Hank, watching the fire grow. "Your son is heartsick," I finally said. "He needs his mother."

Hank tensed up and juggled some coals around. "He needs his father, too."

"Yes, but I think you might have to give in on this one. He decorated the boys' bathroom with spitballs today."

"What?" Hank shot me a look.

"Hank, he's acting out. He desperately wants his mom, and I think . . . I think we have to honor that."

Hank went back to staring into the fire.

When he didn't say anything, I continued. "If your son, in any way, thinks that you're keeping him from his mother, he won't forgive you."

"I'm not keeping him from her," he snapped. There it was—the anger and the hurt. His son had made a clear choice; he wanted June. Hank felt rejected, and his feelings had finally made their way to the surface.

Before the two of us got into a senseless argument, I left Hank alone and went inside to fold laundry. I understood Hank was struggling with what to do. As I dug into our pile of mismatched towels, I suddenly realized how simple—although not easy—this decision was. The Young One needed his mother. Hank was going to have to put his feelings aside and let his boy go.

Minutes later I heard Hank say, "Can we talk for a minute?" He wasn't addressing me; he was down the hall, standing in The Young One's doorway. When Hank disappeared into his son's room and began speaking in hushed tones, I tiptoed down the hall and listened in. (You know you would have done the same thing.)

"You know I love you," I heard Hank say quietly.

"Love you, too" The Young One mumbled back.

"And I want you to be happy."

"I know, Daddy."

Okay, this wasn't right—I was trespassing on their private moment. I quietly tiptoed back to our room and the big heap of laundry on our bed. Hank appeared several minutes later. He shut the door, walked right over to me, and crumbled into my arms.

"I don't want him to go," he choked. "I want him to be with me, and I know it's not about me, but I still *want* him to be with me."

He'd given in. Without Hank explaining anything, I knew that The Young One would be leaving us, and who knew for how long?

As I held on to Hank, I thought about what Piper and Gigi had said about choosing between parents when they were younger—how hard it was for them to make a decision that might hurt someone they loved. I thought about my thirty-five year-old self. To this day, I try to make equal time for both of my parents. When I visit California, I'd rather spread myself thin schlepping all over Sonoma County than leave anyone out. It's really no different from how Piper and Gigi felt two decades ago; if I don't divide my time equally, I worry that it will look like I prefer one parent to the other, and someone I love will get their feelings bruised. Whether or not this is a valid concern, I've convinced myself that because I love them, I need to take care of them; I need to protect them. *But why?* What am I protecting them from? The decision they made to divorce? A decision I had nothing to do with? A decision that seriously complicated my life?

Jesus, Izzy—how long have you been carrying that baggage around?

Of course I empathized with Hank's sorrow—he didn't want to lose his boy—but as a stepkid, I understood how easy it is to confuse your own needs with the desire to please your parents. In this respect, I applauded The Young One's bravery. For weeks now he'd voiced his desire to be with June. Because he was a sweet kid, a sensitive guy who loved his father, I knew this must be a devastating request to make. Yet he'd done it anyway. He'd taken a stand and spoken up for what he needed. And his brother had, too, and made a different choice. I admired the hell out of them for it. For years these kids had been agreeable and unquestioning, and now they wanted to make a few decisions of their own. They wanted some control, and as far as I was concerned, they were entitled.

With that, I formulated

Stepmom Rule Number Nineteen: Say *Hell no* to the status quo! Encourage your stepkids to demand a voice. (All demands subject to parental scrutiny, especially requests that involve throwing *La Belle Mere* out of *La Maison*.)

I felt a strong kinship with the boys takeover. I should tell them about the day I pulled out my orange duffel bag and had a seventeen-year-old psychotic episode. *No more packing! No more schlepping! I can't do this anymore!* That damn bag had taken on a life of its own—it represented seven years of feeling unsettled and split down the middle. I desperately wanted to live in one house, where I could unpack for good, but then what? To this day, I feel crummy about choosing my mom over my dad. I fear that I hurt someone I love. But really, my decision at seventeen had more to do with staying with my sisters and living in the same neighborhood as my friends.

The last thing Hank wanted (even if he didn't know it yet) was for The Young One to continue living with us out of a similar sense of guilt, so I concocted

Stepmom Rule Number Twenty: Don't ask your kids to take care of your feelings. They are not your emotional bellhops.

Hank and I finished folding three loads of towels, and in that time his mournful face softened a bit. "I'll be okay," he finally said. "I'm just going to make the most of the time we have left and not dwell on being sad." He forced a smile. "You never know—maybe he'll end up wanting to come back."

"He might." I smiled back.

The four of us sat outside, passing around a plate of Cowboy Burgers (another Austin carnivore choice)—ground beef, cheddar, bacon, and hatch chiles. (We discovered the premade patties at our neighborhood market and yes, they are worth the heartburn.) It was just another ordinary family dinner, and I guess that's why it felt so bittersweet. I couldn't ignore that soon the boys would be gone for the summer, and in the fall we'd be down to three.

"Mmm, bacon," cooed The Tall One. "We should eat bacon with every meal."

"Have you seen that fancy bacon-flavored chocolate they sell at Whole Foods?" I asked.

"*Bacon*-flavored chocolate?" The Tall One mocked. He shot his brother a look.

"Bacon—*yeah, right,*" The Young One scoffed.

"I'd think you'd love that," Hank teased, "since your favorite food groups are meat and chocolate."

"And toast," I added.

The Young One erupted in laughter. "Don't make me laugh!" he whined. "I'm going to choke on my burger."

"Oh, complain me a river." I smirked and watched him wipe his greasy cheddar-cheese hands all over his shorts. I just let him go for it.

I would miss The Young One, too. Who else would badger me to play Cranium? Who else would teach me how an atomic clock works? A lightning bug shot by, and I looked up at the growing moon. *Will The Tall One step out of the shadows and take center stage?* Maybe this was the silver lining in all of this: The Tall One would have his father's full attention for the first time since The Young One came along. And he'd have all mine. He'd be the most important kid in the house—a kid who was quickly becoming a young man, who needed a strong father figure. I looked at Hank and his oldest kidding around and hoped that their relationship would grow.

The next afternoon I flip-flopped outside in shorts and a cotton tank (the Austin uniform) to fetch the mail. A fat envelope from the United Methodist Church immediately grabbed my attention. I tore it open.

*Dear Hank and Izzy, Here's the service that I traditionally use.
Take a look and let me know what you think. Looking forward
to this special event, Minister Jan.*

Okay, I lied. I told you that every bride suffers one big complication; in my case, it was more than just the ex. Marrying the son of a
preacher also confused another issue—I wasn't necessarily keen on
inviting the Father, Son, and Holy Ghost to my wedding.

Izzy the INFIDEL! *Not quite.* I have my own set of mainstream-
ish beliefs, but to me, a wedding is not the place for proselytizing,
and some of my best friends are Buddhists and Jews, so I was kind of
hoping to keep Jesus on the sidelines. But since I was joining Hank's
more traditional family, I knew it would be smart to compromise.
We'd already passed on a church wedding, so I agreed to have Margaret's friend and colleague, Jan, marry us at the Peabody. I was a tad
hesitant, but when Jan and I spoke on the phone, she assured me that
we could keep the language fairly generic. I said, "Good. I don't
want to hear anything about my being a rib."

But now, as I scanned through her proposed service, I panicked.
This does not sound fairly generic at all. I called Mom.

As soon as she answered the phone I said, "Quick question:
Might I go to hell if I rewrite the service our minister sent us?"

"Izzy, what are you *talking* about?"

"Well, I'm looking at this marriage language, and it doesn't sound
like anything Hank and I would ever say to each other. Like this
thing about a wedding at Galilee? I don't even know what that is."

"Oh, dear," she said. "I really should have sent you to Sunday
school."

"Yeah, really—I think this is all your fault. All your liberal feminist
values have really put me in a bind right now. What am I going to do?"

"Well, why don't you just ask Jan if you can craft something that satisfies you, if that's even possible," she kidded, "and still stays true to her beliefs?"

"You think this is funny, don't you?"

Thankfully, Jan (bless her heart) took me a little more seriously than my own mother did. I called her with my concerns, saying, "Jan, there's a whole lot of God talk in this."

"Well," she said, and I could hear her smiling through the phone, "I *am* a Methodist minister. We like to talk about God."

Right. I couldn't really argue with that—but I tried to anyway. After much cajoling, she agreed to tone it down a bit. She said, "Rework it. Let me take a look, and we'll go from there." As soon as we hung up I started writing an Izzy-sanctioned service that Jan would, I prayed, give her blessing to.

On Saturday Hank and I took the boys to Barton Springs. Lena, like the good friend she is, tagged along. We spread our towels out behind the high diving board and watched a constant line of Austin's bravest crash into the chilly sixty-degree water. When it's scorching out, the spring-fed pool is perfectly refreshing, but since it was the beginning of the swimming season and not yet in triple-digit heat, one needed the proper motivation to get in.

"Come on, hot shot," she said to me. "Those legs need some sun." Lena stood up and trotted off toward the pool, her red hair flashing in the sunlight.

I watched her for a moment before stripping off my shorts and following little miss smart-ass to the water's edge. I'd gotten so lucky scoring Lena as my new BFF. Because of her, I was hardly ever lonely anymore. Plus, through my ladies' book club, bridal boot camp, and short-lived career at Whales, I'd begun to form a Southern sisterhood of women who were smart, brave, and—I now realized—totally necessary to my survival. Girlfriends give you roots. They give your spirit a place to rest, a place to call home. I looked at Lena in the springs, splashing around. I dove right in.

I swam out to the middle of the pool, where off in the distance one can see the tips of the tallest buildings in downtown Austin. I lay back and floated with my eyes closed, listening to a mixture of gurgles and laughter. I let the sun seep in. *Stepparenting is kind of like a day at the pool, isn't it?* Some days the water is quite comfortable, and I float eas-ily on my back looking up at the clouds. Other times I want to grow fins and hide at the bottom of the deep end. Most days I feel like I'm just treading water, but at least I'm buoyant and still breathing. I was enjoying my clever metaphor when something tugged me under and my nose filled with water. *Oh, my God—I'm being attacked by a fresh-water shark!* Once I popped back up to the surface, I was greeted by a splash in the face and The Young One's hysterical laughter.

"Ohhhh, you're in trouble now," I said. I flipped over and kicked up a storm that drenched the little minnow. "Go pick on someone your own size!" I said and swam away.

"Hey, come back," The Young One called after me.

I took a big breath and, just like Fun Monkeys do, dove under the water and disappeared.

After nearly an hour in the chilly springs, I pulled myself out of the pool and wrapped up in a beach towel, overcome with that old familiar fatigue—that achy, heavy feeling we used to get as kids after a full day of playing Marco Polo. I was tickled by the sensation—I was tempted to buy one of those saccharine-laced snow cones just to top off the high. Instead, I curled up next to Hank under an oak tree and fell asleep.

When we got back to the house after many hours of baking in the sun, something very curious occurred.

I was unloading the dishwasher and returning a serving dish to the top shelf when the sharp odor of the Y chromosome wafted my way. I turned around, expecting to greet one of my manly pack, but I was all alone. *That's weird.* Hadn't I just smelled essence of man? With no men in sight, I dismissed the oddity and returned to dish duty. When I reached up to slide an oversized bowl onto a high shelf, there it was again!

Oh, my God. Is that stink coming from me?

Maybe I'm revealing too much here, but as a general rule, I don't tend to excrete much of a scent. For more than thirty years my glands have been very well behaved, so as you can imagine, it gave me great discomfort to think that maybe they were now making up for lost time.

This is impossible! For months now, our house had been relatively stink-free. I lifted up my arm and took a whiff, and sure enough, I smelled just like my man-cubs. *Talk about weird science.*

It didn't take long once the boys moved in for the house to smell like a cross between a horse stable and an onion farm. Instead of holding it against them, I invested in a surplus of Right Guard and tropical breeze–scented air freshener. This seemed to keep the funk at bay, but now the needle on the smell-o-meter was inching back into the danger zone, and as much as I wanted to deny it, my pits were to blame.

The next morning I asked The Evil One if she'd ever heard of this type of transformation. "It's like, all of a sudden, I smell like a dude—the three dudes I'm living with, to be exact."

She gave me a distasteful look and told me to lower my arms and drop the ten-pound weights. She encouraged me to focus on leg strength for the remainder of the session.

Once I got home and showered, I smeared on some of Hank's Right Guard Xtreme—No Gel Is Stronger! How presumptuous I'd been. I was sure that with all my cleanliness rules and regulations I'd shape the boys into perfect, odorless children. But I was outnumbered, and clearly, they were stronger. When I wasn't looking, the boys had changed *me!* As the next couple of weeks passed, I found myself feeling extra sentimental about them leaving, so as not to turn into a dewy-eyed fool, I refocused my attention on the final details of our Memphis ceremony. According to my "wedding workbook," I was right on schedule—so much so that I took the opportunity to ask James at the Peabody to make a minor adjustment to our upcoming event.

"James, here's the problem. I've looked at too many bridal magazines, and I feel like I need to do something different—something you don't see in the magazines. Something spectacular."

"Uh-huh," he said slowly. Poor James. He thought I'd finally crossed over to the dark side. Six weeks before the wedding, and he had another crazy bride on his hands.

"Here's what I want to know: Might I dress the Peabody ducks in mini tuxedos and include them in my ceremony?"

Silence on the other end of the phone.

"James?"

James cleared his throat. True Southern gentleman that he was, I could tell he was reluctant to disappoint.

"I'm just kidding—I don't want the ducks in my ceremony."

"Oh, thank God." He let out a nervous laugh. "Darling, don't *do* that to me."

"What I do want is a pink cake." I still didn't care much what it tasted like, and I didn't need an ornate architectural masterpiece, but I'd decided that white, while traditional, was kind of blah. "Can your pastry chef slather pink icing all over my cake?"

"Like *pink*—pink?"

"Yes. Cotton candy pink. And I want to put sparklers on top, like people wave around on the Fourth of July."

James chuckled. "I'll see what I can do. As long as we're not breaking any of our fire codes, that should be fine. Any other last-minute surprises?"

Uh, I paid off our minister to not touch the trinity. "Nope," I said.

That evening the book club ladies and I sat around in a comfortable circle, drinking wine and talking about everything going on in our lives, instead of discussing the book of the month. The majority of the women in my Austin book group are married with children, so the conversation quickly turned to Mother's Day. I was reminded it was "right around the corner," so I should "make sure your family knows what you want." One woman had ordered breakfast in bed; another would be treated to brunch; and someone else was heading off to the spa.

"What are your guys planning for you?" someone asked me.

"Uh . . ."

"Well, maybe you don't celebrate it?" another said in an effort to help me out.

"Oh, that must be a hard holiday for you," another added.

Before the scene could get any more awkward, the topic was changed to plastic surgery, but for the remainder of the evening I stayed stuck on Mother's Day. This would be the first year I was actually in a position to be honored. *Hmm.* I wondered if Hank and the boys had given this any thought.

On the drive home, I remembered the year when I was about The Tall One's age and I didn't call Crystal on Mother's Day because I was busy celebrating with my mother. Where else would I be? Dad called to say that Crystal's feelings were hurt, and I remember thinking, *She's not my real mom. What does she expect?* I can't remember if I apologized to Crystal or not, but if I did, it was only to please my father. So here we were, twenty years later, and the tables were turned. *Damn karma.* Reminded of my shitty treatment of Crystal, I couldn't really expect anything more from the boys. Except that they live with me full-time, and if anyone had been motherly lately, it had been me. So maybe I did expect a little recognition?

For the next week I tried to put Mother's Day out of my mind, mostly because I didn't want to set myself up for disappointment. I slipped a few times and said things to Hank like, "Don't forget your mother on Mother's Day—she'll never forgive you," but for the most part I stayed cool and by the time the stupid retail holiday rolled around, I'd done a good job of convincing myself that whatever happened I'd be a big girl about it.

On that Sunday morning Hank and I were lying in bed listening to NPR when he took me into his arms and whispered, "Happy Mother's Day." *What a sweet guy. Of course he remembered.*

I can't say the same about the boys.

Not a word at breakfast. Nothing at lunch. It was nearly three o'clock when I blew up at Hank. I found him outside. "So, have the boys called June yet today?"

"Uh," Hank said, not picking up on the edge in my voice. "I'm not sure, babe."

"Well," I snapped, "you might want to make sure your kids call their *mother* and wish her a happy *mother's* day."

"Okay," he said, a little defensively, as he often does when he senses we're on the verge of battle.

"And in the future"—I raised my voice—"you might want to suggest to your boys that they at least acknowledge me, for parenting them."

I hadn't kept my cool.

After I stomped off, I locked myself in our bedroom and cried. I was mad at Hank for acting clueless. I was mad at the boys for being selfish little jerks. And I was mad at myself for feeling so heartbroken. Not only did they forget me on Mother's Day, but I was the one reminding everyone to call June—the one and only. *WTF!*

Hank knocked on the door and I reluctantly let him in.

"I'm sorry," he said. "I didn't know it was so important to you." *Neither did I.* "Do you want us to take you out to dinner?"

"Hank," I said with frustration, "Mother's Day is the busiest day of the year." I knew this from my waitressing days; it was a coveted shift for a single gal supporting herself. "There's no way we'll get in anywhere."

"Well, then, we'll make you a nice dinner." He was trying to fix it, but I'd slipped into a stubborn funk and I wasn't going to help him out. "And I'll make sure the boys say something to you."

"Whatever," I said, crawling deeper into my pathetic cave.

Hank left me lying on the bed, staring up at the ceiling fan. A few minutes later there was another knock on the door.

"Izzy," said The Tall One. I didn't respond. He knocked again. "Izzy?" he said again. *Go away, kid—you're too late.* "Well, if you're in there, Happy Mother's Day." My heart did a somersault. That's all I had wanted—three simple words, some acknowledgment, for flippin' sake. I rolled over and cried into the pillow. I appreciated the belated gesture, but I knew he'd only come to the door because Hank told him to, so actually, no, I didn't appreciate it at all. Neither boy had come to me on his own. *Is this how Crystal felt? Ick— this feels bad.* I'd turned my world upside down for these kids. I'd opened up my fearful, twitchy heart, and I'd spent the past year parenting them, rightly or wrongly, the only way I knew how. And just like I had done to my stepmom, the little creeps had blown me off.

The phone rang, and for some dumb reason I picked it up. Piper, Gigi, and Mom sang in unison, "Happy Mother's Day!"

"Thanks," I whimpered.

"What's wrong?" asked Gigi.

"My dumb stepkids forgot to wish me a Happy Mother's Day."

"What?" blurted Piper. "Unacceptable! Get those boys on the phone right now and let their mean auntie deal with them." This made me crack a smile.

"Izzy," Mom said, "Piper's right—they should have remembered you. But try not to take it too personally."

"How else am I supposed to take it? And this isn't the first time, FYI. They totally glossed over my birthday, and I had to bribe them with doughnuts to acknowledge Hank on his."

"They're *boys*." Gigi sighed. "They just don't always remember stuff like this. It doesn't mean they don't care about you."

I argued, "Just because they're boys? That shouldn't let them off the hook."

"No," Mom said. "But you're probably going to have to train them."

"For God's sake," I cried. "How many life lessons do I need to teach these kids?"

There was a pause, and then all three of them burst out laughing. Mom said, "Sweetie, there's probably a few more things you'll have to educate them on."

"I'd appreciate a list."

As they often did, my favorite women pulled me through a low moment. I had Mom, Piper, and Gigi to raise a glass to me when others, very humanly, missed the mark. Plus, I had my girlfriends in San Francisco, and Lena in Austin. I had Sarah the shrink. I had my Stepmother's Milk sisters, who had coached me through a variety of stepmom quandaries.

And I had Hank. Having a supportive husband was essential.

I was grateful for all of them. They indulged my incessant babbling. I wouldn't have survived the past year if I'd kept my mouth shut. I most definitely would have done a George Bailey off the Congress Street Bridge—screaming the whole way down.

By the time I got off the phone I wasn't feeling so hurt. I was still disappointed in the boys, but I decided that once I left the room, I'd let it go. Of course, next year I expected compensation. An ice sculpture in my likeness, for starters.

Later that evening, after Hank prepared his shrimp etouffée, which the boys enthusiastically served and cleaned up without complaint, I wandered into The Young One's room. Pillows propped him up and his lobster lay by his side. He was buried in a book called *Animals of the Ocean*. When I sat down on his bed he said, "Izzy, if a starfish went through the guillotine it wouldn't get hurt, because starfish can regrow their limbs."

"You really are a weird kid. Time for bed, okay?" I turned out the light. And then, just like he'd been saying it all his life, he said, "I love you."

Really? After ignoring me all day, you're busting out the L word?

I was shocked. I was deeply touched. Ever so faintly, I whispered into the dark, "I love you, too."

A week later the four of us were back on I-35, heading toward the airport. Hank was all business. "Do you have your emergency contact list? Where's the twenty dollars I gave you? Remember to call me as soon as you land, and be polite on the plane."

I stayed out of the way during check-in; one rattled adult was enough. Hank was in stern-daddy mode—his way of covering up his sadness. When we arrived at the gate, he gave each of the boys a lingering hug. And then it was my turn. This time I didn't resist; I hugged them like I meant it, even to the point of embarrassing them. "Okay, Izzy," The Tall One said. "LET GO."

"Any children traveling alone?" a woman in airport garb said over the loudspeaker.

"That's you guys," said Hank. They threw themselves at their father one last time, then turned toward me. Each handed me a folded-up piece of paper. "What's this?" I asked, but they were already skipping down the Jetway, waving good-bye.

Hank and I walked out of the airport hand in hand, without saying a word. *Now that the boys aren't here, who are we again?*

Back in the car, Hank asked, "What are those notes?"

"You don't know? I figured you put them up to this."

"Nope. Not this time."

I unfolded the note from The Tall One. It read: "Out of the blazing sun—back into the cold mist. I'll see you when I come back. Have fun." So our budding chocolatier was also a budding poet.

The Young One wrote, "Izzy, I will miss your voice. I will miss your disgusting jokes."

I choked up and looked out the window. I'd found a man whose charm and tenderness often left me speechless. His sons had turned out to be an even bigger surprise.

Before I hooked up with Hank, I wasn't so sure I ever wanted kids. It wasn't *only* that I thought kittens were cuter than babies, it was that I didn't think I was smart enough. Not together enough. Not qualified. Not yet.

Well, ready or not, here I am.

I had this harebrained idea that I should wait until I knew everything before having a child. And when I say "everything," I mean a working knowledge of every subject, including basic plumbing and the philosophy of Kierkegaard. Wasn't that the responsible thing to do? Children have questions. They need experts to guide them through life, right? But then this wonderful man came along, with two kids in tow. Two kids with minds for *Jeopardy!* What kind of dumb luck is that? Except The Tall One and The Young One don't seem to care that my medieval history is rusty, and they weren't disappointed to learn that I have no lead on the Holy Grail. It turns out they need me for other things.

So, finally,

Stepmom Rule Number Twenty-One: Knowing everything isn't the point. Maybe that's the first thing you learn about parenting.

EPILOGUE

The Wedding

It was time to get dressed. *Oh shit, oh shit, oh shit.* I hopped in the shower. I'd been calm all day, and now it was three o'clock, and I was officially rattled. *Stay cool, Izzy. Everything is on schedule—there is no reason to panic.* I practiced my yoga breathing while the water pounded down on me (I'd traded in bridal boot camp for hatha flow two weeks earlier; a bride needs to be centered, not ripped). I slowly exhaled. *I'm getting married today. What's the big deal? I can do this.* But then, as soon as I picked up my lady razor, my hand started to shake. Oh, this is fantastic. Instead of smooth legs on my wedding night, I'm going to end up with bloody bride ankles that soak through my dress. *Fuck it.* I put the razor down. I'd been living with, and technically married to, Hank for a year. He'd slept with my hairy legs and me tons of times— one more night in the jungle wasn't going to kill him.

As I shampooed, I mentally went over the wedding-show rundown. Hank and I had timed out the event, similar to what a news producer does for an evening newscast. Last night after the rehearsal dinner at the Rendezvous (best ribs in Memphis), we handed out copies of the printed schedule to everyone in the wedding party. The day was broken down into fifteen-minute increments leading up to the five-thirty ceremony. I was proud of our efficiency until I heard Dad mutter under his breath, "Control freak." I pretended not to hear him and said, "Dad, you're in charge of keeping the wedding photographer on time." (To add to the extended family picture, let me explain that the professional photographer is also my dad's girlfriend.) "Christina should start with the guys no later than two-fifteen. That means everyone's in a suit and camera-ready. No dicking around, 'kay?"

Ladies, what did I tell you? TV people make excellent wedding co-ordinators.

The big day began easily enough. I trotted downstairs to the Peabody's spa for a light massage at nine. I liked the idea of being rubbed down celebrity-style while my minions greeted out-of-town guests and took care of last-minute business, like finding someone to cut the boys' hair (the little angels arrived from California with sizable halos). Still, I couldn't afford another sadistic grinding just hours before I was expected to glide down the aisle. "Please keep it gentle," I told the masseuse, cringing a little as her hands came toward me. "Maybe you could just pet me like a cat?" Because I was the bride she obliged, and an hour later I rolled off her table relaxed and unharmed. At 10:45, Piper and Gigi met me in the spa for pedicures.

"Hey, have you guys heard about those fish pedicures?" I said, slipping my feet into the warm, bubbly water.

Gigi, eight months pregnant and ready to burst, propped herself up with a pillow behind her back and gave me a doubtful look.

"I'm not kidding. You put your feet in a tub that has these flesh-eating fish in it—"

Piper burst out laughing. Gigi said, "You're making that up."

"No, I'm serious. These little minnows eat off your dead skin. They're not dangerous—they don't break the skin or anything. They just eat the flaky stuff."

"Okay, stop talking," Gigi demanded. "That's disgusting." Piper chuckled to herself. Her tolerance for nauseating humor rivals mine. (For the record, I wasn't making up the foot-eating fish. I'd read about it in *Glamour* or some other reputable, fashion-forward magazine.)

"Where's Ashley?" Piper changed the subject. "Isn't she supposed to be here?" Ashley was my cheeky sister-in-law (wife of Hank's brother, Garrison), whom we'd welcomed into our sorority of three last night.

"Yeah, where is she?" Gigi added, looking forward to having an even number in the sisterhood, and one who could give her birthing tips.

Hmph. Maybe Ashley was one of those rebel bridesmaids I'd heard about who secretly hate the bride and want to sabotage the wedding? Nah, I was confident she'd turn up. Ashley, as they say in the South, is "good people."

As a gift to my attendants, I'd paid for their fancy mani/pedis. I thought it was a nice gesture, although I heard that brides in Manhattan were splurging on chemical peels, Botox, and liposuction for their thirty-something-year-old maids. And that's not all: Some of the more modern bridesmaids were not only expected to slip into dresses they wouldn't have picked out for themselves, they were encouraged to get "breast augmentation" to fill them out. Sorry, but I'm not spending my money to lift someone else's saggy girls.

My cell phone rang. I answered, "Hello, Bridal Party Central." A minute later I quietly hung up and turned to my sisters.

"What's going on?" Gigi could sense a problem.

"That was Ashley's mom. It seems that Ashley did a handstand in the hotel pool and accidentally kicked her daughter in the head and now they're at the hospital because little Katie might have a concussion."

"Oh, shit," said Piper.

That was the first crisis of the day.

After rationalizing that there was nothing I could personally do to fix poor Katie's head, I left the spa. I had a schedule to keep. I found the florist in the elegant Forest Room, where the ceremony would soon take place—marble floors, grand fireplace, floor-to-ceiling windows, and old-world detail. Germaine was hanging a spiral of vines and sweet-smelling gardenias from the center chandelier. Long-stemmed white tulips, peonies, lilac, and faded blue hydrangeas spilled out of two huge urns at the front of the room. Votive candles were scattered everywhere. I gasped.

"Hey, what are you doing here?" Germaine cracked. "You're supposed to be getting ready."

"I just wanted to check in."

"Go, go, go. Everything's under control."

I shuffled out and found James in the adjoining Venetian Room, where he was overseeing all aspects of the reception. "Well, hello, dear. Shouldn't you be getting ready?"

"Why is everyone trying to get rid of me?"

"Because you're the bride and you're not supposed to be doing any work on your wedding day."

"Okay, *fine*," I grumbled. "Just let me ask a few questions and I'll leave. Has the gospel choir arrived?"

"Yes."

"What about the DJ?"

"He just unloaded his equipment."

I was more disappointed than relieved. I'd kind of hoped our DJ, who went by the name Biggy Bob, would be a no-show and we could resort to Plan B: hooking our iPod up to a pair of speakers and letting Piper run the show. ("McPiedPiper will rock the house!" she'd said last night after eating an entire slab of pig. This unnerved me, but still, I had more confidence in my sister than in Biggy Bob.)

As soon as I'd hired the big music man, I wanted to fire him, but available DJs were hard to find in June and Hank said, "How bad can he be? Let's give him a chance"—although that's exactly what I didn't want to do after reading through his suggested song list. For starters, he wanted to welcome Hank and me into the reception with "Fanfare for the Common Man," complete with pounding drums and clashing symbols. *Kind of hokey, isn't it?*

Biggy Bob explained that "Fanfare" was a classic, a crowd favorite, and he promised it would be "dazzling." I explained to him that Hank and I had a list of songs that were meaningful to us, and that we'd rather stay away from the typical wedding slop. "Maybe I could e-mail you our list and you could just play that?" I asked. Biggy Bob was reluctant, but he agreed to do it our way. Still, I didn't really trust him, and yesterday, in a moment of panic, I'd phoned him and threatened, "If I hear that lame-ass 'Celebration' by Kool and the Gang, I will pull the plug out of the wall and ask you to leave. Same goes for that mushy 'Butterfly Kisses'—are we clear?"

Okay, so maybe Dad was right; I was a bit controlling. Now that I was on wedding soil and could physically touch every detail of the event, I just couldn't keep my hands in my pockets. Or my mouth shut. I was becoming that obsessive-compulsive bride James had warned me about.

"Well," I said to James, pouting, "I guess you don't need *my* help."

James gave me a sympathetic smile. He could sense my unease with the forced downtime. "Izzy, would you like to see your cake?"

"OH, YES!" I clapped.

James led me behind a tall column, and there she was: my pink cake. Three simple stacked rounds covered with bubblegum-pink frosting. A flurry of skinny sparklers stuck out of the top. White peonies dressed the base of the cake.

"Did we get it right?" James asked.

"Yeeeeeessssssss," I said breathlessly. "It's perfect." I turned to James all misty-eyed and said, "I'm going up to my room right now. You're in charge—no more questions. Next time you see me, I will look like a bride."

Now there was nothing more to do, other than walk down the aisle. I got out of the shower and toweled off. A word of advice: Do not attempt to yank on your butt-hugging Spanx when you are still ever so slightly wet. I don't care how fit you are—you will feel like a sausage busting out of its casing, and this is not how you want to feel on your wedding day. I called Mom's room.

"I'm starting to get dressed. Where are you? Is it too soon to start drinking?"

"On my way."

I slipped on the robe hanging in the closet. I may be a certifiable grown-up and all, but I still get downright giddy every time I put on a white, all-cotton terry hotel robe. They make a girl feel glamorous, and I applauded the Peabody for indulging women like me. I applied a base layer of makeup and powder, feeling like a Broadway starlet getting ready to take the stage.

There was a knock on the door. It was Ashley's mom. She looked terrible. "I'm so sorry," she said, "but Katie's still in the hospital, and Ashley probably won't make it back for the ceremony."

"Oh, my God. Is Katie all right?"

"Yes. They just want to keep her for a couple of hours to monitor her. Ashley feels horrible—"

I interrupted, "Tell her not to worry. Of course I understand." (Seriously, attending to your kid in the hospital trumps dress-bustling duty.)

I was officially down one bridesmaid. No problem. I called room service. "I need five turkey sandwiches and some bottled water. And a mint julep, light on the mint, heavy on the bourbon."

I hadn't eaten all day and if I didn't put something in my stomach I might fall over, bang my head, and suffer my own concussion.

There came a second knock on the door. The photographer. Christina is a size zero, with wild hair and the energy of a locomotive. Like me, she's a bit of a control freak—that made two of us in Dad's life.

"Why aren't you dressed?"

"What? I'm not supposed to be dressed for another half hour."

"Well, can you get dressed now? I had to move you up because the guys aren't ready yet."

I counted to ten, and made a mental note to spank Hank later.

The door swung open and Mom and Gigi walked in. Finally, my reinforcements. "The photographer's here. I need to get dressed ASAP."

"All right," Mom said calmly. "I'll help you." Mama Bird to the rescue.

Knock. Knock. Knock.

"I'll get it," said Gigi.

Mom took my gown off its hanger and brought it over to me, saying, "Okay, just step right in."

I looked over at Christina, who had her shot composed and her finger on the trigger. I turned to Mom and said under my breath, "Please explain to her that I do not need to be immortalized in my push-up bra and Spanx."

"Are you sure?" Mom joked. "I'd like a framed copy."

"Who ordered five turkey sandwiches and a bourbon drink?" Gigi called out.

"I did."

Gigi returned carrying a huge tray. "You're going to eat five sandwiches?"

"Not if she wants to fit into this dress," Mom said as she zipped me up.

"We *all* need to eat," I said coolly. "Speaking of—where the hell is Piper?"

"Here I am!" Piper announced, briskly walking through the door. "I have a big problem. 'McPiedPiper' got lipstick on the front of her dress, and it won't come out."

"Oh, Jesus," Gigi said, inspecting the damage. "What color is this, by the way?"

"Kiss and Tell." Piper was in one of her flirty moods and had developed a crush on the Peabody concierge ever since he'd gone out of his way to open all doors for her once she'd arrived at the hotel. I tried to tell her, "This is what men do in the South," but she didn't buy it. She was convinced they had a special connection.

"Hi, y'all—can we come in?"

"Hi, Margaret," Mom called out. Margaret walked in with superbly styled hair, wearing a vintage beaded top and a black silk organza skirt. What did I tell you? She's one hip minister. Gram followed behind her in a periwinkle dress, pearls, and silver pumps. She made herself comfortable on the sofa.

Mom announced, "We have a minor crisis. How do you get lipstick off fabric?"

"Well," said Margaret, "my mama always used soda water to get stains out." Gram nodded in agreement.

"Call room service," I said to Piper.

"And ask for some mustard, too," Gigi said. "I can't eat this turkey sandwich dry."

"Put down your sandwiches. We do not have time to eat," Mom said. "Get over here and start helping me with all these buttons." My slim-fitting mermaid dress had close to one hundred teeny-tiny buttons running up the back.

"The baby is hungry." Gigi pointed to her belly.

"So am I," Piper chimed in.

"*You* don't get to eat." I pointed at Piper. "You already got lipstick on your dress. There's no room left on the front of that thing for turkey."

So there I was, standing still (and Spanx firm) while my mother and my two sisters buttoned me up from behind. Piper kneeled on the floor and Gigi pulled up a chair and tackled the midsection while Mom worked the top of the dress. The first camera flash of the day captured the scene.

"SHIT!" Piper exclaimed. "I just messed up my manicure."

"Oh. My. God." Gigi laughed out loud. "You are having some serious issues."

I took a deep breath and counted from ten to twenty.

"Stop breathing," Mom said.

"It's all these *buttons,*" Piper complained. "They're taking off the polish. Do I have time to go get it fixed?"

"NO!" we all screamed.

"Uh, excuse me, girls." All four of us looked at Margaret, who was standing with the room-service guy. We'd been so busy bickering that we hadn't heard him knock on the door.

"This nice gentleman has your soda water and mustard," she said in her sugary, genteel drawl. "Do y'all need anything else?"

"You got any nail polish remover?" Piper asked.

* * *

After Christina captured the "money shot," lying on the floor while I balanced like a contortionist above her, we were finally ready to head downstairs. I took one last look at myself in head-to-toe ivory, with my double-tier veil. Hold on to this image—Izzy the bride, the wife, the stepmom. *You just never know, do you, how your life will unfold?* Maybe we'd done it all backward—the City Hall quickie, the house, the kids down the hall, and then, *finally*, the wedding, but our unique timing felt right. The truth was, a year of marriage had only convinced Hank and me that we wanted to do it all over again. *Were we nuts?*

Sure, the past year had been hard. Marriage isn't always pretty, and family dinners can be a grind, but Hank and I were stronger as a couple because we'd been able to laugh at the absurd (such as lice on Thanksgiving Eve) and push through the gunk. Hank and I were dedicated partners, and I'm going to let you in on a little secret: Being unified with your husband is a big turn-on. I know, I know— I'm nauseating you with this mushy-gush. But isn't that what you want to hear? That sometimes the right guy comes with baggage— kids, an ex-wife, and questionable fashion sense—and the roof will not necessarily cave in if you let him unpack. You can make it work, if you really want it to.

I sure did—I wasn't about to add the D word to my list of lifelong achievements. And Hank felt the same way. This was his second time around, and he wanted a happy ending. "I'm not going to screw it up twice," he'd told me almost a year ago when he got down on one knee and proposed to me in the lobby downstairs. And now it was time to hop on the elevator and remarry my fine Southern man. There was just one obstacle—the ducks.

At promptly five o'clock every evening, the famous Peabody ducks leave the lobby fountain they've been splashing around in all day. Accompanied by the Duckmaster, a man in a red jacket with a cane, they take the elevator up to their rooftop penthouse to get their beauty sleep. As in the morning when the little quackers descend from their crash pad and make a showy entrance, the elevators tend to jam up for the rest of the hotel guests. So when my entourage and I hit the down button at 4:50 P.M., we were forced to wait.

"What's taking so long?" I said.

"The ducks," said my father, walking up in a sleek black suit. "They're holding the elevators downstairs until the ducks get out of the fountain." He was clearly amused. "You should see it—there are about a hundred people down there taking pictures."

Damn ducks! Maybe I should have included them in the wedding; then they wouldn't be stealing my show.

"What do we do?" I said.

"Wait." Dad smirked. Was he enjoying this moment of unplanned chaos?

I considered taking my shoes off while we waited; they were already pinching my feet. I hadn't broken them in by wearing them around the house like they tell you to do in the wedding magazines. I just felt silly every time I slipped them over my gym socks and matched them with my pajama bottoms. But it really didn't matter now; I'd be fine. All I had to do was make it down the aisle and do some light mingling afterward. I was thankful that Hank and I had decided to pass on a highly choreographed first dance. I knew a lot of couples did this and that guests often expected it, but I hate these performances. It's like watching figure skating; it's nerve-wracking. Someone always screws up and slides across the ice on her ass. Given the likelihood of an accident, Hank and I agreed not to waste our money on dance lessons. Instead, we planned to slow dance like we both used to in junior high, swaying back and forth to the sounds of Spandau Ballet. If our guests felt let down, tough shit. This was our wedding, not *Dancing with the Stars*.

Ding! The elevator doors opened and, of course, it was full of duck-hunting touristas. Mom kicked it into high gear. "Make room— bride coming through!" Piper and Gigi led me into the elevator, corralling people to the back. Dad followed behind, bringing up the rear.

He pressed the elevator's down button and I relaxed. My dad has a calming effect on me. It's his competence—a trait that Hank shares. In many ways, they're similar men. Responsible. Passionate. And always putting me in first place. When Hank and I realized we needed a witness for our City Hall nups in San Francisco, Dad was the one I wanted. He could appreciate the practical aspect of getting married early for the sake of health care, along with our backward way of doing things (Dad has always embraced the unconventional). Still, it had been a rushed job. The entire event lasted about five minutes, and besides taking a few pictures there hadn't been a whole lot for him to do. I was happy now that he'd be playing the traditional role, delivering his only child into the hands of a man he respected and trusted and who shared his appreciation for a calming shot of José Cuervo.

As soon as we reached the mezzanine level, my entourage led me to a hideout until the ceremony began. Everyone minus Hank was there. Margaret, Big Hank, and Stanton; and Gigi's husband, Jack; plus Ashley and Garrison, back from the hospital in time. And, of course, the boys.

The Tall One and The Young One were dressed in black pinstriped suits (yes, with collared shirts) that accentuated their gorgeous features and chestnut curls. (Warning to all girls: These two are bound to break hearts.) The Tall One saw me first and gasped. "Look at Izzy," he said. Naturally, I blushed like a bashful bride.

The recognizable first notes of "Seasons of Love" from *Rent* quieted our jittery group. Above the sound of the piano, the voices of our Memphis gospel choir sang out:

Five hundred twenty-five thousand six hundred minutes,
How do you measure, measure a year?

That was our cue to begin. Margaret and Big Hank went first . . .

Mom and Stanton followed, with Ashley and Garrison right behind them . . .

Gigi hooked The Tall One's arm and went next . . .

Piper reported later that she said to The Young One, "Okay, it's our turn. What did I tell you?"

"No talking?"

"Excellent—let's go."

When the choir swelled, and all I heard was one resounding word—LOVE—Dad turned to me. "Ready to do this?"

"Yep." He took my arm and we walked together. Candlelight flickered throughout the Forest Room and the natural glow coming in from the windows threw a splash of scattered late-afternoon light on the black-and-white marble floor. I spotted my TV pals from San Francisco right away, along with my longtime girlfriends from the West Coast and my new pal Lena and her boyfriend from the Gulf Coast. And there, at the front of the room, was Hank. I fixed my gaze on him when I noticed the tears in his eyes. This is why I love this man—he's just the right balance of jagged edges and sweet spots.

As soon as Dad and I reached the front of the room, Reverend Jan began. "The marriage of Hank and Izzy unites many families and creates a larger one. Do all those who represent the families of Hank and Izzy bless this marriage?"

There was a unanimous "WE DO."

Jan said, "The union of Hank and Izzy creates a new and extended family for Hank's two sons." She looked directly at Hank and me. "Do you promise to love, encourage, and protect the boys and live together as a family?"

I looked over at the boys, who, although not biologically mine, were in other ways becoming my own. Hank and I said, in unison, "We do."

Jan turned to The Tall One and The Young One and said, "Do both of you bless this marriage and promise to love and live with one another as a family?"

The boys shuffled in their dress shoes and nodded, saying, "We do." Jan winked at them.

Next, Mom, who was already standing by my side, took a step forward. Hank and I had asked both mothers to contribute some wise words about marriage. Mom said something like this:

"Weddings are Christmas mornings and Saturday nights. Marriage is Tuesday mornings and Thursday nights—when there's nothing good on TV. Weddings are a day you'll always remember, and marriage is one day after another—sometimes tough, sometimes fun, sometimes boring, but hopefully with a person you alternately adore and find enraging, but who knows how to make you laugh and when to bring you flowers."

Next, Margaret addressed the guests. "This isn't so easy, even for a preacher. I can't say I really know how a marriage works. I'm still learning after forty-three years! I know it isn't what you read in a romance novel. It's deciding to stay, even when we feel like leaving sometimes. It's a commitment to making it work, and for that you need patience, tolerance, forgiveness, flexibility, and passion— don't forget the passion."

This got a few chuckles from the room, including a snort from The Young One, who covered his mouth and looked down at the ground.

Jan handed me an index card, on which were scribbled my vows. She nodded for me to begin. "Before everyone here tonight, I take you, Hank, to be my husband. I choose you, a man with fire and strength; a man who makes me laugh; a man who listens and is kind. With you I am at home, and my world finally makes sense. I marry you because I believe in you, I believe in us, and I believe in the family we've created."

As Hank read his vows—"I can see in your green eyes a love and a connection I've never had" (words that got every woman in the room crying into her cocktail napkin)—I looked over at The Tall One and The Young One, absorbing the scene with a mixture of acceptance and uncertainty, not unlike a photograph of Piper, Gigi, and me taken the day Mom and Stanton got married over twenty-five years ago.

I couldn't tell my men now, but I would be sure to tell them later: *We're going to be all right. All of us.*

ACKNOWLEDGMENTS

First and foremost, let me thank my kick-ass agent, Yfat Reiss Gendell, and her awesome posse of gals at Foundry Literary + Media: Kendra Jenkins, Rebecca Serle, Hannah Brown Gordon, and Stephanie Abou. Thanks for believing in this project and holding my hand through the whole process. You make me feel like a rock star and really, what more can a girl ask for? Thanks to longtime friend Dan Dion for introducing me to Foundry. I owe you. I'm not sure what—but something. Hugs to Lindsay Orman, my editor at Three Rivers Press, who convinced me that, even in sweatpants, I'm glamorous and this story deserved to be told. I am especially grateful to Philip Patrick, publisher of TRP, and Carrie Thornton, who put their time and energy into this project. Big thanks to my awesome TRP publicity and marketing team: Donna Passannante, Jay Sones, Melanie DeNardo, Niki Sprinkle. Mucho praise goes to Patricia Shaw and Kevin Garcia, as well as to JoAnna Kremer for your skillful copyediting (without you I may have been asked if English was my second language); and finally, to Laura Duffy for the superstylish cover art. It was a pleasure and *a dream* to work with "the pros." I'm especially thankful to all the smart and wise stepmoms who visit me at my blog, www.stepmothersmilk.com. Your honesty and humor inspired this book. And to all my girlfriends and colleagues on the West Coast and the Gulf Coast—I have included many of you in these pages because you've taught me something important (or said something I couldn't resist exploiting).

But to Hank—this book would never have happened without your support and encouragement. There were many mornings when I was whimpering into my coffee mug, complaining about the loss of my TV career, when you could have said, "Get over yourself and hit the pavement," but you gave me the space to find myself and find my voice. *The Package Deal* is a direct result of your unwavering belief in me. I could not have finished this book without my brilliant mother, Susan, who read every line of every draft multiple times and contributed a few of the best zingers in the book. Anything I know about writing, I learned from her. Thanks for letting me include you as a major character even though you thought I made you sound like a drunk and a lunatic. You are neither, BTW. I am grateful to the rest of my family—my dad, sisters, and stepdad for being my constant cheerleaders. And to my classy gram, who would be so tickled to know that her rum cake recipe was getting national attention. Special thanks to my in-laws Margaret and Big Hank—I hope what you've read here doesn't give you second thoughts about welcoming me into the family. If it's any consolation, I never threw out any of the Christmas ornaments and I'm working on my tolerance of bears. A big acknowledgment goes to the traveling circus, for which there would be no story to tell had I not got on board the *Big Love* caravan. Finally, a round of applause goes to the boys, who gave me the green light to write this book and who often refer to me as "weird" but now have proof that I'm truly a mess. Thanks for letting me stick around despite my imperfections. I love you guys.

ABOUT THE AUTHOR

Ms. Rose is an Emmy Award–winning writer and television producer from the San Francisco Bay Area. At thirty-five she married and became a stepmom—her two most challenging projects to date. She currently lives in Austin, Texas, with her husband and his two man-cubs. *The Package Deal* is her first book.

Visit her popular blog at www.stepmothersmilk.com.

READER'S GROUP GUIDE

While *The Package Deal* is one woman's adventure as a new step-mother, at its heart it is a story about today's stepfamilies, modern-day marriage, negotiating family and career, the necessity of friend-ships, the constant search for identity, and the many ways to make a home.

1) What aspects of your life now would be hardest to change or give up for love and marriage? What would you absolutely not sacrifice? What parts are negotiable?

2) Has *The Package Deal* challenged any notions you used to have about getting involved with a man who has kids? Would children and an ex-wife be automatic deal-breakers?

3) Statistics tell us that there are more than 15 million stepmothers in the country today, yet many of them feel isolated and alone. Why do you think this is? Like Izzy asks, *"Why isn't stepparenting a mainstream discussion?"*

4) Has this book changed your image of the modern stepmom? How does *The Package Deal* challenge what Izzy calls the "wicked lame" stepmother stereotype and our romantic ideal of the "perfect guy"?

5) When it comes to girlfriends, how do women find their new BFF, particularly in a new and unfamiliar city?

6) Is it true that the mommy club is often closed to non–bio mothers? Why is this?

7) As the newest member of the traveling circus, Izzy struggled with how to fit into Hank's existing family. *"I'm not an extension cord. You can't just plug me into the family power strip."* How does a blended family successfully create the right mix and whose job is it to make sure everyone has a place?

8) Just before the boys move to Austin, Izzy dreads the "impending threat of dirt" until she realizes her apprehension has less to do with boy grime and more to do with her deep fears. Discuss what yours might be if you were Izzy.

9) In your opinion, what *is* the proper etiquette in dealing with your boyfriend/fiancé/husband's ex-wife? How important is it to have a relationship with her and how close are you willing to get?

10) How do you think Izzy's life would have been different had she been a co-parent with June in Texas? Discuss the differences between full-time and part-time step-parenting.

11) Izzy used her own stepkid experiences to shape her stepmom role. How was Izzy's perspective an advantage or a disadvantage in raising her two stepkids?

12) If you are also a stepchild, how did your experiences compare with Izzy's?

13) When it comes to discipline, what *is* the role of the stepparent? And who makes this determination?

14) For Izzy, her stepkids were enough of a responsibility, but many "instant mothers" still want to have kids of their own someday. Discuss the dynamics of adding a new baby to the mix.

15) If you are a stepparent, how long was it before you said the L-word to your stepkids? Do you think Izzy's reluctance to "pour on l'amour" was justified?

16) What's in a name? What do your stepkids call you? Was this your choice or theirs? How do you introduce each other?

17) Discuss "Stepmom Rule Number Seventeen: No one gets it all." Do you agree that this is the reality for every stepfamily?

18) Do you have a Stepmom Rule of your own to add to the list?